Quantitative
International
Economics

QUANTITATIVE INTERNATIONAL ECONOMICS

Edward E. Leamer
Harvard University

Robert M. Stern
The University of Michigan

Allyn and Bacon, Inc.   Boston

Contents

List of Figures and Tables   vii

Preface   xi

Chapter 1   Introduction   1

PART I   THE BALANCE OF PAYMENTS   5

Chapter 2   Time-Series Estimation of Import and Export Demand Relationships   7

Choice of Variables, 8.   *Functional Form*, 17.   *Time Dimension*, 19.   *Special Problems in Estimation*, 28. *Reporting Results*, 36.   *Conclusion*, 40.   *Appendix to Chapter 2*, 41.   *References*, 51.

Chapter 3   Theory and Measurement of the Elasticity of Substitution in International Trade   56

Theoretical Foundation, 57.   *Measurement*, 63. *Interpretation and Use of Results*, 64.   *Pooled Time-Series and Cross-Section Estimation*, 69.   *Conclusion*, 71.   *Appendix to Chapter 3*, 72.   *References*, 74.

Chapter 4   The Estimation of International Capital Movements   76

The Theory of International Capital Movements, 77. *The Measurement of International Capital Movements*, 92. *Conclusion*, 104.   *References*, 105.

v

Chapter 5   Forecasting and Policy Analysis with Econometric
                   Models   108

                   Economic Forecasting, 109.   *Policy Analysis*, 117.
                   A Model of the World Economy, 118.   *Evaluation
                   of Econometric Models of the U.S. Balance of Payments*,
                   122.   *Conclusion*, 132.   *Appendix to Chapter 5*, 133.
                   References, 140.

PART II   INTERNATIONAL TRADE AND
                   WELFARE   143

Chapter 6   Theory and Measurement of Trade Dependence
                   and Interdependence   145

                   *The Theory and Measurement of General Equilibrium
                   Trade Sectors*, 147.   *The Theory and Measurement
                   of Trade Flows*, 157.   *Conclusion*, 168.
                   References, 168.

Chapter 7   Constant-Market-Share Analysis of Export
                   Growth   171

                   Theory and Measurement, 171.   *The Choice of
                   "Standard,"* 176.   *Further Implications*, 177.
                   Conclusion, 179.   *A Numerical Illustration*, 179.
                   References, 182.

Chapter 8   Estimating the Welfare Effects of Trade
                   Liberalization,   184

                   The Welfare Effect of a Prohibitive Tariff, 185.
                   The Welfare Effect of a Nonprohibitive Tariff, 190.
                   Statistical Estimation of Welfare Effects, 194.
                   Customs Unions and Trade Preferences, 195.
                   Conclusion, 196.   *References*, 197.

                   Index   201

Figures and Tables

FIGURES 2.1 Demand for Imports: Perfect Substitutability
              Between Home and Foreign Goods   11

         2.2 Linear Regression Fit to Curviliniar Demand
              Schedule   19

         2.3 Adjustment of Quantity to a Change in Price
              20

         2.4 Adjustment of Quantity to Successive Price
              Changes   20

         2.5 Linear Regression Fit to Quantities Adjusted
              to a Change in Price   22

         2.6 Unacceptable Configuration of α_i 26

         2.7 Alternative Configuration of α_i 27

         2.8 Downward Bias in the Estimated Price
              Coefficient   30

         2.9 Unbiased Estimate of Price Coefficient   31

         2.10 Errors of Observation in Quantity   32

         2.11 Errors of Observation in Price   32

         2.12 Confidence Intervals for Income and Price
              Elasticities for U.S. Import Demand   35

3.1   The Elasticity of Substitution Along a Single
        Indifference Curve   58

3.2   The Elasticity of Substitution Between Two
        Indifference Curves   59

3.3   Income and Substitution Effects   66

3.A.1   Range of Values of Elasticity of
        Substitution   73

4.1   The Effect of Capital Controls   97

4.2   The Effect of Credit Rationing   98

5.1   Probability Forecasts   113

6.1   Consumption Possibilities in the Absence
        of Trade   148

6.2   Consumption Possibilities with Trade   148

6.3   Resource Endowment Skewed Towards
        Export Production   149

6.4   Resource Endowment Skewed Towards
        Home Goods Production   150

6.5   Balanced Resource Endowment   150

6.6   Hypothetical Growth Paths of Imports in
        Relation to GNP   154

8.1   Welfare Effect of a Prohibitive Tariff   185

8.2   Welfare Gain in a Simple Exchange
        Situation   186

8.3   Measurement of Welfare Gain: A 187

8.4   Measurement of Welfare Gain: B 187

8.5   Compensated Demand Curve   188

8.6   Welfare Effect of a Nonprohibitive
        Tariff   190

8.7   Welfare Triangles   191

8.8   The Impact of Terms-of-Trade
           Changes   193

TABLES   2.1   Explanatory Variables Used in Import
                        Demand Analysis   13

             4.1   International Investment Position of the
                        United States at Year-End, 1967   99–100

             4.2   Short-Term Claims on Foreigners Reported
                        by Banks in the United States at Year-End,
                        1967   101

             5.1   Changes from 1961 to 1968 in U.S. Current
                        Account   124

             5.2   Prachowny's Quarterly Model of the Foreign
                        Sector of the U.S. Economy, 1953–59
                        126–127

             5.A.1   Estimates of the Trade and Savings
                        Gaps   138

             7.1   Illustration of the Constant-Market-Share
                        Analysis of Changes in Italian Exports,
                        1955–59   180–181

             8.1   Estimated Direct Welfare Effects of Trade
                        Liberalization in the Kennedy Round   196

Preface

Our interest in the subject of quantitative international economics developed in the course of drafting some chapters of a book by Mr. Stern, *The Balance of Payments: Theory and Economic Policy*. It was thought that it would be worthwhile to include in that book some discussion of empirical work and statistical methods for estimating relationships of various kinds that are relevant to international financial matters. As the work progressed, it became increasingly evident how difficult it was to report on what had been done because of the diverse statistical specifications and methods used and the comparatively few reliable results that pertained to particular countries.

As a result, we decided to write something more general on this subject that could serve as a guide and reference work for economics graduate students, academicians, and practicing economists in private and governmental circles. The object was to set forth on a reasonably advanced level the various methods for quantitative measurement of what we considered to be the most important relationships at issue in the areas of international finance and trade, to give some flavor of the results achieved in studies done in recent years, and to indicate directions for new research.

The level at which we have aimed is that of first- and second-year economics graduate students who have had a one- or two-semester course in international economics and in econometrics as an integral part of their training. A number of our chapters contain extensive discussions of the economic theory underlying the relationships to be measured. The reason for this is that many published contributions have lacked a clear theoretical rationale, with the consequence that sometimes inadequate or incorrect statistical specifications have been employed. Although we feel very strongly that valid empirical work must have a solid theoretical base, our intent is not to cover all international economic theory. We are not concerned, moreover, with the development per se of the econometric methods to be discussed. Abundant references are supplied on both of these scores in the individual chapters in case the reader wants to delve more deeply into some particular problem. While we do offer some concrete advice on what and how things should be done, our primary goal is to enhance the reader's understanding of what the important relationships are and the problems he may encounter in attempting to measure these relationships statistically. We employ on the whole relatively simple algebraic and geometric formulations, reserving for footnotes and appendixes the somewhat more advanced material.

All of the chapters have benefited greatly from the criticisms and suggestions for improvement offered by members of the Research Seminar in International Economics at The University of Michigan. We are indebted especially to J. David Richardson for his extensive comments on the entire manuscript and to Giorgio Basevi, Ralph Bryant, Kevin Collins, John Cross, Alan Ginsburg, Jay Levin, Norman Miller, Th. Peeters, Martin Prachowny, Thomas Willett, Sidney Winter, Charles Wolf, and Kunio Yoshihara for comments on individual chapters.

We are grateful to the National Science Foundation and the Ford Program Development Fund of The University of Michigan for providing financial assistance in undertaking this research. We would also like to thank Jacqueline Parsons and Patricia Rapley for their patience and good humor in typing the various drafts of the manuscript.

Edward E. Leamer
Robert M. Stern

Ann Arbor, Michigan
March 1969

Introduction

Our concern in this book is with the quantitative measurement of international economic relationships. The relationships we discuss were selected in terms of their theoretical importance and policy relevance in the areas of international finance and trade. We follow the procedure of beginning each chapter with a discussion of the theoretical rationale underlying the particular relationship. We then treat measurement considerations, drawing in this regard upon some of the most noteworthy studies published in recent years. We try insofar as possible to offer concrete suggestions on research methodology and to point out the directions in which we think future research might profitably go.

Part 1 dealing with the balance of payments consists of Chapters 2 through 5. The longest of these by far is Chapter 2, in which we treat at length the time-series analysis of the demand for imports and exports from the point of view of an individual country. This subject has a long and somewhat checkered history dating from the 1940's, when a number of estimates using least squares multiple regression methods were made of import and export demand functions for the interwar period. The noteworthy feature of many of these estimates was that they suggested relatively low price elasticities of demand in international trade. The implication was thus drawn that the international price mechanism could not be relied on for balance-of-payments adjustment purposes.

However, this implication was shown by Orcutt in his pathbreaking 1950 article not to be altogether valid since there were tendencies for the regression methods and statistical specifications employed to bias the measured elasticities downward towards zero. In the years following Orcutt's work, there was great hesitation in using traditional least squares regression in the time-series analysis of demand. This situation has since been altered by further theoretical inquiry into the statistical issues raised by Orcutt. It is now believed that Orcutt's arguments were not so conclusive and general as they first appeared to be. In addition, as more data points became available for the post–World War II period, a number of studies using least squares regression were made of import and export demand functions with results that seemed quite plausible in view of a priori theoretical considerations concerning price elasticities. It seems therefore that while there were special characteristics in the interwar period that made this period unconducive to the use of least squares analysis, these characteristics are much less important today.

Our object in Chapter 2 is thus to discuss at some length the most important points that an investigation using least squares analysis should be concerned with in estimating import and export demand functions. Considerable evidence has already accumulated regarding the demand factors that determine the international flow of goods, thereby providing information useful to policymakers concerned with the balance of payments. However, further improvements are possible.

Chapter 3, dealing with the measurement of the elasticity of substitution in international trade, represents a bit of a digression. This is justified in our judgment by the amount of effort in the past that has gone into such measurement. Much of this effort was motivated by a search for alternative specifications that would yield more reliable and larger price elasticities than those obtained in estimating demand functions directly. However, given our increased understanding of statistical and data problems and the fact that the elasticity of substitution in international trade lacks a clear theoretical rationale, we take the position that there may be a greater payoff in direct estimation of the demand functions in question. It may be nevertheless that measurement of the elasticity of substitution is useful in models of relative export performance that embody both price and nonprice factors.

The measurement of factors determining international capital movements is treated in Chapter 4. This poses more difficult problems than trade in real goods and services especially because of the greater importance of expectational variables and the impingement of institutional practices and constraints. Moreover, some of the first works on capital movements in the early 1960's were limited by an inadequate theoretical framework, which resulted in improper selections of variables. The fact that the confusion over the appropriate variables has lasted as long as it has is attributable to a premature preoccupation with statistical problems of secondary importance. Much remains then to be done as far as the empirical examination of the capital account of the balance of payments is concerned.

In Chapter 5, we attempt to bring the current and capital account relationships to bear on the problems of forecasting and policy analysis of the balance of payments. While this is a burgeoning subject, due especially to the great advances that have been made in computer technology, we are nevertheless still at a stage where there are somewhat divergent views on exactly what should go into the construction of econometric models and the uses to which these models should be put in forecasting and policy analysis. Much of our discussion in this chapter is therefore somewhat tentative and suggestive. We have reviewed the treatment of the foreign sector in some of the existing econometric models of the United States economy. Since this treatment is quite simple at the present time, there remains much to be done, at least in the United States, to integrate the domestic and foreign sectors into a comprehensive model capable of yielding reasonably accurate forecasts and serving as the basis for analyzing alternative economic policies.

Part II dealing with international trade and welfare consists of Chapters 6 through 8. There is of course a large body of empirical literature dealing with the different aspects of trade theory. In general, much of this literature is aimed at particular implications of the theory, such as comparative advantage, the validity of the factor endowments model of international trade, and, more recently, the explanation of trade according to the "product-cycle" and "technological-gap" hypotheses. Since most of these studies have not raised important questions of conceptual design and statistical methodology and since they have been in large measure reviewed at length elsewhere, we have chosen to restrict ourselves to a narrower range of topics that appeared to us important and not always well understood. Perhaps at some later time we may expand our scope to include the other topics mentioned.

In Chapter 6 we are concerned with providing a general equilibrium framework into which can be fitted the analysis of factors determining the size of a country's foreign sector and the flows of goods between pairs of countries. Of all the topics treated in the various chapters, the material in Chapter 6 is perhaps the most unfamiliar, at least to American readers, since the bulk of the work involved has been carried on in continental Europe. The lack of an explicit theoretical framework has been the greatest failure of these studies. Without such a theory the analysis tends to degenerate into a search for meaningless empirical regularities. It thus is quite important to bring international trade theory to bear upon the role the variables may play and thereby provide some rationale for the otherwise ad hoc empirical impressions that such studies convey.

The material contained in Chapter 7 has grown out of a concern for analyzing the component factors that affect a country's export growth over time. The basis for the analysis is the assumption that a country's share in world markets should be constant over time. The application of an identity based on the constant-share norm highlights the importance to a country of concentrating its exports in high-growth commodities and markets and indicates whether the country has been successful in competing with other sources of supply during the period in question.

Chapter 8 deals with estimating the welfare effects of trade liberalization. This analysis is relevant for analyzing the consequences for economic welfare of unilateral and multilateral tariff changes from the standpoint of individual countries. It can also be applied to cases of preferential tariff changes in the context of customs unions and trade preferences of various kinds. Most of the discussion of this chapter is concerned with the theoretical derivation of the compensated demand curve, which serves as the conceptual basis for analyzing the welfare effects of tariff changes in terms of consumer surplus. The price elasticities required for the actual calculations can in principle be obtained by using the procedures described in Chapter 2, although in practice "guesstimates" of the relevant elasticities are usually employed. The assumptions underlying the compensated demand curve are shown to be rather restrictive. However, the changes involved in trade liberalization are usually relatively small so that the calculation of the welfare effects may provide a reasonable assessment of the order of magnitude of these effects.

Rather than list all the bibliographic items together, we have chosen instead to list them separately with each chapter. These bibliographies contain the most important works of about the past decade, but they are by no means exhaustive.

PART I

The Balance of Payments

Time-Series Estimation
of Import and Export
Demand Relationships

In the present chapter we shall discuss the application of traditional multivariate least squares regression methods to the analysis of import and export time series. Our object is not to review regression methods in detail, since there are many standard books on the subject.[1] Rather, our primary concern will be to bring together the many questions with which a researcher must cope in planning his own work and in evaluating the work of others.

The foundation of the statistical research to be discussed in this chapter is a hypothesized behavioral relationship on the demand side between the level of imports (exports) of goods and services and several explanatory variables.[2] This relationship is assumed to have held consistently throughout the data period. When forecasting is performed, the relationship is extended by assumption into the future as well.

The central problem at issue is the specification of the import (export) demand relationship in a form suitable for statistical fitting. In this regard, we will be concerned with selection of appropriate dependent and independent variables, choice of functional form, and method for handling response lags. We shall also discuss certain special problems of estimation that may be relevant for particular countries and classes of goods, and appropriate formats for the presentation of results.

Some readers may be disturbed by the multitude of questions that will be posed in our discussion in comparison with the sparseness of definite answers. If this is indeed the case, we will have succeeded in our purpose, for it is far too common for the important questions to be glossed over and for research

---

[1] For introductory, intermediate, and advanced discussions of regression analysis, see for example the works by Suits [71], Johnston [29], and Goldberger [19].

[2] There will be a behavioral relationship between imports (exports) and several explanatory variables on the supply side as well. Much of the discussion to follow is relevant to the supply side. Unfortunately, the rather meagre empirical attempts to uncover supply relationships do not warrant extensive comment. See Rhomberg [62, 65] for examples of supply functions.

decisions to be fallen into rather than arrived at by explicit design. The fact that we shall concentrate mainly on statistical questions should not be interpreted to mean that knowledge of the institutions and the economic characteristics of the markets to be analyzed is unimportant. This surely is not the case, and any research design will be measurably improved if the investigator takes the time to learn about these matters.

CHOICE OF VARIABLES

The Dependent Variable   As already mentioned, our focus here will be on import and export demand relationships. The most readily available data on imports (exports) are in value rather than quantity terms. However, the theory of demand suggests that quantity is the appropriate dependent variable, and we will have to divide or deflate the value series by a measure of prices to obtain the proper dependent variable. Thus the dependent variables are given by

$$M = \frac{V_M}{p_M} \tag{2.1}$$

and

$$X = \frac{V_X}{p_X} \tag{2.2}$$

where M = quantity of imports of some commodity class; p_M = price of imports; V_M = value of imports and X, p_X, and V_X are defined analogously for exports.

It should be obvious that for goods that are homogeneous in quality, M and X will be accurate measures of quantity. But when goods differ in quality and when classes of goods are combined into aggregates, M and X may bear little or no relation to real quantity.[3] In such cases the price variables are index numbers and the quantity variables are values in constant dollars. The defining relationship (2.1) is expressed explicitly by

$$M_t = \sum_i p_{i0}q_{it} = \frac{\Sigma_i p_{it}q_{it}}{\Sigma_i[(p_{i0}q_{it})/(\Sigma_i p_{i0}q_{it})](p_{it}/p_{i0})} = \frac{V_M}{p_M} \tag{2.3}$$

---

[3] Since countries import and export typically thousands of different types of goods, it is necessary to employ index numbers of prices for purposes of deflation and, as will be noted shortly, as explanatory variables in the analysis. This suggests the importance of precisely defining the characteristics of the goods to be included in the index in order to minimize the variations in prices due to quality differences. Needless to say, this is a very difficult thing to accomplish and one should be continually on guard therefore in the use of published price indexes and in the calculation of average prices or unit values. This point is further discussed in the appendix. A useful general source on index number construction is Mills [47]. See also Kravis and Lipsey [41] and Lipsey [44].

where p_{i0}, q_{i0}, p_{it}, q_{it} are the price and quantity of imports of commodity i in the base period and period t respectively. Interpreting this relationship, we observe that the dependent variable M_t is the value of imports at base-year prices, which may be expressed as current value divided by a price index. M and X are interpreted as the "real values" of imports and exports in the same way that the deflated value of gross national product (GNP) is called "real income."

Occasionally, researchers have used the value of imports in current dollars as the dependent variable. On theoretical grounds this should be avoided. In the appendix to this chapter we demonstrate that if the definition (2.3) is used, then there is a macro relation between M_t and several explanatory variables, including income and price indexes. For other definitions of M, the proper weights to be used in the import price index become somewhat more complicated.[4] However, when only a crudely constructed price index is available, it may be preferable to use the current-value variable and avoid the error introduced by deflating by the crude price variable. In addition, there will be cases when it is extremely difficult to express imports and exports in real terms, as for example with services, tourism, and banking charges. It is common in these circumstances to carry out the analysis using current-value data.[5]

Independent or Explanatory Variables The basic explanatory variables are suggested by the theory of demand, according to which the consumer allocates his income among consumable commodities in an effort to achieve maximum satisfaction. The quantity of imports purchased by any consumer will thus depend on his income, the price of imports, and the price of other consumable commodities. This suggests that for an economy we may write import demand as

$$M = \frac{V_M}{p_M} = f(p_M,\ p_Y,\ Y) \tag{2.4}$$

[4] The reader may verify this by demonstrating that (2.A.19) in the appendix would include a $q_{j'}$ term.

[5] It might be argued, as Branson [7] does, that our ultimate interest is in the balance of payments and consequently in the *value* of imports. When the constant-dollar variable is used, a second equation to explain prices will be needed to predict the import value. It remains an open empirical question whether a single equation with value as the dependent variable would provide a better prediction than the two-equation explanation that is theoretically preferable.

There is one theoretically acceptable alternative to the variable defined by (2.3). It may be the case that disturbances to our hypothesized behavioral relationship will grow in size as M grows, perhaps maintaining a proportionality to M. Least squares procedure, in contrast, assumes that the disturbances maintain their absolute size. This conflict can perhaps be dealt with by dividing M by real income. The ratio of imports to real income is not likely to change significantly, and the assumption of constant-sized disturbances to a relationship explaining this ratio thus seems acceptable. The importance of the foregoing point will depend on the growth of M over the data period. We will not dwell on it further.

where Y is domestic money income, p_M is the price level of imports, and p_Y is the price level of other goods, in this case domestic goods. The fact that the demand relations for individual consumers can be aggregated over individuals and over commodities to yield (2.4) is supported by theorems on aggregation that are presented in the appendix to this chapter.

The theory of demand proceeds one step further in suggesting that the demand relationship (2.4) may actually be written as

$$M = f\left(\frac{p_M}{p_Y}, \frac{Y}{p_Y}\right) \tag{2.5}$$

or

$$M = g\left(\frac{p_Y}{p_M}, \frac{Y}{p_M}\right) \tag{2.6}$$

This transformation is based on the assumption that individual consumers display the absence of money illusion; that is, a doubling of all prices and money income will leave the quantity demanded unchanged. In that event, either (2.5) or (2.6) should be preferred to (2.4). The point at issue is whether we are so confident concerning the absence of money illusion that we will impose this presumption on the data, or whether the data should be allowed to support or to contradict the absence of money illusion hypothesis. In our judgment, the theoretical support for the absence of money illusion is not sufficiently strong to justify Equation (2.5) or (2.6), and we therefore prefer Equation (2.4).[6] It may be noted nonetheless that Equation (2.5) is the form which has traditionally been employed in demand analysis in international trade. In deference to tradition and with simplification as a side product, we will employ Equation (2.5) as the basic description of demand throughout the remainder of the chapter.

The export-demand function can be written analogously as

$$X = \frac{V_X}{p_X} = g\left(\frac{Y'}{p_{Y'}}, \frac{p_X}{p_{Y'}}\right) \tag{2.7}$$

where the primed values refer to income and prices in the rest of the world.

---

[6] Researchers will sometimes shy away from the more general form (2.4) due to the enlarged standard errors inherent in using a third explanatory variable that is likely to be correlated with the other two. While such reasoning is understandable, it is in our judgment unacceptable. In the first place, the proper statistical method does not allow for the choice of specification on the basis of standard errors. Secondly, the comparison of the standard errors obtained via Equations (2.4) and (2.5) is not particularly relevant to the question at hand. That is, the coefficient on the price term from (2.5) describes the effect of a change in p_M/p_Y holding Y/p_Y constant. A comparable statistic from (2.4) will be a combination of all three of the basic coefficients, the standard error of which will include covariance terms and cannot be read directly from the standard errors of the basic coefficients.

The theory of import demand we have just discussed is based on the proposition that imports and domestic goods are not perfect substitutes. Suppose, however, as illustrated in Figure 2.1, that imports and domestic goods are perfect substitutes, or equivalently that the price elasticities are very large. In Figure 2.1, DD is the domestic demand for some good while SS is the domestic supply. The difference between these schedules MM represents an excess demand or equivalently a demand for imports, where imports are the same good as that produced domestically. From an empirical point of view, the very important difference between the situation discussed earlier in connection with Equations (2.4) et seq. and that depicted in Figure 2.1 is that in the former case domestic supply will influence imports only through its impact on domestic prices, while in the latter case domestic supply will directly influence imports. Figure 2.1 suggests accordingly that the import demand function should include domestic supply variables.

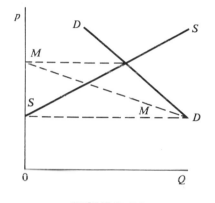

FIGURE 2.1

Demand for Imports: Perfect Substitutability
Between Home and Foreign Goods

To illustrate this point further, suppose that the international supply of the good in question is infinitely elastic at the given price and that domestic investment increases the capacity of import-competing industries. In our first situation, domestic prices will fall and imports will be reduced. In the second situation, the domestic and import prices must be the same as long as some of both goods is being sold. Accordingly, no price change is observed, yet at the same time imports will be reduced. The only way to account for this is to include the capacity of the import-competing industries as an explanatory variable in the import-demand function. The basic import-demand function suggested by our second situation is given by

$$M = f(S,\ Y,\ p,\ p_A) \tag{2.8}$$

where S is a variable that shifts the domestic supply function, Y is money income, p is the common price of the good from domestic and foreign sources of supply, and p_A is the price of an alternative domestic good that is not a perfect substitute for the good in question. If M is total aggregate imports, then there will be no p_A at all.

We have therefore two quite different descriptions of import demand. In the first instance, prices will be observed to move and will allocate income among the alternative consumable commodities, imports and domestic goods. In the second instance, the effect of a price change is so great that no price change can occur and the only way to account for changes in imports due to competition between the sources of supply is through supply variables.[7]

Virtually all of the statistical studies of import demand that have come to our attention have used some variant of Equation (2.5).[8] What our discussion suggests, however, is that a more proper approach would be to distinguish commodities that are perfect substitutes from those that are not and to adopt the appropriate specification of the import function in each case. Any particular commodity may be placed in one class or the other according to how well the competing specifications in Equations (2.5) and (2.8) explain the data.

Inasmuch as there have been no efforts, of which we are aware, to explore relationship (2.8), we shall not pursue it further at this point, beyond indicating the sort of variable that is associated with S. The variable S should represent those factors that will affect the supply of import-competing goods. What comes to mind particularly in this regard is the capacity of the import-competing industries that may be reflected in recent investment. Other possible factors include the cost of inputs such as labor or raw materials.

A similar description of import demand will be needed to describe imports of raw materials and unfinished goods. These are inputs into productive activities and may be explained by

$$M = f(p_M, p_A, O) \tag{2.9}$$

where p_M is the price of the import, p_A is the price of an alternative domestic input, and O is the level of production or output of the industries in question. This is seen to be analogous to the finished-good demand function (2.4). In the case of infinite price elasticities, there will also be a function analogous to Equation (2.8).

---

[7] This discussion illustrates, incidentally, a consideration that will work against relatively high estimates of price elasticities. When elasticities are in fact high, little or no price movement is observed, making estimation of the elasticities subject to inaccuracy.

[8] Branson's [7] theory suggests that he is describing imports as an excess demand function, but it should be noted that he has in addition the relative price variable associated with the other theory.

Both the consumer and the producer items may be further divided into durables and nondurables. There are quite a number of studies that have examined the demand for consumer durables and investment goods (producer durables). While in principle these studies might well be adapted in dealing with import demand, they have unfortunately not yet had much impact on the international trade field. The importance of these considerations will of course depend on the extent to which the demand for durables is motivated differently from nondurables and also on the importance of durables in total imports (exports).

Let us now consider other possible explanatory variables. Some of these will be seen simply to represent variations of the basic real income and relative price variables to make allowance for particular categories of imports, while others are acknowledgements on the part of the researcher that understanding a complex demand phenomenon requires more variables than the usual two. Examples of variables commonly used in import-demand analysis are indicated in Table 2.1.

It will be noted in line 1 of Table 2.1 that the income or "activity" variable is chosen to conform with the particular import category and that further subdivisions of these variables can be used for more refined categories. This suggests that the use of an aggregate income or an aggregate production term

TABLE 2.1

Explanatory Variables Used in Import-Demand Analysis

Total Imports	Imports of Finished Goods	Imports of Unfinished Goods
1. Real GNP; degree of capacity utilization	1. Real disposable income; real expenditure components; degree of capacity utilization	1. Industrial production; real change in inventories; degree of capacity utilization
2. Relative price of imports [a]	2. Relative price of imports [a]	2. Relative price of imports [a]
3. Dummy variables for unusual periods	3. Dummy variables for unusual periods	3. Dummy variables for unusual periods
4. Dummy variables for seasonal variation	4. Dummy variables for seasonal variation	4. Dummy variables for seasonal variation
5. Lagged variables	5. Lagged variables	5. Lagged variables
6. Foreign exchange reserves	6. Foreign exchange reserves	6. Foreign exchange reserves
7. Credit	7. Credit	7. Credit

[a] Measured as import price divided by the price of domestic goods in general or as import price divided by the price of close domestic substitutes. The specification will depend especially on the level of aggregation employed.

in the aggregate import function is improper insofar as increases in particular categories of income or output may generate significantly more imports than similar increases in other categories. This is especially true for the aggregate production variable. The differences in the import requirements of the various productive activities are likely to be quite substantial. In order to take such differences into account, as noted in the detailed discussion of aggregation in the appendix to this chapter, the components of the aggregate activity variables ought to be reweighted according to their marginal contribution to imports. These weights may be approximated in the case of the production variable by the average import content of the commodity class. The use of the inventory variable separately may be interpreted to reflect the assumption that increases in GNP due to changes in inventories have a unique and separable impact on imports.

The capacity-utilization variable represents an amendment to the traditional theory of demand insofar as it gives cognizance to the idea that queues as well as prices may be used to allocate goods among consumers. Thus, an increase in domestic demand may not be met immediately by price increases. Rather, domestic producers may ration the available supply by delaying deliveries or, in other words, forcing the consumer into a queue to await servicing of his order. In such a period, the consumer may look to foreign sources of supply to avoid the delay in delivery. The consumer therefore pays two prices for the good he desires: the quoted price as well as an imputed cost of waiting in a queue. He will seek the supply source that provides the good at minimum total cost, including the cost of waiting.

What this suggests accordingly is that the import-demand function should include variables that reflect the length of queues at home and abroad. Capacity utilization is a proxy for queue-length. When production is close to capacity, queues are likely to be long. In periods of excess capacity, orders are likely to be filled rapidly. The inventory variable may be interpreted as a proxy for queue-length as well. Increases in demand may be met initially by a drawing down of inventories and later by increases in queue-length. Accordingly, a disinvestment in inventories in one period may be a signal for increased queue-length in the next.

The two-good description of demand is misleading in discussion of the relative price term noted in line 2 of Table 2.1. The dependent variable, imports, typically represents, as we have noted, a conglomerate of goods that substitute freely for some domestic goods, not so freely for others, and not at all for still others. Ideally one would use a price relative for each of the first two classes of goods. The specification of these two classes of goods will of course depend on the goods that make up the dependent variable, imports, and consequently on the level of aggregation. When aggregate imports is the dependent variable, the use of only the price index for GNP in the price relative involves the assumption that imports substitute generally the same with all domestic goods. Such an assumption is rarely warranted, and the procedure will surely impair the price relative's explanatory power. This is again a problem of aggregation, which is treated extensively in the appendix.

Another complication is introduced when price indexes are not available, and unit-value indexes are used instead. A unit value may be calculated for particular commodity classes of imports (exports) by dividing the value of imports (exports) of that class by the unweighted sum of the quantities imported. A unit-value index is thus a weighted average of such unit values, and it may change because of the commodity composition of any of the commodity classes quite independently of any price changes. Since a unit-value index is thus not ordinarily a true price index, one must exercise great care in its use and interpretation.

The dummy variables in line 3 are designed to allow for the effects upon imports of unusual occurrences such as a strike, war, or natural disaster. Such variables would assume a value of one for the duration of the unusual period and zero otherwise. If quarterly or monthly data are being used, it may be desirable, as indicated in line 4, to employ dummy variables to reflect the seasonal variation in the relationship.[9] The alternative here would be to use data that were already seasonally adjusted. However, this might have the disadvantage of imposing possibly arbitrary regularities on the data, which might be inappropriate for the particular demand function being estimated.[10]

Line 5 of Table 2.1 referring to lagged variables is of particular importance in measuring the influences of past changes in the independent variables on the current behavior of imports. The effects of lags will be more important the shorter the time-period units utilized in the analysis. Thus, for example, in a quarterly analysis current imports may be influenced more by the prices of preceding quarters than by current prices. This is because of such factors as the lag between orders and shipments and the speed with which imports are adjusted to changes in prices. A common way of introducing lagged influences is by including as an independent variable the value of the dependent variable lagged one quarter.[11]

The level of foreign exchange reserves indicated in line 6 may be relevant in particular to less developed countries, where the reserve position can be considered indicative of the strictness of controls affecting imports. That is,

---

[9] See Suits [72] or Johnston [29] for a discussion of the uses and interpretation of dummy variables.

[10] A point worth mentioning here is that seasonal adjustment will use up the same number of degrees of freedom whether performed before or during the import regression. Thus, those who use adjusted data should reduce their degrees of freedom by the appropriate numbers. It is then clear that any argument in favor of adjusted data may not appeal to degrees-of-freedom restrictions.

[11] This would correspond to the so-called Koyck distributed lag, in which the weights of past influences are assumed to decline geometrically. We shall have much more to say on these matters later in this chapter.

imports may respond in these countries more to foreign exchange availability than to the level of real income. A similar variable would be foreign exchange earnings. In the case of developed countries, the reserves variable can be used as a proxy for the degree of official restraints. Thus, for example, as the U.S. has lost more and more reserves, government officials spend more and more time persuading consumers and producers to "buy American."

The "credit" variable indicated in the last line of Table 2.1 has been neglected in most studies to date. This variable is meant to indicate the availability and terms at which credit is provided for the financing of imports. Such a variable will play an important role especially in linking the current and capital accounts of the balance of payments. Increasing interest in the capital account will surely provide a stimulus to increased examination of the effect of credit on imports and exports.[12]

A table could be constructed for exports that would be analogous in principle to Table 2.1. Data do not exist, however, for world income and world prices, which would be determining variables. In cases when the country in question exports primarily to countries or regions that have published and reliable income and price data, export demand may then be viewed as primarily the demand for imports by these important countries or regions.[13] It is necessary otherwise to seek proxy measures for world income and world prices.

The most common choices are to use real world exports (less those of the country in question) as a proxy for world income and a measure of the price of world exports as a proxy for the price of world goods. This amounts roughly to assuming that the country exports a certain fraction of world exports and that this fraction is altered by the country's relative export prices.[14] The interpretation of the export-demand relationship will thus differ from the one for imports because in the case of exports neither world income nor world prices is being measured directly. There may in addition be a complication introduced by relying on unit values rather than on actual prices in the construction of the indexes used to measure relative prices.

The variables discussed above are in general the most important ones, although the list is by no means all-inclusive. Many other explanatory variables will suggest themselves in particular situations, and the choice among these

[12] See Houthakker and Magee [27] and Prachowny [57] for an analysis that incorporates credit considerations.

[13] Examples of this approach are to be found in the work of Rhomberg and Boissonneault [64] for the United States and Davis [11] for Canada.

[14] Polak [56, especially pp. 47–51] has argued that the aggregate of world exports is in fact preferable to the use of aggregate world income on two grounds: (1) it makes allowance for intercountry differences in marginal import propensities; and (2) it is not affected by any general shift in the relationship between income and imports vis-à-vis the country in question. See also Prachowny [57]. Houthakker and Magee [27] have recently constructed a measure of world income that apparently gives reasonably good results.

variables will depend significantly on the intimacy of the researcher's knowledge concerning the demand phenomena he is attempting to explain. Thus, the importance of close contact with the markets being investigated cannot be overemphasized.[15]

FUNCTIONAL FORM

The general functional relations for import and export demands ignoring all but the two basic variables have already been noted in Equations (2.4) and (2.7). Thus, the import-demand function was

$$M = f\left(\frac{Y}{p_Y}, \frac{p_M}{p_Y}\right)$$

where M is the quantity of imports, Y/p_Y is real income, and p_M/p_Y is the relative price of imports. In order to fit such a relationship statistically using least squares regression, a particular functional form must be chosen. The most common forms are linear, as in Equation (2.10), and log-linear, as in Equation (2.11)

$$M = a + b\frac{Y}{p_Y} + c\frac{p_M}{p_Y} + u \tag{2.10}$$

$$\log M = \log a_1 + b_1 \log \frac{Y}{p_Y} + c_1 \log \frac{p_M}{p_Y} + \log u \tag{2.11}$$

which is equivalent to

$$M = a_1\left(\frac{Y}{p_Y}\right)^{b_1}\left(\frac{p_M}{p_Y}\right)^{c_1} u \tag{2.12}$$

In Equation (2.10), a is the constant term in the regression, b is the marginal propensity to import, c is the import coefficient of relative prices, and u

---

[15] The following quotation from Lewis [43, p. 579] is particularly suggestive in the present context:

Every successful drive for trade in manufactures contains five elements: keen prices, a flood of salesmen, large scale organization of selling, attention to customers' wishes and liberal credit. Econometricians usually put all the emphasis on the first element, prices, because this is easiest to measure. Businessmen, however, usually attribute much greater importance to sales effort, and it is clear that success or failure in selling is not always attributable to prices.

It will be noted in our later discussion, particularly of factors determining export-market shares, that Ginsburg [18] has attempted quantitatively to assess the importance of price and nonprice factors and found the latter to be especially important in the case of American and British exports of manufactures in the interwar and postwar periods.

is an error term reflecting other minor influences, which is assumed to be uncorrelated with the explanatory variables.[16] In the linear form the income and price elasticities of import demand will depend on the levels of these variables,[17] while in the log-linear form the income and price elasticities will be measured by the constants b_1 and c_1, which are read directly from the regression result.

There are unfortunately no clear-cut criteria that can be relied on in choosing a functional form. The researcher is more or less left to select a functional form according to his own theoretical leanings with the hope that his choice does not adversely affect his result. Some comments on the linear and log-linear forms may nevertheless be in order. One drawback of the linear form is that the price elasticity will diminish as income grows. Under such circumstances the log-linear form, which constrains the elasticities to be constant, might be preferred.[18] A characteristic of the linear and log-linear forms worth noting is that they both presume the basic demand relationship to be linear. Thus, consider Figure 2.2, in which the true underlying demand schedule *DD* is curvilinear. Assuming income effects already to have been removed, a linear or log-linear relation fitted to the data points on price and quantity would produce a demand schedule like *EE*. Statistical tests might indicate a poor fit and possibly a regression coefficient on price that was not statistically significant. The use of the linear or log-linear form might therefore be looked on as testing the significance of a particular functional form rather than the significance of the particular explanatory variable.[19]

[16] It will be noted below that if this assumption is violated, the least squares estimates of b and c will be biased.

[17] This is the same thing as saying that the price elasticity of demand will vary along a straight-line demand schedule. When the linear form is used, the relevant elasticities are often computed at the point of the sample means.

[18] From time to time some investigators have used an inverted price term (p_Y/p_M) instead of the usual one (p_M/p_Y). The coefficients and elasticities reported are therefore positive in such cases rather than negative as we generally think of them. This need not create confusion, however, since the elasticity with respect to the inverted price term is simply the negative of the usual elasticity. This can be seen as follows by considering the demand function $q = f(p)$. Letting $p^* = p^{-1}$ we would like to calculate the following demand elasticities

$$\eta = \frac{dq}{dp} \cdot \frac{p}{q} \quad \text{(usual elasticity)}$$

$$\eta^* = \frac{dq}{dp^*} \cdot \frac{p^*}{q} \quad \text{(inverted elasticity)}$$

We can write $\eta = f'p/q$, where $f' = dq/dp$. Note also that $q = f(p) = f[g(p^*)]$, where $g(p^*) = 1/p^*$. Then we can write

$$\eta^* = f'\left(-\frac{1}{p^{*2}}\right)\frac{p^*}{q} = \frac{-f'}{p^*q} = -\frac{dq}{dp} \cdot \frac{p}{q} = -\eta$$

[19] The problem of functional form is common to all econometric research and has unfortunately not been handled adequately, perhaps because it has not been thought to

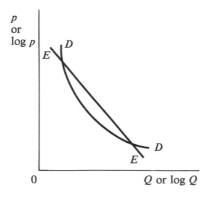

FIGURE 2.2

Linear Regression Fit to Curvilinear
Demand Schedule

TIME DIMENSION

The time dimension poses quite serious problems generally in economic analysis. The econometric analysis of demand is no exception. We can begin our discussion by recalling the well-known distinction between short-run and long-run elasticities of demand. That is, whenever a demand schedule is drawn in theory, it refers to some specified period of time. In the very short run when habits are persistent, the demand schedule will be completely inelastic with respect to changes in price. The more time we permit for adjustment to price changes, the more elastic the demand schedule will be. What time period should we have in mind therefore in demand analysis?

---

be very important. Thus, for example, even the comparatively simple problem of choosing between the linear and log-linear forms is often decided in an ad hoc manner. The only statistically proper method currently available to make this selection is presented by Zarembka [79]. This approach however discards the niceties of least squares.

In practice, once a particular form is chosen, the investigator is often content to explore the residuals from the estimating equation for regularities that would suggest other forms. If ambiguity is revealed in the choice of function, it is often not considered important. This is surely ascientific in character.

It might be desirable therefore to introduce special variables into the function that are designed to reflect curvilinearity in the relationship. Some suggestions in this regard are given in the appendix to this chapter.

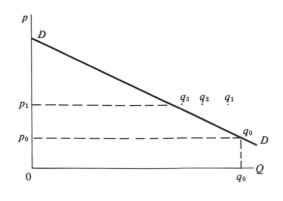

FIGURE 2.3

Adjustment of Quantity to a Change in Price

Suppose that point q_0 at price p_0 in Figure 2.3 lies on the long-run demand schedule DD, which indicates the level of demand after complete adjustment has occurred. If the price now rises from p_0 to p_1, we could imagine a sequence of decisions affecting quantity such as q_1, q_2, and q_3, where the subscripts indicate the appropriate time period. It would appear that short-run elasticities can be calculated for each of three periods of varying length. We would expect these elasticities to increase as the length of period was increased.

Let us now consider Figure 2.4, in which two successive price changes

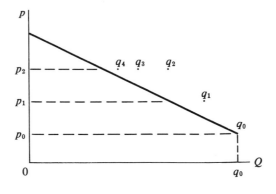

FIGURE 2.4

Adjustment of Quantity to Successive Price Changes

occur from p_0 to p_1 to p_2. What is noteworthy now is that the adjustment indicated by q_2–q_3–q_4 results from the first price change as well as the second. The q_1–q_2 adjustment appears for this reason to involve a larger elasticity than the q_0–q_1 adjustment. The point we are trying to illustrate is that the adjustment of quantity depends on the past history of price changes and the sequence of price changes within the relevant period as well as the total price change within the period. The concept of short-run elasticity is not meaningful in this context unless we can assume that the initial period's price–quantity point falls on the underlying long-run demand schedule and that the relevant price changes occur totally before any adjustment begins to take place.

Should the assumptions just mentioned be invalid, we may conclude that the concept of short-run elasticity is misleading and, regardless of the assumptions made, unnecessary. It is misleading in the sense that it implies the existence of several demand schedules that differ by the amount of time allowed for quantity to adjust, when in actuality there is only a single long-run demand schedule.[20] The concept is unnecessary insofar as the long-run demand schedule and the associated adjustment process fully describe the system.

The central question that concerns us here is the effect the time pattern of adjustment of quantity to changes in price has on the statistical estimating procedures. Thus, suppose our estimating equation is

$$M_t = f\left[\left(\frac{Y}{p_Y}\right)_t, \left(\frac{p_M}{p_Y}\right)_t, \cdots\right] \tag{2.13}$$

[20] There is one sense, however, in which time should be associated with a demand schedule. The term long-run demand schedule has been used to indicate the quantity demanded that would occur if a price change persisted indefinitely and allowance was made for complete adjustment. The quantity demanded in this equilibrium situation is a flow that will clearly depend on the length of the time period. That is, if we double the time period, we will double the quantity demanded and therefore move the long-run demand schedule proportionately to the right. This will not affect the elasticity, however. To illustrate this, let us compute the elasticity as a function of time

$$\frac{q}{t} - D(p)$$

or

$$q = tD(p)$$

where q refers to quantity, t to time, and p to price. Differentiating the foregoing expression, we have

$$\frac{dq}{dp} = tD'(p)$$

which in elasticity form is

$$\frac{dq/q}{dp/p} = \frac{pD'(p)}{D(p)}$$

which is independent of time t. Thus at any level of p, the greater slope just cancels the increased quantity, thereby maintaining the same elasticity. This conclusion is of course not startling when we recall that an elasticity is a dimensionless measure.

where each period's quantity of imports depends on the levels of the explanatory variables in the same period. Assume an adjustment process such that any period's quantity purchased is midway between the quantity in the last period and the quantity indicated by the long-run demand schedule. This is the situation in Figure 2.5, which depicts a price change from p_0 to p_1 that persists indefinitely. The dots in Figure 2.5 indicate the price–quantity points

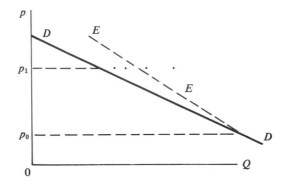

FIGURE 2.5

Linear Regression Fit to Quantities Adjusted
to a Change in Price

for each period and the dashed line EE represents the regression estimate fitted to these points. This regression line conveys little or no information about the underlying demand schedule or the process of adjustment, since it is an unknown mixture of these two things.[21]

We must endeavor in the light of the foregoing discussion to grapple explicitly with the process of adjustment. The proper approach will depend on the length of the data period. While time lags may be unimportant when annual data are used, this will not be the case when quarterly or monthly data are used. Our discussion will thus presume data periods of relatively short length. The most straightforward procedure in dealing with the adjustment process is to add lagged explanatory variables

$$M_t = \gamma + \sum_{i=0}^{n} \alpha_i \left(\frac{Y}{p_Y}\right)_{t-i} + \sum_{i=0}^{n} \beta_i \left(\frac{p_M}{p_Y}\right)_{t-i} \qquad (2.14)$$

[21] We would also get a lower elasticity estimate if we assumed p_0 to move to p_1 in a series of steps and that quantity adjusted by half the distance between last period's quantity and the quantity measured along the true long-run demand schedule DD.

In this formulation, an income change at time t induces a quantity change of $\alpha_i \Delta Y/p_Y$ in time period $(t+i)$. If the income change is maintained, the total or long-run effect is $(\Sigma\alpha_i)\Delta Y/p_Y$. Implicitly we have assumed, and shall continue to assume, that the nature of the response lag is fixed. Other than for this assumption, Equation (2.14) is completely general.

Unfortunately, Equation (2.14) meets with two rather severe difficulties. The economic researcher typically has a scarcity of observations and an equation such as (2.14) requires many observations because of the number of explanatory variables. More important, there is almost surely substantial collinearity among the various lagged explanatory variables. The result of such "multicollinearity" is well known: large standard errors on the coefficients.

Some investigators have approached this problem by including lagged values until they assumed the incorrect sign or had statistically insignificant coefficients. Such a procedure is improper, however, for it is sure to exclude lagged values that should properly be included, to overestimate the coefficients on the more recent terms, and furthermore to yield misleading statistical tests. Alternatively, it might be observed that if we are interested in the long-run response and not the distribution of the response over time, then large standard errors on individual coefficients are unimportant. We should be interested instead in standard errors on $\Sigma\hat{\alpha}_i$ and $\Sigma\hat{\beta}_i$ which would generally be smaller because of the negative covariances between the individual estimators associated with the multicollinearity of the lagged variables.

The two procedures just mentioned represent attempts to work within the framework of Equation (2.14). However, given the generality involved in that equation, it can be argued that it does not adequately represent our theoretical knowledge of the lag structure. Rather, if we restrict the values which the α_i and β_i can assume, smaller standard errors will be obtained. The simplest procedure in this regard is to replace the terms in (2.14) with weighted averages such as

$$\alpha_0 \left(\frac{Y}{p_Y}\right)_t + \alpha_1 \left(\frac{Y}{p_Y}\right)_{t-1} + \alpha_2 \frac{(Y/p_Y)_{t-2} + \cdots + (Y/p_Y)_{t-5}}{4}$$

This embodies the idea that most of the response occurs in the first two periods, with the remainder being so small that the last four periods can be treated identically.

A currently very popular procedure is to describe the demand phenomenon in "stock-adjustment" terms.[22] Thus, the long-run demand is

$$M_t^* = a + b\left(\frac{Y}{p_Y}\right)_t + c\left(\frac{p_M}{p_Y}\right)_t + \epsilon_t \qquad (2.15)$$

[22] See Nerlove [52] for further discussion.

The current demand adjusts only δ 100% to the long-run level, with $0 \leq \delta \leq 1$:

$$M_t = M_{t-1} + \delta(M_t^* - M_{t-1})$$
$$= \delta M_t^* + (1 - \delta)M_{t-1} \qquad (2.16)$$

Substituting (2.15) into (2.16) we have

$$M_t = \delta a + \delta b \left(\frac{Y}{p_Y}\right)_t + \delta c \left(\frac{p_M}{p_Y}\right)_t + (1 - \delta)M_{t-1} + \delta\epsilon_t \qquad (2.17)$$

The constant δ is to be interpreted as a coefficient of adjustment and should fall between zero and one. If δ is equal or close to zero, the adjustment process is very slow as is evident from Equation (2.16). Rapid adjustment is associated with values of δ close to one.

When Equation (2.17) is used as a regression, the long-run coefficients a, b, and c are easily calculated by dividing the regression coefficient by one minus the coefficient of M_{t-1}. As argued earlier, the results are most meaningfully reported in terms of the long-run coefficients and δ, the coefficient of adjustment. Some researchers, such as Rhomberg and Boissonneault [64], report the unadjusted or impact elasticities on the grounds that the assumptions underlying Equation (2.16) are untested. However, it should be noted that if these assumptions are improper, the impact as well as the long-run elasticities will be incorrectly estimated.

Equation (2.17) can be derived in still another way that is illuminating. Suppose

$$M_t = \sum_{i=0}^{\infty} \gamma_i f\left[\left(\frac{Y}{p_Y}\right)_{t-i}, \left(\frac{p_M}{p_Y}\right)_{t-i}\right] + \epsilon_t \qquad (2.18)$$

with the long-run demand

$$M_t^* = (\Sigma\gamma_i)f\left[\left(\frac{Y}{p_Y}\right), \left(\frac{p_M}{p_Y}\right)\right]$$

and an adjustment γ_i in the $(t+i)$th period.

Assume the γ_i to decline geometrically

$$\gamma_{i+n} = (1 - \delta)^n \gamma_i \qquad (2.19)$$

Thus

$$(1 - \delta)M_{t-1} = \sum_{i=0}^{\infty} (1 - \delta)\gamma_i f\left[\left(\frac{Y}{p_Y}\right)_{t-i-1}, \left(\frac{p_M}{p_Y}\right)_{t-i-1}\right] + (1 - \delta)\epsilon_{t-1}$$

$$= \sum_{i=0}^{\infty} \gamma_{i+1} f\left[\left(\frac{Y}{p_Y}\right)_{t-i-1}, \left(\frac{p_M}{p_Y}\right)_{t-i-1}\right] + (1 - \delta)\epsilon_{t-1} \qquad (2.20)$$

$$= \sum_{i=1}^{\infty} \gamma_i f\left[\left(\frac{Y}{p_Y}\right)_{t-i}, \left(\frac{p_M}{p_Y}\right)_{t-i}\right] + (1 - \delta)\epsilon_{t-1}$$

$$= M_t - \gamma_0 f\left[\left(\frac{Y}{p_Y}\right)_t, \left(\frac{p_M}{p_Y}\right)_t\right] - \epsilon_t + (1 - \delta)\epsilon_{t-1}$$

and

$$M_t = \gamma_0 f\left[\left(\frac{Y}{p_Y}\right)_t, \left(\frac{p_M}{p_Y}\right)_t\right] + (1 - \delta)M_{t-1} + \epsilon_t - (1 - \delta)\epsilon_{t-1} \quad (2.21)$$

which except for the error term is the same as Equation (2.17).

This derivation illustrates three points. Evidently from Equation (2.18) the nature of the adjustment lag is the same for both variables. This is a disturbing assumption for it may well be that adjustment to income changes will be more rapid than adjustment to price changes. Thus, for example, information concerning price changes is disseminated relatively slowly and the alteration of buying habits may be quite slow. In contrast, the awareness of an income change must occur at receipt and adjustment to new income levels may be rapid, perhaps even anticipatory.

The second observation is that the adjustment has been assumed to decay in a geometric fashion given by Equation (2.19). This is a very restrictive form, which is open to criticism. It seems reasonable that adjustment to a price change would build up slowly rather than decay. A price change is probably met at first by a refusal to alter buying habits on the grounds that the price change may be transitory. Only after the permanence of the change has been accepted will adjustment begin. When the perfect substitutability description of demand is used and import demand is the difference between home demand and home supply, adjustment to price changes will occur partly on the supply side, which will require the transfer of resources between sectors of the economy. Geometric decay is most unlikely to be an adequate description of such a supply response.

Finally, we should notice the difference in the error terms in Equations (2.17) and (2.21). The error $\delta\epsilon_t$ in (2.17) has all the classical properties except that it is correlated with succeeding values of the explanatory variable M_{t-1}: M_t, M_{t+1}, ... This will cause bias in the estimates, although the desirable properties of unbiasedness and minimum variance are preserved for large samples. Somewhat worse is that the error $\epsilon_t - (1 - \delta)\epsilon_{t-1}$ in Equation (2.21) is correlated with earlier error terms, with later values of the explanatory variable M_{t-1}, and with the explanatory variable M_{t-1} as well. In such a situation, the estimators will not retain even their large sample properties. More complicated estimating procedures have been suggested to deal with this situation, as in Johnston [29, pp. 211–12]. The question as to whether the stock-adjustment or the geometrically decaying lag description is preferable is best left open. It should be emphasized, however, that the use of lagged dependent variables as explanatory variables is an extremely tricky business that requires knowledgeable exploitation in order to be effective.

After the discussion of the question of lags in terms of stock adjustment and geometric decay, it may be useful to consider the somewhat more general approaches attributable to Jorgenson [31] and Almon [3]. According to

Jorgenson, if we include lagged values of the explanatory variables and additional lagged values of the dependent variables, we can produce a very general lagged response. Thus, for example

$$M_t = a + b_0\left(\frac{Y}{p_Y}\right)_t + b_1\left(\frac{Y}{p_Y}\right)_{t-1} + c_0\left(\frac{p_M}{p_Y}\right)_t + c_1\left(\frac{p_M}{p_Y}\right)_{t-1} + \delta M_{t-1} \quad (2.22)$$

allows the current coefficients to be completely free, while all lagged responses form a geometrically declining series governed by the adjustment coefficient δ. Clearly both the multicollinearity and the degrees-of-freedom pinch have been mitigated. Unfortunately, the problems concerning the error term and the associated statistical properties of the estimators discussed above still apply.

The procedure suggested by Almon [3] is to observe that the perfectly general form

$$M_t = \gamma + \sum_{i=0} \alpha_i\left(\frac{Y}{p_Y}\right)_{t-i} + \sum_{i=0} \beta_i\left(\frac{p_M}{p_Y}\right)_{t-i} \quad (2.23)$$

allows the coefficients an amount of freedom that is quite unjustified. For instance the α_i can assume a sawtooth of values as in Figure 2.6. But if this

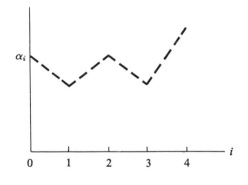

FIGURE 2.6

Unacceptable Configuration of α_i

is not believed to be possible, we ought to restrict the values of α_i. If we use this extra information, we will improve our estimates of the α_i's.

Suppose, for instance, that we expect the α_i to look something like Figure 2.7. We observe that such a configuration may be well approximated by a quadratic form: [23]

$$\alpha_i = a + bi + ci^2 \quad (2.24)$$

[23] This derivation of the Almon technique is based on remarks made by D. B. Suits.

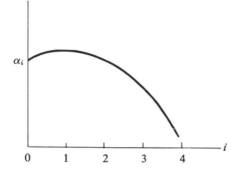

FIGURE 2.7

Alternative Configuration of α_i

We observe further that assumption (2.24) is not particularly restrictive. All it says is that α_i must be relatively close to α_{i-1} and α_{i+1}, and that if there is a hump (or a trough, for that matter) in the distribution of the α_i, it is the only one. Also, the response after five periods is negligible.

We can now use assumption (2.24) to express Equation (2.25)

$$\sum_{i=0}^{4} \alpha_i \left(\frac{Y}{p_Y}\right)_{t-i} = a\left(\frac{Y}{p_Y}\right)_t + (a+b+c)\left(\frac{Y}{p_Y}\right)_{t-1}$$

$$+ (a+2b+4c)\left(\frac{Y}{p_Y}\right)_{t-2} + \cdots$$

$$+ (a+4b+16c)\left(\frac{Y}{p_Y}\right)_{t-4} \tag{2.25}$$

$$= a\left[\sum_{i=0}^{4}\left(\frac{Y}{p_Y}\right)_{t-i}\right] + b\left[\sum_{i=0}^{4} i\left(\frac{Y}{p_Y}\right)_{t-i}\right]$$

$$+ c\left[\sum_{i=0}^{4} i^2\left(\frac{Y}{p_Y}\right)_{t-i}\right]$$

We see, therefore, that by using a very plausible assumption we have reduced the number of explanatory variables from $n+1$ to three. The number of variables can be further reduced by adding other assumptions such as $\alpha_4 = 0$. Alternatively, a larger number of variables will be required if a higher-degree polynomial for α_i is used. Precisely the same procedure can, of course, be used for the β_i.

In theory this Almon technique is the most promising method for attacking the problem of lagged responses. The researcher is free to choose from a wide variety of polynomials to restrict the α_i. Even when such an assumption is made, the distribution of the α_i is usually quite free. Finally, the error term remains agreeable to ordinary least squares. However, experimentation with the Almon technique is required before its efficacy can be established in the kinds of analysis we have been discussing.

One final approach worth mentioning is to express the variables in terms of first differences

$$\Delta M = f\left[\Delta\left(\frac{Y}{p_Y}\right), \Delta\left(\frac{p_M}{p_Y}\right)\right] \qquad (2.26)$$

where

$$\Delta M = M_t - M_{t-1}, \Delta\left(\frac{Y}{p_Y}\right) = \left(\frac{Y}{p_Y}\right)_t - \left(\frac{Y}{p_Y}\right)_{t-1}, \cdots$$

The use of first differences is often recommended when it is desired to reduce the effects of serial correlation.[24] First differences do not constitute a solution to the adjustment problem, however, since no allowance is made for the adjustment of quantity in relation to the changes that have occurred historically in income and prices. The first-difference equation form is consequently no different from the naive form in which no explicit allowance is made for the process of adjustment.

In our earlier discussion of the choice of explanatory variables, extensive familiarization with the details of the relationships under study was urged in order that a judicious selection of explanatory variables could be made. The same point applies to the selection of adjustment processes.

SPECIAL PROBLEMS IN ESTIMATION

There appeared during the 1940's a number of studies in which statistical estimates, using ordinary least squares regression methods, were made of the income and price elasticities of demand for the imports and exports of individual countries during the interwar period.[25] The price elasticities in particular were estimated to be substantially less than unity. This suggested in the context of exchange-rate adjustment that a devaluation would tend to worsen rather than improve the trade balance because the sum of the elasticities of demand for an individual country's imports and exports might together

---

[24] If such effects are believed to be serious, it may be desirable to employ some type of adjustment scheme. Some success with the first-order Cochran–Orcutt iterative technique is reported by Houthakker and Magee [27].

[25] See Cheng [8] for a description of these studies.

add up to less than unity.[26] This "elasticity pessimism" suggested that measures other than changes in relative prices might have to be relied upon for purposes of adjusting the balance of trade.

In a pathbreaking article published in 1950, Orcutt [53] sought to demonstrate that the statistical results obtained in the aforementioned studies were subject to very serious reservations because the method and data employed tended to bias the calculated price elasticities towards zero. He gave five reasons why this might be the case:

(1) Lack of independence between relative prices and the random deviation in the import-demand function.

(2) The data may reflect errors of observation.

(3) The use of data aggregates may give undue weight to goods with relatively low elasticities.

(4) Short-run elasticities were measured and these are typically lower than long-run elasticities.

(5) Devaluation elasticities were larger than the estimated short-period elasticities, which reflect adjustment to small price changes.

It is worthwhile to discuss each of these points in turn. In doing so, we shall find it convenient to use the linear form of the regression equation for import demand noted earlier in Equation (2.10):[27]

$$M = a + b\left(\frac{Y}{p_Y}\right) + c\left(\frac{p_M}{p_Y}\right) + u$$

where M is the quantity of imports, Y/p_Y is real income, p_M/p_Y is the relative price of imports, and u is a random deviation associated perhaps with variables that have been inadvertently excluded. According to the theory underlying ordinary least squares regression, the estimate of the relative price coefficient c will be unbiased only if the random deviation u is independent of p_M/p_Y.

Since income and relative prices tend to move together, the estimate of the price coefficient c will be biased if real income is excluded from the relationship. In this case the random disturbance includes the excluded income term and would necessarily be correlated with the only explanatory variable, relative prices. The problem is not solved, however, by including both real income and relative prices in the relationship because the relative price variable and the random variable u may continue to move together rather than independently. This can be seen with the aid of Figure 2.8.

Thus suppose that we have a demand DD and supply schedule SS as in Figure 2.8, in which the quantities indicated are net of what can be explained

---

[26] That is, if we assume infinite supply elasticities, the Marshall–Lerner condition that is necessary for a devaluation to improve the trade balance would not be satisfied.

[27] The remarks to be made apply equally to the log-linear form or any other function employed.

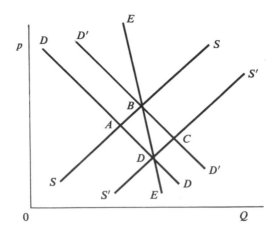

FIGURE 2.8

Downward Bias in the Estimated
Price Coefficient †

† Adapted from G. H. Orcutt, "Measurement of Price Elasticities in International Trade," *Review of Economics and Statistics*, XXXII (May 1950), 123.

linearly by variations in income. Now if we assume that there is a random disturbance that results in a shift of the demand schedule up to the right to $D'D'$, there will be an increase in price with SS unchanged. What this means therefore is that high values of the random variable u are associated with high values of price. This violates the requirement that u be independent of p_M/p_Y, with the result that the estimate of the price coefficient c will be between the true negative elasticity of demand and the positive elasticity of supply.[28]

The bias in the estimate can be illustrated by supposing that there are random disturbances that cause the demand schedule to shift up and down between DD and $D'D'$, and similarly that there are random disturbances that cause the supply schedule to shift up and down between SS and $S'S'$. This will yield the parallelogram $ABCD$, within which the data points for prices and quantities will be confined. If we were now to fit a regression line through these points that would minimize the deviations in a horizontal direction with respect to the dependent variable, quantity demanded, we would get a line such as EE. It will be evident that the elasticity calculated from EE will be underestimated in comparison to the true elasticity on the underlying demand schedule.

[28] For a rigorous demonstration of the downward bias in the price as well as in the income coefficients, see Orcutt [53].

A bit of experimenting with Figure 2.8 will show that if the shifts of the demand schedule were large relative to those of the supply schedule, the regression line fitted would have a positive slope approximating that of the supply schedule. By the same token, if the shifts of the supply schedule were large relative to those of the demand schedule, a regression line closer to the demand schedule would be obtained. In either case the estimate of the price coefficient c would be less than the true one. If, however, the elasticity of supply can be taken as infinite, the estimated and true coefficients will coincide. This situation is depicted in Figure 2.9.

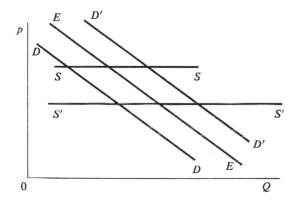

FIGURE 2.9

Unbiased Estimate of Price Coefficient

This discussion suggests that the use of ordinary least squares regression may be appropriate when the shifts in the supply schedule are large relative to those of the demand schedule, and/or when the supply schedule is highly elastic. In employing ordinary least squares, care should be taken therefore of the particular economic conditions affecting the relationship. Thus, in the case of a small country that imports only a relatively small fraction of total world exports, it may be quite realistic to assume an infinitely elastic supply schedule. In contrast, a country like the United States may face a rising supply schedule because of its relatively large size.[29]

[29] An obvious way to deal with the problem of biased estimates is to use simultaneous equation estimating techniques. The problem here, however, is that we have very little knowledge of supply relations. The little experimentation that has been done along these lines—see especially Morgan and Corlett [49]—has not been particularly successful. Alternatively, one can seek to approximate the shifts in the schedules as Harberger [24] has done, although it is by no means clear that this can be accomplished in a nonarbitrary manner.

Orcutt's second point was that when the data contain errors of measurement due to misclassification, falsification, and faulty methods of index-number construction, the effect may be to bias the coefficients toward zero. This point is illustrated in Figures 2.10 and 2.11, in which the underlying demand DD has no error term associated with it. We may contrast Figure 2.10,

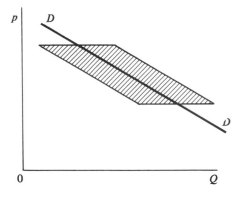

FIGURE 2.10

Errors of Observation in Quantity †

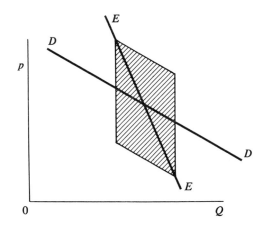

FIGURE 2.11

Errors of Observation in Price ‡

† Adapted from G. H. Orcutt, "Measurement of Price Elasticities in International Trade," *Review of Economics and Statistics*, XXXII (May 1950), 124.
‡ Adapted from G. H. Orcutt, "Measurement of Price Elasticities in International Trade," *Review of Economics and Statistics*, XXXII (May 1950), 124.

in which it is assumed that there are errors of observation in quantity and not in price, with Figure 2.11, in which the errors are in price but not in quantity. In Figure 2.10 the true demand schedule would be measured by the regression line. This would not be the case, however, with Figure 2.11, in which the regression line implies a lower elasticity than the true underlying demand schedule. Observation errors in the explanatory variables are thus seen to produce biased estimates. The importance of this point is essentially an empirical question and is therefore hard to assess. Moreover, we have implicitly assumed a certain relationship between the observation error and the true value. Other assumptions about this relationship will lead to other conclusions.[30]

In his third point Orcutt argued that goods with relatively low elasticities may exhibit the greatest price variation and will therefore exert a predominant effect on the aggregative price indexes. The use of such aggregative indexes may thus understate the true elasticity to the extent that goods with lower elasticities are given undue weight.[31] It would thus appear on these grounds that a strong argument can be made against using aggregative

---

[30] Suppose that the true description of demand is

$$Q = \alpha + \beta p + \epsilon$$

where ϵ is the usual error. Suppose further that we do not observe p but rather Π, which is p plus an independent error term u

$$\Pi = p + u$$

A regression of Q on Π

$$Q = \alpha + \beta\Pi + (\epsilon - \beta u)$$

will yield a biased estimate of β because of the correlation of the independent variable Π and the error term $(\epsilon - \beta u)$. This is clear, since Π is the sum of the true value p plus an error u, and must be correlated with that error u.

If, on the other hand, the measurement error is independent of the observed value we can write

$$p = \Pi + u$$

to express the fact that the observed value Π and the measurement error u are independently generated and add to p, the true value. A regression of Q on Π in this case

$$Q = \alpha + \beta\Pi + (\epsilon + \beta u)$$

will yield an unbiased estimate of β, since Π and $(\epsilon + \beta u)$ are independent.

Observation error is typically described by the first model and is therefore associated with biased coefficients. Although the second model casts some doubt on such statements, it does not seem to make much sense. In Prais's [58, p. 576] words, however, ". . . it is not easy to know which of these hypotheses is closer to the truth, but the case for supposing a downward bias to be inevitable is clearly not as strong as at one time thought." Johnston [29, Chap. 6] provides an extensive discussion of the treatment of errors in variables.

[31] This point is demonstrated in the appendix to this chapter, in which we indicate that the price indexes should be reweighted proportionally to the individual demand elasticities.

indexes. This may be reinforced more generally by the fact that a price index, being a weighted average, tends to show less variation than any of its components insofar as price increases are offset against price declines. As a consequence, there will tend to be an increase in the estimated standard error. An aggregative price index is likely, moreover, to be highly correlated with income.

The foregoing points suggest that disaggregation may be desirable, although whether or not the results will be improved significantly is an empirical question. What little evidence is available—see Ball and Marwah [4], DaCosta [10], and Dutta [13]—indicates that the returns to the use of fine subcategories of data may be limited.

Orcutt's fourth point related to the fact that what was calculated in most studies was a short-run elasticity that would be expected to be lower than the long-run elasticity. We shall not dwell on this point here since it was already argued in the preceding section dealing with the time dimension that the concept of the short-run elasticity is not particularly meaningful, and, further, that ignoring the time dimension in the analysis would bias downward the estimate of the long-run price elasticity.

Orcutt's final point was that the price elasticity of demand for large price changes will generally be higher than for small price changes. His reasons were that it takes time for habits to adjust and that the price changes must be large enough to overcome the costs of switching. This point is in direct opposition either to our assumption of a long-run demand function that depends only on current prices and not on the history of prices, or to our assumption that the nature of the response lag is fixed independent of the type of price movement that is occurring. Since in our judgment the assumption of an underlying long-run demand relationship seems absolutely basic, we assume Orcutt's point is really that adjustment to large price changes is more rapid than adjustment to small changes. This will be especially true in the case of a devaluation when the price changes are clearly going to be permanent and there will be no adjustment delay in anticipation of a reversal of the price change. However, if this is the case, we will underestimate the speed of adjustment but not the total adjustment. The long-run elasticity will be properly estimated.

The upshot of Orcutt's five points was to cast grave doubts on the usefulness of least squares procedures for the time-series analysis of demand. It led Neisser [51, p. 130], for example, to declare in 1958 that: "The traditional multiple regression analysis of time series . . . is dead." This conclusion was overly pessimistic, however, since Orcutt's reservations about least squares procedure are not quite as devastating as they may appear. That is, there may be many cases in which this procedure is reasonably applicable. This will be true when countries are relatively small and also when demand is relatively stable. It is also possible to use data specifications that will avoid lumping together commodities with widely varying elasticities. Explicit allowance can be made, moreover, for lags in the adjustment process. Finally, it may well be that the interwar period had special characteristics that made for unreliable statistical results. The postwar period has in contrast been much more stable, with the result that the effects of changes in income and prices may be more readily isolated. These conclusions seem to be borne out, it may be noted, in a number of studies using postwar data. Typical results from two of these studies are given in confidence-interval form in Figure 2.12.[32]

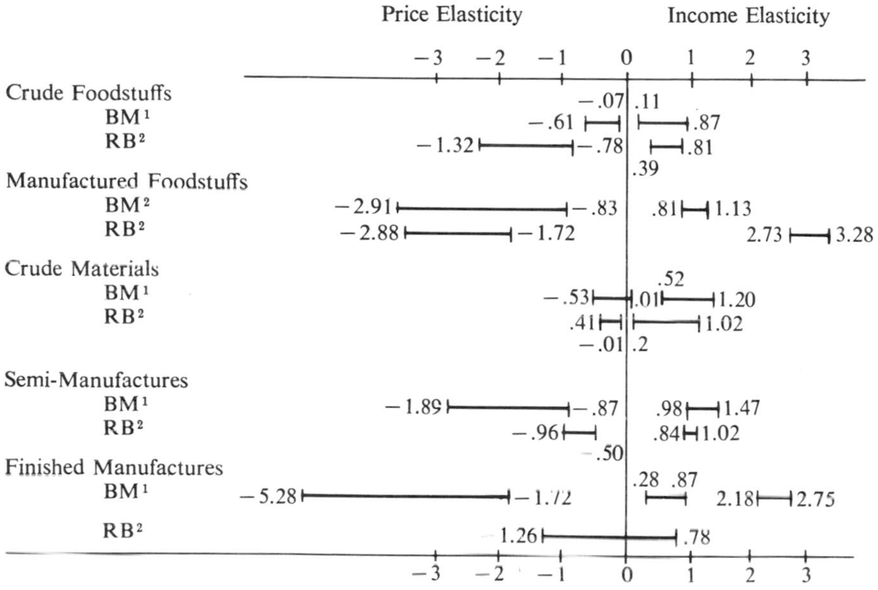

FIGURE 2.12

Confidence Intervals for Income and Price
Elasticities for U.S. Import Demand †

[1] BM refers to Ball and Marwah [4].
[2] RB refers to Rhomberg and Boissonneault [64].
† Based on Harley [25, p. 19]; original data from R. J. Ball and K. Marwah, "The U. S. Demand for Imports, 1948–1958," *Review of Economics and Statistics*, XLIV (November 1962), and from R. R. Rhomberg and L. Boissonneault, "The Foreign Sector," in J. S. Duesenberry et al., eds., *The Brookings Quarterly Econometric Model of the United States*. Chicago: Rand McNally & Company, 1965.

[32] The evident differences in results noted may be due largely to differences in the time periods and data classifications employed in the two studies cited. Results for fifteen major industrialized countries and twelve developing countries for 1951–66 are to be found in Houthakker and Magee [27]. Alternative formats for presentation of data are treated in the next section, which deals with the reporting of results.

In closing, two additional matters deserve comment. These concern the presence of multicollinearity in the explanatory variables and the types of statistical tests performed in conjunction with least squares regression. When two explanatory variables are statistically correlated, least squares regression divides the explanatory power between them and both may take on relatively large standard errors. When one variable is removed from the regression, the other will gain in significance but the coefficient becomes biased. A situation of this kind is due largely to data inadequacy, and it is very difficult to overcome since explanatory variables respond jointly to similar underlying forces, as for example when income and prices tend to move together over time. Multicollinearity thus will plague most time-series analysis of demand relations and there is often not much that can be done to cope with it. One possibility worth mentioning, however, is to employ extraneous estimates—see Kaliski [33]—which amounts to fixing a particular coefficient at a level determined by exterior knowledge, obtained perhaps from a cross-section estimate.

Finally, some caution appears necessary in placing excessive faith in the statistical tests employed in least squares regression. It is of course quite important to attach levels of confidence to any estimates that are made, provided that the assumptions upon which the tests are predicated are reasonably good approximations.[33] But it should be noted that the final results in any study often represent the best of many experiments that are all based upon the same data. This means that out of the many experiments that may have been done, some of the significant results may only be random. This might be taken into account when specifying the width of confidence intervals.

REPORTING RESULTS

Two points that have been mentioned just briefly are worthy of additional comment. These involve the reporting of experimentation and the use of significance tests.

It is altogether too common for researchers to report only their best results without indicating the trial-and-error process by which they were obtained. It is statistically improper in principle to experiment freely, select the best fit, and report confidence intervals and/or significance tests. When none of the experimentation is reported, it becomes very difficult to assess the quality of the research effort in terms of its approach to the many important

---

[33] For example, standard errors will not be reliable when there is serial correlation in the residuals of the regression.

methodological issues we have discussed earlier. It is also the case that one researcher's experimental failures are of considerable importance in the design of future research by others.

As far as significance tests are concerned, the economist's general obsession with them leads one to the belief that often sight has been lost of just exactly what significance means. A thorough discussion of this subject is well outside the scope of the present undertaking, but it is hoped that the brief discussion below will serve to clarify the issues involved.

We will first consider the question of inference within the classical statistical framework. When, for example, a price elasticity is reported to be statistically significant at the 95 percent level, the following statement is being made: "A procedure has been followed such that if the true value of the price elasticity were zero, 95 percent of the time we would say the value is not significantly different from zero, while the other 5 percent of the time we would say that it *is* significantly different from zero, that is, we would be making a mistake." This is all that is being asserted. For instance, the statement says nothing about the situation when the price elasticity is different from zero. Nor does it allow us to accept any useful hypothesis; thus a rejection of the value zero does not imply acceptance of some value different from zero, nor does failure to reject zero imply acceptance of zero.

The obvious weakness in significance tests has led enlightened researchers to report confidence intervals. They have argued that there are really two distinct reasons why an estimate is deemed not significant. In the one case, standard errors are small but the point estimate is near zero. In the other case, standard errors are large and the point estimate may be anywhere. The general feeling is that in the first case the value of the elasticity is truly near zero while in the second case its value is unknown. This same idea is sometimes expressed by pointing out that "not significant" does not mean "insignificant." In other words, "not significant" does not mean "near zero." On the contrary, "not significant" means that the data have been unable to answer the question that has been posed. This is not to say that the data can answer no questions. It is up to the researcher to ask other questions and thereby get "significant" answers. Confidence intervals are meant to contain all the answers the data will yield. It is well known that the set of points exterior to the confidence interval includes all those points that would be rejected by a significance test.

At this juncture we should ask just what a confidence interval means. The appropriate description is: "A procedure has been followed to generate a set of points that 95 percent of the time will include the true value of the elasticity." This should not be taken to mean that the true value is a member of the set of points; nor should we necessarily believe that it is. For instance, the interpretation that a short interval "nails down" the estimate is inappropriate in this setting. Such a statement requires that we turn the above statement around to "the probability that the true value lies in the interval is

0.95." To the classical statistician the probability that the true value lies in the interval is zero or one. In other words, the true value is a parameter and does not have a probability distribution.[34]

Economic researchers generally do not behave in this classical manner, as they are more than willing to bestow the reward of belief on their confidence intervals. This puts them, perhaps unknowingly, into the Bayesian school of inference. The Bayesian has a probability distribution of the true parameter and does make the statement that the probability is 0.95 that the true value lies in the confidence (credence, to him) interval. Perhaps, more important, he can make statements such as, "The probability that the price elasticity exceeds one is 0.85." This is the kind of information, for example, that is needed by the policymaker who must choose to devalue or not.

Quite apart from one's statistical school, the central issue in reporting results is how to convey the information contained in the study as completely and concisely as possible. Confidence intervals are clearly the proper vehicle. To expand on this let us consider five possible formats for reporting on a simplistic aggregate import function for the U.S.

The formats are listed in the increasing order of our preference. Thus Format 2 conveys much more information than Format 1. Although confidence intervals could be calculated from the information in Format 2, Format 3 saves the reader the trouble. The summary statistics of Format 2 can easily be added to 3, 4, and 5 if necessary. Format 4 is preferred to Format 3 only because it is more readable. Although Format 5 may be prohibitively space-consuming, it contains an additional but quite important bit of information. A high price elasticity can be traded for a low income elasticity because of the correlation between the two. This is evident from the slanted confidence area.[35]

---

[34] If this discussion is unconvincing, consider the following situation. Two researchers take independent samples from the same process. Each provides us with a confidence interval for the value of the price elasticity. We must choose between these two intervals and are told only that one is longer than the other. Which should we choose? If you prefer the shorter one, then you have improperly turned the confidence statement around. It is easy to show that the longer interval is more likely to fall over the true value than the shorter one (from independence of the position and length of the interval). Accordingly, one should be quite indifferent between the two intervals. The length of the interval in this example should not be associated with the quality of the information afforded by the interval.

[35] Goldberger [20, p. 175] shows that an α-confidence set for a subset of the coefficients, denoted by vector β_2, is given by

$$\frac{(b_2 - \beta_2)'D(b_2 - \beta_2)}{(K - H)s^2} \leq F_{T-K-1}^{K-H}(\alpha)$$

where T is the number of observations; K is the number of explanatory variables; H is the number of variables in β_2; b_2 is the estimated value of β_2; D is the inverse of the appropriate submatrix of $(X'X)^{-1}$; s^2 is the estimated standard error; and $F(\alpha)$ is the value of the Snedecor F distribution at level α.

FORMAT 1

Price Elasticity	−0.77*
Income Elasticity	1.27*

* Significant at the 95 percent level.

FORMAT 2

$$\log M = 15.2 - .77 \log \frac{p_M}{p_Y} + 1.27 \log \frac{Y}{p_Y}$$
$$(.13) \qquad\qquad (.08)$$

$$\text{d.w.} = .56 \qquad \sigma = .04 \qquad R^2 = .997$$

FORMAT 3

95% Confidence Intervals

	Lower Limit	Point Estimate	Upper Limit
Price Elasticity	−0.99	−0.77	−0.55
Income Elasticity	1.14	1.27	1.40

FORMAT 4

95% Confidence Intervals
Price Elasticity
Income Elasticity

FORMAT 5

95% Confidence Area

In the example in the text, β_2 has two components, D is a two-by-two matrix, and the formula above describes an ellipse centered at the estimates of the elasticities. The slope of the major axis of the ellipse is given by θ, where

$$\tan \theta = \frac{2d_{12}}{(d_{11} - d_{22}) - \sqrt{(d_{11} - d_{22})^2 + 4d_{12}^2}}$$

and d_{ij} are the elements of D. The denominator is necessarily negative; thus the slope of the major axis will be positive when d_{12} is negative, and the converse. In our example, d_{12} is simply the covariance between the price and income terms, and is negative. The slope of the confidence region is consequently positive. If the price and income terms are positively correlated, the confidence region would slope the other way.

There are two reasons why the confidence-region information is important. Low price elasticities are often attributed to the collinearity between the price and income terms. This statement is supported by the slope of the confidence region. Secondly, inferences and decisions such as a devaluation will involve the price elasticity and income elasticity jointly. Such a decision will be incorrectly made if it is based on the two intervals separately rather than on the confidence region. The 95 percent confidence region implied by the two intervals is a box bordered by the interval limits. This is evidently quite different from the true confidence ellipse in Format 5. If the researcher prefers one of the other formats, he should by all means report the covariance terms between the estimates. This will allow the reader to perform any sort of test he might desire.

CONCLUSION

In conclusion, we may briefly review the salient points of this chapter. From a theoretical point of view, import (export) demand should be distinguished according to (1) consumer demand and (2) producer demand. In addition, these may both be subdivided into durables and nondurables. Each of these categories represents a unique economic phenomenon that requires a unique set of explanatory variables. We may disaggregate further within each of these groups according to the nature of domestic substitutes, with a special treatment when there is an almost perfect substitute available domestically.

In addition to deciding on the level and nature of the disaggregation and the proper explanatory variables, the researcher will have to select a functional form and a method for handling response lags. The choice of functional form is largely arbitrary. Current thinking on response lags tends to favor the Almon approach.

Finally, the researcher must decide how best to convey the results of his efforts to the reader. We have argued that any and all experimentation should be reported, and that the statistical evidence is best summarized in confidence intervals and regions.

We have seen that a long list of indictments of the traditional least squares method drawn up by Orcutt caused considerable skepticism during the 1950's concerning the reliance on this method. Since then, however, reconsideration of Orcutt's points has suggested that they were not as damaging to the use of least squares procedures as was initially believed. Thus, used with proper care, these procedures may yield valid and meaningful measures of the income, relative price, and other influences on the demand for a country's imports (exports).

APPENDIX TO CHAPTER 2

INDEX NUMBERS AND THE PROBLEM OF AGGREGATION

The validity and relevance of all that has been discussed in Chapter 2 rest fundamentally on the existence of the macroeconomic relationship (2.4) describing the demand for a quantity of imports as a function of a price and an aggregate income term. We have mentioned in the text that the quantity and price variables are not raw observations but rather index numbers made necessary by the aggregation over commodities. In this appendix we will be interested in defining precisely the index numbers and discussing the effects of aggregation, with an aim toward understanding the occasions when aggregation should be avoided and the procedures by which its bad effects might be alleviated.

Index Numbers   The point of an index number is to reduce a large set of data describing a complex economic event into a single number that somehow captures the essential features of that event. Thus, for example, we would like to express a set of price observations p_{io} and p_{it}, $(i = 1, \ldots, n)$ in a single number or index, which is able to indicate whether prices have generally risen or fallen from year o to year t. An apparently good candidate for such a number is a weighted average of the price relatives

$$P_{to} = \sum_i w_i \frac{p_{it}}{p_{io}}, \qquad w_i \geq 0, \qquad \sum_i w_i - 1 \qquad (2.A.1)$$

The index P_{to} has the property that if all prices fall, remain the same, or rise, P_{to} will be less than, equal to, or greater than one. We might hope therefore that the index P_{to} captures the average movement of prices. We have not as yet selected the appropriate values of the weights and might do so by observing that for the ith commodity

$$\frac{V_{it}}{V_{io}} = \frac{p_{it}}{p_{io}} \times \frac{q_{it}}{q_{io}} \qquad (2.A.2)$$

That is, the increase in the value from year o to year t has been separated into the price change p_{it}/p_{io} and the quantity change q_{it}/q_{io}. The same thing can be done for the aggregates

$$V_{to} = \frac{V_t}{V_o} = \frac{\sum_i V_{it}}{\sum_i V_{io}} = \frac{\sum p_{it}q_{io}}{\sum p_{io}q_{io}} \times \frac{\sum p_{it}q_{it}}{\sum p_{it}q_{io}}$$

$$= \left(\sum w_{io}\frac{p_{it}}{p_{io}}\right) \times \left(\sum w_{it}\frac{q_{io}}{q_{it}}\right)^{-1}$$

(2.A.3)

where

$$w_{io} = \frac{p_{io}q_{io}}{\sum p_{io}q_{io}} \quad \text{and} \quad w_{it} = \frac{p_{it}q_{it}}{\sum p_{it}q_{it}}$$

The first term reflects the change in prices while the second reflects the change in quantities. The price term using base year weights is a Laspeyres price index and the quantity term using current year weights is a Paasche quantity index.

An alternative index scheme is

$$V_{to} = \frac{V_t}{V_o} = \frac{\sum_i V_{it}}{\sum_i V_{io}} = \frac{\sum p_{it}q_{it}}{\sum p_{io}q_{it}} \times \frac{\sum p_{io}q_{it}}{\sum p_{io}q_{io}}$$

$$= \left(\sum w_{it}\frac{p_{io}}{p_{it}}\right)^{-1} \times \left(\sum w_{io}\frac{q_{it}}{q_{io}}\right)$$

(2.A.4)

where the first term using current year weights is a Paasche price index and the second term using base year weights is a Laspeyres quantity index.

There is of course a wide variety of other possible weights and other possible formulas for the construction of index numbers. While it is not our intention to review index numbers in general, we do wish nevertheless to impress on the reader the often rather arbitrary methods used in constructing index numbers. The properties that make an index number useful in some contexts may work to a disadvantage in other contexts. We will presently be discussing the properties that seem desirable in the time-series analysis of demand.

The Problem of Aggregation An aggregate demand relationship such as Equation (2.5) is meant to reflect the reaction of the constant dollar value of imports M to the changes of aggregate income Y/p_Y and changes of a price index p_M/p_Y. It accordingly involves the reactions of rather diverse individuals purchasing rather diverse commodities. We therefore must ask if it is possible to condense such a heterogeneous collection of responses into a single function such as Equation (2.5).

Let us begin by expressing the dependent variable, imports, in the following manner

$$M = \sum_j p_{jo}q_j = M(y_1, \ldots, y_m, p_1, \ldots, p_n, \pi_1, \ldots, \pi_p) \qquad (2.A.5)$$

This expresses the fact that the value of imports at base year prices depends on $y_i (i = 1, \ldots, m)$, the income going to the ith individual, $p_j (j = 1, \ldots, n)$, the price of the jth import, and $\pi_k (k = 1, \ldots, p)$, the price of the kth domestic good. The income terms y_i can also be thought of as including the productive activity of various industries, thereby allowing for the importation of raw materials and unfinished goods. Henceforth we will call the y_i "activity variables" to indicate either income or output.

Equation (2.A.5) is quite general and is hardly disputable. Unfortunately it is not manageable as the number of explanatory variables will ordinarily far exceed the number of available observations. To deal with this problem we will summarize the effects of income and prices in a set of index numbers.

Equation (2.A.5) can be linearized (using the Taylor series approximation) to yield

$$M = k + \left[\sum_i \frac{\partial M}{\partial y_i} y_i \right] + \left[\sum_j \frac{\partial M}{\partial p_j} p_j + \sum_k \frac{\partial M}{\partial \pi_k} \pi_k \right] \qquad (2.A.6)$$

To a first-order approximation, the level of imports is seen to depend on an activity term and on a price term. This suggests that an appropriate aggregate activity term is

$$Y = \sum_i \frac{\partial M}{\partial y_i} y_i \qquad (2.A.7)$$

One-unit increments in Y will induce one-unit increments in M. We may wish to normalize this expression so that the weights add to one

$$Y_N = \sum_i \frac{\partial M / \partial y_i}{\sum_i \partial M / \partial y_i} y_i \qquad (2.A.8)$$

In this case a one-unit increase in Y_N results in a $\sum_i \partial M / \partial y_i$ increment in M.

The important point to notice is that the appropriate aggregate activity term is not the simple unweighted $\sum y_i$, but is rather a summation weighted by the marginal contribution to imports $\partial M / \partial y_i$. Although the marginal responses are unknown, there are three possible approaches that may be followed with regard to them. In the case of the importation of inputs, it may be argued that the marginal responses are closely approximated by the import content of the GNP final-demand components, which are then used as weights. Alternatively one can argue that aggregate output and income are distributed among producers and individuals according to a rule such as

$$y_i = f(\sum_i y_i) = \alpha + \beta \sum y_i \qquad (2.A.9)$$

In other words, as aggregate activity increases, every component of it increases in a regular fashion. This can be substituted into (2.A.7) to yield

$$Y' = \left(\sum_i \frac{\partial M}{\partial y_i} \right) \left(\alpha + \beta \sum_i y_i \right) \qquad (2.A.10)$$

The unweighted activity term would then be sufficient to indicate changes in imports induced by activity changes. Finally, if the marginal responses are similar for all activity components, the unweighted aggregate can be used. This suggests that we use several activity terms, indicating the output/incomes accruing to producers/consumers with widely different marginal import coefficients. The choice among these three alternatives is an empirical issue that has not, as yet, been resolved. Any answer that might be obtained would unfortunately apply only to that particular set of data.

By a similar argument the price term suggested by (2.A.6) is

$$P = \sum_j \frac{\partial M}{\partial p_j} p_j + \sum_k \frac{\partial M}{\partial \pi_k} \pi_k \qquad (2.A.11)$$

One-unit increments in P will induce one-unit increments in M. This expression can be made more familiar in the following manner

$$P_t = M_o \left[-\sum_j \left(-\frac{\partial M}{\partial p_j} \frac{p_{jo}}{M_o} \right) \left(\frac{p_{jt}}{p_{jo}} \right) + \sum_k \left(\frac{\partial M}{\partial \pi_k} \frac{\pi_{ko}}{M_o} \right) \left(\frac{\pi_{kt}}{\pi_{ko}} \right) \right]$$

$$= M_o \left[-\left(\sum_j - e_j \right) \sum_j \left(\frac{-e_j}{\sum_j - e_j} \right) \left(\frac{p_{jt}}{p_{jo}} \right) \right. \qquad (2.A.12)$$

$$\left. + \left(\sum_k e_k \right) \sum_k \left(\frac{e_k}{\sum_k e_k} \right) \left(\frac{\pi_{kt}}{\pi_{ko}} \right) \right]$$

where the subscripts t and o indicate the time period, and where the letter e indicates the elasticity of M with respect to the appropriate price term. We therefore have P_t expressed as the weighted difference in two price indexes for import and domestic goods

$$P_t = -M_o \left(\sum_j - e_j \right) \sum_j w_j \frac{p_{jt}}{p_{jo}} + M_o \left(\sum_k e_k \right) \sum_k w_k \frac{\pi_{kt}}{\pi_{ko}} \qquad (2.A.13)$$

$$= -M_o(\sum_j - e_j) P_M + M_o(\sum e_k) P_Y$$

where the constants w are the appropriate elasticities normalized to sum to one. It should be noted that in order to combine P_M and P_Y into a single index, we will have to know $\sum - e_j$ and $\sum e_k$ or be confident that they are equal. We will soon be evaluating these expressions and will argue that they cannot be known a priori. The implication of this remark is that our aggregate import equation must have two price terms, one for imports and one for domestic goods.

This discussion implies that the appropriate price term is a weighted sum of the individual prices for home and foreign goods. Actually a price ratio is more often used. We can produce a price-ratio term by changing (2.A.7) into a multiplicative relation. The linear relation that we have constructed to this point is

$$M = k + \left(\sum_i \frac{\partial M}{\partial y_i}\right) Y_N - M_o \left(\sum_j - e_j\right) P_M + M_o \left(\sum_k e_k\right) P_Y \quad (2.A.14)$$

We can easily calculate the following elasticities

$$\frac{\partial M}{\partial Y_N} \frac{Y_{No}}{M_o} = \left(\sum_i \frac{\partial M}{\partial y_i}\right) \frac{Y_{No}}{M_o} = \sum_i \frac{\partial M}{\partial y_i} \frac{y_{io}}{M_o} = \sum_i e_i$$

$$\frac{\partial M}{\partial P_M} \frac{P_{Mo}}{M_o} = -M_o \left(\sum_j - e_j\right) \frac{P_{Mo}}{M_o} = -\sum_j - e_j \quad (\text{since } P_{Mo} = 1)$$

$$\frac{\partial M}{\partial P_Y} \frac{P_{Yo}}{M_o} = \sum_k e_k$$

These elasticities imply the multiplicative approximation

$$M = k Y_N^{\Sigma e_i} P_M^{-(\Sigma - e_j)} P_Y^{\Sigma e_k} \quad (2.A.15)$$

At this point it is typical to appeal to the absence of money illusion to argue that the function is linearly homogeneous of degree zero, and therefore

$$\sum_i e_i + \sum_j e_j + \sum_k e_k - 0 \quad (2.A.16)$$

If this is true, we can alter (2.A.15) to

$$M = k \left(\frac{Y_N}{P_Y}\right)^{\Sigma e_i} \left(\frac{P_M}{P_Y}\right)^{-(\Sigma - e_j)} \quad (2.A.17)$$

These two explanatory variables, real income and relative prices, are the ones typically chosen to explain imports. If, however, condition (2.A.16) does not hold, then three explanatory variables must be used: *money* income, import price, and domestic price. We will argue shortly that the absence of money illusion, condition (2.A.16), is too strong a proposition to be known a priori and imposed on the data. All three explanatory variables should therefore be used.

Let us now turn to the evaluation of the elasticities e_j and e_k, which are also the appropriate weights in the price indexes. From (2.A.5) we have

$$M = \sum_j p_{jo}q_j = \sum_j p_{jo}q_j(y_1, \ldots, y_m, p_1, \ldots, p_n, \pi_1, \ldots, \pi_p) \quad (2.A.18)$$

where q_j is the demand function for commodity j.

Thus we have

$$
\begin{aligned}
e_{j'} &= \frac{\partial M}{\partial p_{j'}} \frac{p_{j'o}}{M_o} = p_{j'o} \frac{\partial q_{j'}}{\partial p_{j'}} \frac{p_{j'o}}{M_o} + \sum_{j \neq j'} p_{jo} \frac{\partial q_j}{\partial p_{j'}} \frac{p_{j'o}}{M_o} \\
&= \left(\frac{p_{j'o} q_{j'o}}{M_o} \right) \left(\frac{\partial q_{j'} p_{j'o}}{\partial p_{j'} q_{j'o}} \right) + \sum_{j \neq j'} \left(\frac{p_{jo} q_{jo}}{M_o} \right) \left(\frac{\partial q_j}{\partial p_{j'}} \frac{p_{j'o}}{q_{jo}} \right)
\end{aligned}
\tag{2.A.19}
$$

The proper weights to use in the import price index are seen to be the sum of direct and cross elasticities of demand weighted by the share of the commodity in total imports. A judicious mixture of skill and luck may allow us to define the commodity classes such that the cross elasticities are negligible. In this case all but the first term would drop out and the appropriate import price index can be seen to be the common Laspeyres price index, reweighted by the direct elasticities. Of course these elasticities are not known, else we would not be concerned with estimating them, and we shall have to content ourselves with the standard Laspeyres price index. If, however, we are careful to include commodities in the aggregate import variable with roughly similar elasticities, then the Laspeyres index is the appropriate choice. Alternatively, if such disaggregation is undesirable, we may mitigate the bad effects by including several price terms, one for each disaggregated class of commodities. These classes are to be chosen so that the elasticities differ between classes much more than within classes.

In the main text we mentioned that when an import good and a home good are perfect substitutes, we have to handle them somewhat differently. The same point can be made in the context of the present discussion. A perfectly substitutable good would have an infinite or very large price elasticity. To conform with the weights indicated by (2.A.19), this good would receive all or most of the weight in the index. The appropriate approach would be in this instance to exclude this commodity's direct elasticity from the index and include in the relationship variables that explain the domestic supply. Alternatively, as suggested in the text, we should run separate regressions for these commodities.

Similarly we may evaluate e'_k

$$
\begin{aligned}
e'_k &= \frac{\partial M}{\partial \pi_{k'}} \frac{\pi_{k'o}}{M_o} = \sum_j p_{jo} \frac{\partial q_j}{\partial \pi_{k'}} \frac{\pi_{k'o}}{M_o} \\
&= \sum_j \left(\frac{p_{jo} q_{jo}}{M_o} \right) \left(\frac{\partial q_j}{\partial \pi_{k'}} \frac{\pi_{k'o}}{q_{jo}} \right)
\end{aligned}
\tag{2.A.20}
$$

Once again we have an inner product of a vector of elasticities and a vector of import shares. This time, however, we do not have a direct elasticity that is likely to dominate the expression. We might nonetheless be able to specify a group of imports that are close substitutes for the particular domestic good. Ignoring the effect of the elasticities as we did to obtain the Laspeyres index earlier, the weight we give to the kth domestic good would be the import share of foreign substitutes for the kth domestic good. If the commodity composition of imports were similar to the commodity composition of domestic goods, we would be able to use the usual GNP price deflator, with domestic weights. It would be clearly advantageous, however, to remove from the index prices of goods that do not substitute for imports, for instance, services.

We pointed out earlier that the specification of imports as a function of real output and relative prices rests on the absence of money illusion in the aggregate relation (2.A.15). This event is expressed quite formally by condition (2.A.16). To evaluate this expression we shall have to define demand functions for individuals as

$$q_{ij} = q_{ij}(y_i, p_1, \ldots, p_n, \pi_1, \ldots, \pi_p) \qquad (2.A.21)$$

which expresses the purchases of imports of the jth commodity by the ith individual as a function of his own income y_i and the set of prices. The commodity demand function q_j, which we have used earlier, is simply the sum of q_{ij} over all i. It is tedious, but not difficult, to show that if the individual demand functions q_{ij} are homogeneous of degree zero, then the aggregate relation (2.A.15) is likewise, or equivalently that condition (2.A.16) holds. We will content ourselves with the intuitive proof that if no individual suffers from money illusion (that is, if no individual alters his buying habits in response to a doubling of his income and all prices), then the sum of all individuals must behave similarly.

We have seen, therefore, that the homogeneity postulate in the aggregate rests upon the homogeneity postulate for individuals. But can we be so certain of that postulate that it can be imposed on the data by using the relative price term P_M/P_Y and Y/P_Y? We think not. In the first place, the homogeneity postulate is only a postulate and not a necessary description of reality. It describes how people, in seeking to maximize a utility function, ought to behave. Whether they do that or not is quite another question. Secondly, import demand includes the importation of raw materials and unfinished goods. Whereas the postulate has some appeal on the demand side, it is quite a bit more doubtful for the demand for inputs. Finally, even if we firmly believe in the homogeneity postulate, we can use it to justify the relative prices and real income only when the three measures are weighted properly. As the weights are quite impossible to know, we can expect that the approximations that are used will affect the three terms differently. We therefore ought to use the price terms and money income individually.

At this point it is interesting to compare the effect of aggregation on the income and price terms. We have seen with regard to the income term that a rather reasonable assumption concerning income distribution was sufficient to eliminate aggregation effects. When this assumption is unwarranted, comparatively simple cures are available. This is not the case when we explore the price term. We have already discussed the difficult problems and complex solutions surrounding the price term. There is a strong presumption that the price term is more severely damaged by aggregation than the income term.

Conclusion The points made in this appendix are summarized below for reference:

I. Income Term
   A. Weight income components by marginal contribution to imports. Import content may be used for weights on the assumption that the marginal propensity is well approximated by the average import content.
   B. Weighting is unnecessary when all income components behave similarly over time.
   C. Weighting is unnecessary when all income components have similar marginal propensities. Alternatively, use several income terms reflecting incomes accruing to groups with widely different marginal import propensities.

II. Import Price Term
   A. Proper weights are quite complicated; see (2.A.19).
      1. Laspeyres price index is probably the best available approximation.
      2. Disaggregation and/or the inclusion of several price terms will mitigate the bad effects.

III. Domestic Price Term
   A. Proper weights are quite complicated; see (2.A.20).
      1. The readily available Laspeyres index with domestic weights is unlikely to be a good price index.
      2. In the absence of information to the contrary, an unweighted index is as good as any other.
      3. A minimal step toward a proper weighting scheme would exclude prices of domestic goods that clearly do not substitute with imports.

THE USE OF DUMMY VARIABLES IN THE ANALYSIS OF CURVILINEARITY

Some suggestions for handling curvilinearity have been given by Ginsburg [18] and Goldberger [19]. Let us define the following variable

$$W_i = \begin{cases} 1, & \text{if relative price is in interval } i \\ 0, & \text{otherwise} \end{cases}$$

The regression equation would then be

$$M = f\left(\frac{Y}{p_Y}, \frac{p_M}{p_Y}\right) + \sum_i a_i W_i + \sum_i b_i W_i \frac{p_M}{p_Y} \qquad (2.A.22)$$

This function has different levels a_i and different marginal response to price b_i in each of the selected price intervals W_i. The functional form f in this expression becomes the dominant characteristic of the demand equation while the dummy variables indicate the interval-by-interval deviation from that dominant form. In a sense, the data determine the proper functional form. It would appear, especially on the basis of Ginsburg's interesting results [18], that this method of handling curvilinearity should be explored more fully.

In practical application the dummy-variable method for handling curvilinearity may be severely limited by lack of data in much the same sense that the number of explanatory variables is often limited in time-series analysis. An alternative is to use the Durbin–Watson test for serial correlation in the residuals of the regression equation. Usually the residuals are arranged by time period and the Durbin–Watson test compares successive time periods for correlation. This procedure will be ineffective for discovering problems of functional form, however, unless the explanatory variables exhibit a trend over time. An alternative to the Durbin–Watson test would be to specify domains of the explanatory variables and with the use of variance analysis to test for internal homogeneity and external heterogeneity of the residuals within the domains. This alternative is in effect the same procedure as the dummy variable method discussed above.

It is also worth noting that the dummy variable method described does not make the determination of the functional form completely dependent on the data. Cross-product or interaction terms have been excluded. Let us now indicate how such terms can be taken into account.

THE INTRODUCTION OF INTERACTION TERMS IN THE ANALYSIS OF CURVILINEARITY BY MEANS OF DUMMY VARIABLES

We have just noted that curvilinearity in the import demand function may be handled by specifying dummy variables W_i, which permit the function to have different slopes or elasticities for the particular price intervals chosen. This formulation made no allowance, however, for cross-product interaction terms, such as $(p_M/p_Y \cdot Y/p_Y)$. The situation can be remedied by defining dummy variables as indicated already, but specifying their values in domains of the $(p_M/p_Y \cdot Y/p_Y)$ space rather than in intervals along the p_M/p_Y and Y/p_Y axis.

It is of interest to compare the two approaches for the W variables that take on the values of zero or one. Thus, with no interaction we have

$$W_i^p = \begin{cases} 1, & \text{if } p_M/p_Y \text{ is in interval } i \\ 0, & \text{otherwise} \end{cases}$$

$$W_j^Y = \begin{cases} 1, & \text{if } Y/p_Y \text{ is in interval } j \\ 0, & \text{otherwise} \end{cases}$$

This can be seen diagrammatically as follows

Allowing for interaction we have

$$W_i = \begin{cases} 1, & \text{if the point } (p_M/p_Y, Y/p_Y) \text{ is in region } i \\ 0, & \text{otherwise} \end{cases}$$

This is seen diagrammatically as follows

If the price variable is divided into k intervals and the income variable into m intervals, then $k + m$ explanatory dummies are needed when there are no interaction terms present. When interaction is allowed for, $k \times m$ explanatory dummies are required. It should be evident that $k \times m$ will ordinarily be substantially larger than $k + m$, which implies that we may select either short intervals or make allowance for interactions, but not both.

REFERENCES

The following list of references contains most of the important works completed since 1958 on the subject of estimating demand relationships for imports and exports. Earlier works are summarized for convenient reference in Cheng [8]. The reader should also consult the references to Chapter 3 since there is some degree of overlap in the material in that chapter and in the present one. The most significant contributions (in our judgment) are denoted by *; and the principal surveys by **.

1. Allen, R. G. D., *Mathematical Economics*. London: Macmillan, 1965. Chap. 20.

2. Allen, R. G. D. and J. E. Ely, eds., *International Trade Statistics*. New York: John Wiley and Sons, 1953. Chap. 10.

*3. Almon, S., "The Distributed Lag Between Capital Appropriations and Expenditures," *Econometrica*, 53 (January 1965), 178–96.

*4. Ball, R. J. and K. Marwah, "The U.S. Demand for Imports, 1948–1958," *Review of Economics and Statistics*, XLIV (November 1962), 395–401.

5. Ball, R. J., et al., "The Relationship Between United Kingdom Export Performance in Manufactures and the Internal Pressure of Demand," *Economic Journal*, LXXVI (September 1966), 501–18.

6. Bannerji, H., "Analysis of Import Demand," *Artha Vijnana*, 1 (September 1959), 259–70.

7. Branson, W. H., "A Disaggregated Model of the U.S. Balance of Trade," Board of Governors of the Federal Reserve System, Staff Economic Studies, No. 44 (February 29, 1968).

**8. Cheng, H. S., "Statistical Estimates of Elasticities and Propensities in International Trade: A Survey of Published Studies," International Monetary Fund, *Staff Papers*, VII (August 1959), 107–58.

9. Choudry, N. K., "An Econometric Analysis of the Import Demand Function for Burlap (Hessian) in the U.S.A., 1919–53," *Econometrica*, 26 (July 1958), 416–28.

10. DaCosta, G. C., "Elasticities of Demand for Indian Exports—An Empirical Investigation," *Indian Economic Journal*, 13 (July–September 1965), 41–54.

11. Davis, T. E., "A Model of the Canadian Current Account," *The Canadian Journal of Economics and Political Science*, XXXII (November 1966), 468–88.

12. Detomasi, D. D., "Elasticity of Demand for Canadian Imports to the United States," *Canadian Journal of Economics*, II (August 1969), 416–26.

13. Dutta, M., "A Prototype Model of India's Foreign Sector," *International Economic Review*, 5 (January 1964), 82–103.

14. Dutta, M., "Measuring the Role of Price in International Trade: Some Further Tests," *Econometrica*, 33 (July 1965), 600–07.

15. Dutta, M., "Import Structure of India," *Review of Economics and Statistics*, XLVII (August 1965), 295–300.

16. Ferguson, C. E. and M. Polasek, "The Elasticity of Import Demand for Raw Apparel Wool in the United States," *Econometrica*, 30 (October 1962), 670–85.

17. Gehrels, F., "The Effect of Price on Europe's Exports to the United States," *Kyklos*, XXIV (Fasc. 1, 1961), 47–59.

*18. Ginsburg, A. L., *American and British Regional Export Determinants.* Amsterdam: North-Holland Publishing Company, 1969.

19. Goldberger, A. S., *Econometric Theory.* New York: John Wiley and Sons, 1964.

20. Goldberger, A. S., *Topics in Regression Analysis.* New York: The Macmillan Company, 1968.

21. Gray, H. P., "The Demand for International Travel by the United States and Canada," *International Economic Review*, 7 (January 1966), 83–92.

*22. Griliches, Z., "Distributed Lags: A Survey," *Econometrica*, 35 (January 1967), 16–49.

23. Haq, W., "An Econometric Model for International Trade," *Pakistan Economic Journal*, IX (March 1959), 1–13.

*24. Harberger, A. C., "A Structural Approach to the Problem of Import Demand," *American Economic Review*, Papers and Proceedings, XLIII (May 1953), 148–60.

**25. Harley, C. K., "Empirical Literature on the U.S. Balance of Trade," Board of Governors of the Federal Reserve System, Staff Economic Studies, No. 35 (July 1967).

26. Heien, D. M., "Structural Stability and the Estimation of International Import Price Elasticities," *Kyklos*, XXI (Fasc. 4, 1968), 695–711.

*27. Houthakker, H. S. and S. P. Magee, "Income and Price Elasticities in World Trade," *Review of Economics and Statistics*, LI (May 1969), 111–25.

28. Islam, N., "Experiments in Econometric Analysis of an Import Demand Function," *Pakistan Economic Journal*, XI (September 1961), 21–38; XI (December 1961), 1–19.

29. Johnston, J., *Econometric Methods.* New York: McGraw-Hill, 1963.

30. Johnston, J. and M. Henderson, "Assessing the Effects of the Import Surcharge," *Manchester School*, XLV (May 1967), 89–110.

31. Jorgenson, D. W., "A Rational Distributed Lag Function," *Econometrica*, 32 (January 1966), 135–49.

32. Kaliski, S. F., "Some Recent Estimates of the Elasticity of Demand for British Exports—An Appraisal and Reconciliation," *Manchester School*, XXXIX (January 1961), 23–42.

33. Kaliski, S. F., "Extraneous Estimates and Goodness of Fit: A Problem in Empirical Economics," *Manchester School*, XXXVIII (January 1960), 59–71.

34. Kemp, M. C., "Errors of Measurement and Bias in Estimates of Import Demand Parameters," *Economic Record*, 38 (September 1962), 369–72.

35. Kemp, M. C., *The Demand for Canadian Imports 1926–55*. Toronto: University of Toronto Press, 1962.

36. Klein, L. R. et al., *An Econometric Model of the United Kingdom*. Oxford: Oxford University Press, 1961.

37. Koo, A. Y. C., "Marginal Propensity to Import as a Forecaster," *Review of Economics and Statistics*, XLIV (May 1962), 215–17.

38. Koo, A. Y. C., "On Measuring European Tariff Changes and United States Exports Based on Cross Section Data," *Review of Economics and Statistics*, XLV (August 1963), 323–28.

39. Koyck, L. M., *Distributed Lags and Investment Analysis*. Amsterdam: North-Holland Publishing Company, 1954.

40. Krause, L. B., "United States Imports, 1947–1958," *Econometrica*, 30 (April 1962), 221–38.

41. Kravis, I. B. and R. E. Lipsey, *Price Competitiveness in World Trade*. New York: Columbia University Press, forthcoming.

42. Kreinin, M. E., "United States Imports and Income in the Postwar Period," *Review of Economics and Statistics*, LXII (May 1960), 223–25.

43. Lewis, W. A., "International Competition in Manufactures," *American Economic Review*, XLVII (May 1957), 579.

44. Lipsey, R. E., *Price and Quantity Trends in the Foreign Trade of the United States*. Princeton: Princeton University Press, 1963.

*45. Lovell, M. C., "Seasonal Adjustment of Economic Time Series and Multiple Regression Analysis," *Journal of the American Statistical Association*, 58 (December 1963), 993–1010.

**46. Magee, S. P., "Theoretical and Empirical Studies of Competition in International Trade: A Review," an unpublished study for the Council of Economic Advisers (1968).

47. Mills, F. C., *Statistical Methods.* New York: Henry Holt and Company, 1955. Chaps. 13 and 14.

48. Moore, L., "Factors Affecting the Demand for British Exports," *Bulletin of Oxford University Institute of Economics and Statistics,* 25 (1963), 343–59.

*49. Morgan, D. J. and W. J. Corlett, "The Influence of Price in International Trade: A Study in Method," *Journal of the Royal Statistical Society,* Series A (General), CXIV (Part III, 1951), 307–58.

50. Murakami, A., "Import Behavior in Asian Countries," *Kobe University Economic Review,* 7 (1961), 101–14.

51. Neisser, H., "Comment" on "Some Evidence on the International Price Mechanism," *Review of Economics and Statistics,* XL (February 1958, Supplement), 129–32.

52. Nerlove, M., "Distributed Lags and Estimation of Long-Run Supply and Demand Elasticities: Theoretical Considerations," *Journal of Farm Economics,* XL (May 1958), 301–11.

*53. Orcutt, G. H., "Measurement of Price Elasticities in International Trade," *Review of Economics and Statistics,* XXXII (May 1950), 117–32.

54. Organization for Economic Co-operation and Development, Department of Economics and Statistics, "Statistical Import Functions and Import Forecasting: An Empirical Study of Import Determination in Seven Member Countries," DES/NI/F(66)4 (17 October 1966).

55. Organization for Economic Co-operation and Development, F. G. Adams, et al., *An Econometric Analysis of International Trade.* Paris: OECD, 1969.

*56. Polak, J. J., *An International Economic System.* Chicago: University of Chicago Press, 1953.

*57. Prachowny, M. F. J., *A Structural Model of the U.S. Balance of Payments.* Amsterdam: North-Holland Publishing Company, 1969.

**58. Prais, S. J., "Econometric Research in International Trade: A Review," *Kyklos,* XV (Fasc. 3, 1962), 560–79.

59. Preeg, E. H., "Elasticity Optimism in International Trade," *Kyklos,* XX (Fasc. 4, 1967), 460–69.

60. Rao, S. V., "Elasticities of Demand for Imports During the Period 1920–21 to 1929–30," *Artha Vijnana,* 2 (December 1960), 307–12.

61. Reimer, R., "The United States Demand for Imports of Materials," *Review of Economics and Statistics,* XLVI (February 1964), 65–75.

*62. Rhomberg, R. R., "A Model of the Canadian Economy Under Fixed and Fluctuating Exchange Rates," *Journal of Political Economy,* LXXII (February 1964), 1–31.

63. Rhomberg, R. R., "Canada's Foreign Exchange Market," International Monetary Fund, *Staff Papers*, VII (April 1960), 439–56.

*64. Rhomberg, R. R. and L. Boissonneault, "The Foreign Sector," in J. S. Duesenberry et al., eds., *The Brookings Quarterly Econometric Model of the United States*. Chicago: Rand McNally & Company, 1965.

65. Rhomberg, R. R. and L. Boissonneault, "Effects of Income and Price Changes on the U.S. Balance of Payments," International Monetary Fund, *Staff Papers*, XI (1964), 59–124.

66. Robinson, T. R., "Canada's Imports and Economic Stability," *Canadian Journal of Economics*, I (May 1968), 401–28.

67. Roy, P. N., "Some Export Demand Functions for India," *Arthanti*, IV (July 1961), 129–37.

68. Sasaki, K., "Quantitative Effect of the United States Economy on Japan's Foreign Trade Between 1950–1956," *Review of Economics and Statistics*, XLI (August 1959), 320–24.

69. Scott, M. FG., *A Study of United Kingdom Imports*. Cambridge: Cambridge University Press, 1963.

70. Stern, R. M., *Foreign Trade and Economic Growth in Italy*. New York: Praeger, 1967. Chap. 2.

71. Suits, D. B., *Statistics: An Introduction to Quantitative Economic Research*. Chicago: Rand McNally, 1963.

*72. Suits, D. B., "Use of Dummy Variables in Regression Equations," *Journal of the American Statistical Association*, 52 (December 1957), 548–51.

73. Swamy, D. S., "A Quarterly Econometric Model of Demand for and Supply of Exports," *Indian Economic Review*, I (April 1966), 79–103.

74. Taylor, W. B., "Short Term Factors Influencing New Zealand Lamb Prices in the United Kingdom," *Economic Record*, XXXVI (December 1960), 568–80.

75. Turnovsky, S. J., "International Trading Relationships of a Small Country: The Case of New Zealand," *Canadian Journal of Economics*, I (November 1968), 772–90.

76. Von Böventer, E., "The Production Elasticity of U.S. Raw Material Imports," *Economia Internazionale*, XII (August 1959), 470–91.

77. Wemelsfelder, J., "The Short-term Effect of the Lowering of Import Duties in Germany," *Economic Journal*, LXX (March 1960), 94–104.

78. Wilkinson, B. W., *Canada's International Trade: An Analysis of Recent Trends and Patterns*. Montreal: Private Planning Association of Canada, for the Canadian Trade Committee, 1968.

79. Zarembka, P., "Functional Form in the Demand for Money," *Journal of the American Statistical Association*, 63 (June 1968), 502–11.

Theory and Measurement
of the Elasticity
# of Substitution in
International Trade

The theoretical presumption of relatively high price elasticities in international trade has frequently not been borne out in empirical studies using ordinary least squares analysis of time series. There has as a consequence been a search for conceptual alternatives, the measurement of which would yield results more in concert with the a priori presumption. One such alternative commonly employed has been the "elasticity of substitution," which is defined simply as the percentage change in relative quantities demanded divided by the percentage change in relative prices

$$e = \frac{\partial(q_1/q_2)}{q_1/q_2} \div \frac{\partial(p_1/p_2)}{p_1/p_2} = \frac{\partial(q_1/q_2)}{\partial(p_1/p_2)} \cdot \frac{p_1 q_2}{p_2 q_1} = \frac{\partial \log (q_1/q_2)}{\partial \log (p_1/p_2)}$$

where q_1 and q_2 are exports from two competing supply sources to some third market (perhaps the rest of the world), and p_1 and p_2 are their respective prices. The partial derivatives in the definition are the mathematical analogue of the economist's *ceteris paribus* assumption. In the case of the utility analysis of demand, it is real income that is being held constant. We will see that when applied statistically the *ceteris paribus* phrase may be conveniently implemented in the present context with regard to money income and other prices.

It is evident that if q_1 and q_2 are absolute complements (such as right shoes and left shoes), no change can occur in q_1/q_2 and e will be zero. Whereas if q_1 and q_2 are perfect substitutes, consumers will purchase only the lower-priced item, in which case e will be $-\infty$ at $p_1 = p_2$ and zero elsewhere. Our interest is in cases lying between these limits, and we naturally would like to be able to specify ranges of values that could be considered large, medium, or small. Unfortunately, as we will see, values of the elasticity of substitution other than zero and $-\infty$ pose serious problems in interpretation. Worse yet, the method used to estimate the elasticity of substitution may yield a result unrelated to the valid theoretical concept. In general, we look on the estimation of the elasticity of substitution with considerable skepticism. We will establish rather strong doubts concerning both the statistical method and the theoretical usefulness of the concept.

We will address ourselves accordingly in the following discussion primarily to three fundamental questions: (1) What is the theoretical foundation of the elasticity of substitution? (2) Can we devise a method of analyzing the data which is likely to disclose the numerical value of the theoretical concept? (3) Assuming we knew the true value of the elasticity, how would it be interpreted and used? In most of what follows, we shall have time series in mind. While cross-section estimation will be treated explicitly later in the chapter, it should be emphasized that many of the points to be made concerning time series apply equally to cross sections.

THEORETICAL FOUNDATION

The elasticity of substitution is rigorously defined with respect to movement along a single indifference curve.[1] Such a situation is depicted in Figure 3.1, with II as the indifference curve, AB as the original price line, and $A'B'$ as the final price line.

In this case the elasticity may be estimated by

$$e = \frac{\Delta(q_1/q_2)}{q_1/q_2} \div \frac{\Delta(p_1/p_2)}{p_1/p_2} = \frac{q_1/q_2 - q_1'/q_2'}{q_1/q_2} \div \frac{A'/B' - A/B}{A/B}$$

In general, the value of e will depend on the particular indifference curve that is selected, as well as on the value of p_1/p_2. Such a situation is cumbersome from a theoretical point of view and, as will be shown, can be crippling to any empirical work. It will behoove us, therefore, to determine the conditions under which the value of the elasticity of substitution depends on the value of p_1/p_2 alone. The proper requirement suggests itself immediately: the slope of the indifference curve must depend on q_1/q_2 and not on any scale factor.[2] Another way of saying this is that the income elasticities of the two goods are identical.

For the sake of realism, we should take other goods besides q_1 and q_2 into account. The additional requirements affecting e in such an event are

[1] See Morrissett [17] for a historical sketch and careful theoretical discussion of the concept. Another source of insight is Morgan and Corlett [16].

[2] See Morrissett [17] for a proof. Linear homogeneous functions have this property. Monotone transformations of linear homogeneous functions do as well.

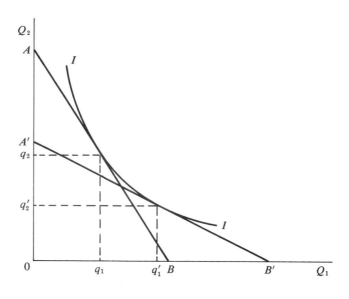

FIGURE 3.1

The Elasticity of Substitution
Along a Single Indifference Curve

similar to the one just mentioned: the proportional responses of q_1 and q_2 to changes in the levels of all other variables should be equal.[3]

The point just made is troublesome since it seems as if we are trying to say that q_1 and q_2 are the same commodity. Yet if they were, the indifference curves would be straight lines and the analysis would degenerate. The most we can say therefore is that e will depend only on relative prices when the two commodities in question are so similar that the reaction of demand for each to all other economic variables is identical, yet at the same time are dissimilar enough to induce the purchase of some of both.

The measurement of the elasticity of substitution has invariably been attempted using a log-linear regression

$$\log \frac{q_1}{q_2} = a + b \log \frac{p_1}{p_2} \tag{3.1}$$

where the coefficient b is the elasticity of substitution, which by virtue of the logarithmic form is constrained to be constant. We can consider this con-

---

[3] To put this in another way, one can think of the indifference curves in Figure 3.1 drawn with the other variables held constant. The condition for e to depend on p_1/p_2 alone is then that the indifference map appears the same for all choices of the other variables.

stancy to result not from explicit assumption but rather from ignoring the problems surrounding the choice of functional form on the basis of the general relationship

$$\frac{q_1}{q_2} = f\left(\frac{p_1}{p_2}\right) \tag{3.2}$$

Besides the fact that Equation (3.1) is open to criticism for ignoring the problem of functional form, an important additional criticism concerns the implicit assumption that q_1/q_2 is dependent only on p_1/p_2, which requires the rather strong symmetry assumptions discussed above.

Thus suppose for the moment that the symmetry assumptions do not hold, yet we persist in running the regression suggested in Equation (3.1). As evident from Figure 3.2, the resulting estimate need bear no relationship

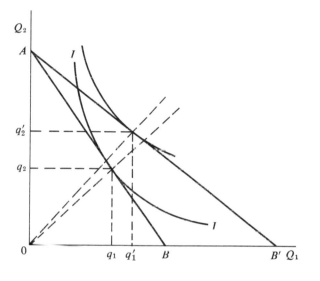

FIGURE 3.2

The Elasticity of Substitution
Between Two Indifference Curves

to the theoretical concept. That is, a fall in the price of q_1, indicated by the shift in the price line AB to AB', has resulted in a fall in q_1/q_2 to q_1'/q_2'. The measured elasticity of substitution would thus turn out to be positive rather than negative in this instance and would provide no insight into the true elasticity of substitution defined along the indifference curve.[4]

---

[4] See Stern and Zupnick [22, pp. 484–86] for a similar demonstration using partial equilibrium demand and supply schedules.

To this point our discussion has implicitly assumed that the importing country has a well-behaved indifference map. In view, however, of the well-known conceptual difficulties involved in such community indifference maps, it may be more fruitful to examine the elasticity of substitution in the framework of conventional demand analysis. Let us write the following export-demand functions

$$q_1 = f(p_1, p_2, y, p_n) \quad \text{and} \quad q_2 = g(p_1, p_2, y, p_n) \tag{3.3}$$

where y is money income in the importing country and p_n is the general price level in this country of commodities other than 1 and 2, including perhaps competing imports. For purposes of simplification we will assume constant-elasticity approximations to (3.3)

$$q_1 = a \, p_1^{\alpha_1} p_2^{\alpha_2} y^{\alpha_y} p_n^{\alpha_n} \quad \text{and} \quad q_2 = b \, p_1^{\beta_1} p_2^{\beta_2} y^{\beta_y} p_n^{\beta_n} \tag{3.4}$$

where the α's and β's refer to the elasticities of the respective variables. We can then write

$$\frac{q_1}{q_2} = \frac{a}{b} \frac{p_1^{\alpha_1 - \beta_1}}{p_2^{\beta_2 - \alpha_2}} y^{\alpha_y - \beta_y} p_n^{\alpha_n - \beta_n} \tag{3.5}$$

The elasticity of substitution may now be conveniently defined holding money income y and other prices p_n constant.

It should be evident from Equation (3.5) that q_1/q_2 will be functionally related to p_1/p_2 only if the exponents of the price variables are equal

$$e = \alpha_1 - \beta_1 = \beta_2 - \alpha_2$$

or $$\tag{3.6}$$

$$\alpha_1 + \alpha_2 = \beta_1 + \beta_2$$

Equation (3.6) asserts that the sum of the direct and cross elasticities of demand be the same for each commodity.[5] This is quite similar to the symmetry

---

[5] Since Equation (3.4) is meant to be an approximation to the general demand equation (3.3), we should be thinking of the exponents of (3.4) as being dependent on the arguments of the functions (3.3). For example, in approximating f we will pick a particular set of values for p_1, p_2, y, and p_n. In a neighborhood around this point, f will be well approximated by $a \, p_1^{\alpha_1} p_2^{\alpha_2} y^{\alpha_y} p_n^{\alpha_n}$. Were we to select a different point, say (p_1', p_2', y', p_n'), we would no doubt have to choose different values of a, α_1, α_2, α_y, α_n to yield a good approximation. In this sense, a, α_1, α_2, α_y, and α_n depend on the values of p_1, p_2, y, p_n. In this situation an additional requirement is needed for q_1/q_2 to be functionally related to p_1/p_2. Not only must (3.6) hold, but also the values of the exponents α_1, α_2, β_1, β_2 must be either independent of p_1 and p_2 or dependent on the ratio p_1/p_2 only.

It is illuminating in this context to consider linear functions for (3.3)

$$q_1 = \alpha_1 + \beta_1 \frac{p_1}{p_2} + \gamma_1 \frac{y}{p_1} + \delta_1 \frac{p_n}{p_1}$$

$$q_2 = \alpha_2 + \beta_2 \frac{p_1}{p_2} + \gamma_2 \frac{y}{p_2} + \delta_2 \frac{p_n}{p_2}$$

conditions discussed earlier in connection with the utility analysis, and the same conclusion holds. Commodities q_1 and q_2 must be quite similar but not too similar.

It will be further evident from Equation (3.5) that there are two variables, y and p_n, that do not appear in the regression equation (3.1). This is justifiable only when $\alpha_y = \beta_y$ and $\alpha_n = \beta_n$, that is, when the income elasticities of each commodity are comparable and when the cross-price elasticities with respect to other goods are also comparable.

The points just made are essentially empirical problems, and it would seem advisable to test their validity in a regression of the form

$$\log \left(\frac{q_1}{q_2}\right) = a + b_1 \log p_1 + b_2 \log p_2 + c \log y + d \log p_n \qquad (3.7)$$

The hypothesis represented by Equation (3.6) would then be examined by testing whether $b_1 = -b_2$. Similarly, $\alpha_y = \beta_y$ and $\alpha_n = \beta_n$ could be examined by testing whether $c = 0$ and $d = 0$.[6]

The question arises again as to what happens if we insist on regressions of the form (3.1) when the condition (3.6) is unwarranted. The answer is that the concept of the elasticity of substitution as a demand phenomenon degenerates since the observed value depends on the particular paths taken by the individual prices. Suppose, for example, that $\alpha_1 - \beta_1 = -1.0$, $\beta_2 - \alpha_2 = -0.1$, $\Delta p_1/p_1 = 0.9$, and $\Delta p_2/p_2 = 1.0$. Since p_1 has risen by a smaller percentage than p_2, the ratio p_1/p_2 has fallen, and we expect q_1/q_2 to rise. However, from Equation (3.5) we see that

$$\frac{\Delta(q_1/q_2)}{(q_1/q_2)} = (\alpha_1 - \beta_1)\frac{\Delta p_1}{p_1} - (\beta_2 - \alpha_2)\frac{\Delta p_2}{p_2}$$
$$= 1.0(0.9) - (-0.1)(1.0)$$
$$= -0.9 + 0.1 = -0.8$$

Contrary to what is expected, a fall in p_1/p_2 has resulted in a fall in q_1/q_2 and the observed elasticity of substitution is positive. The observed elasticity of

---

These functions have the desirable property that if all prices and money income are multiplied by the same factor no change in demand occurs. Equation (3.5) then becomes

$$\frac{q_1}{q_2} = \frac{\alpha_1 + \beta_1(p_1/p_2) + \gamma_1(y/p_1) + \delta_1(p_n/p_1)}{\alpha_2 + \beta_2(p_1/p_2) + \gamma_2(y/p_2) + \delta_2(p_n/p_2)}$$

With use of this function, the elasticity of substitution depends not only on the levels of all the variables but also on the paths taken by p_1 and p_2, which will depend on supply conditions. In other words, q_1/q_2 is not functionally dependent on p_1/p_2, and the concept of the elasticity of substitution degenerates.

[6] If the variables y and p_n are excluded, the resulting estimate of the elasticity of substitution will necessarily be inefficient, statistically speaking. It will be unbiased only if y and p_n are uncorrelated with p_1/p_2. See Morgan and Corlett [16] for some not-too-encouraging experiments with an income term.

substitution will depend in general on the particular choice of $\Delta p_1/p_1$ and $\Delta p_2/p_2$, that is, on the paths taken by the individual prices.[7] An elasticity of substitution estimated during one period will hold for another period only if the paths of these variables are retraced.

The particular paths followed by the explanatory variables will depend, in general, on the interaction of all the other economic variables. But it may be noted that if it were possible to specify other economic relationships that completely determine the paths of the explanatory variables, the effect will be to make the elasticity of substitution unique. Supply functions come to mind immediately.[8] For example, it may be that monetary inflations in Countries 1 and 2 behave similarly and in consequence p_1/p_2 follows the same path. Thus, Country 1 may undergo approximately a 6 percent rate of inflation while Country 2 suffers only a 3 percent rate consistently over time. In this case, p_1/p_2 would grow consistently at a 3 percent rate, and the observed elasticity of substitution would be roughly constant over the period. Such an estimate would only be useful of course if we could be confident of a continuance of the inflation rates in the two countries. But even though it is quite possible that the interaction of demand and supply will create a close relationship between q_1/q_2 and p_1/p_2, such a relationship is only a description of the time series and not an analysis useful in understanding the underlying economic forces or in predicting future events. What can be concluded from our discussion of the theoretical foundation of the elasticity of substitution is that a regression of the form

$$\log \frac{q_1}{q_2} = a + b \log \frac{p_1}{p_2} \qquad (3.8)$$

requires the following assumptions:

(i) The algebraic sum of cross and direct elasticities of demand for the two commodities must be equal.

(ii) The income and any other price elasticities of demand for the two commodities must be equal.[9] This implies roughly that the two commodities be alike in all economic respects except that they are not perfect substitutes. If they are perfect substitutes then b becomes $-\infty$ and $p_1/p_2 \equiv 1$ as long as some of both commodities is being sold. In this case, $\log p_1/p_2$ is a constant (as a is) and Equation (3.8) cannot be estimated.

---

[7] See the Appendix to this chapter for further discussion of this matter.

[8] Polak [20] introduces supply functions for q_1 and q_2 to calculate the observed elasticity of substitution in terms of demand and supply elasticities. Stern and Zupnick [22] discuss the elasticity of substitution within the framework of supply functions as well as demand.

[9] When Condition (ii) holds, Condition (i) can be replaced by the absence of money illusion in the demand functions

$$\alpha_1 + \alpha_2 + \alpha_y + \alpha_n = 0 \qquad (a)$$
$$\beta_1 + \beta_2 + \beta_y + \beta_n = 0$$

The foregoing objections may be met by a regression of the form

$$\log \frac{q_1}{q_2} = a + b_1 \log p_1 + b_2 \log p_2 + c \log y + d \log p_n \qquad (3.9)$$

which is what we suggest be used, with form (3.8) being avoided. However, form (3.9) has the disadvantage that data must be collected on income y and other prices p_n. Inasmuch as the coefficients c and d are likely to be small, we may on grounds of economy drop these two terms and fit

$$\log \frac{q_1}{q_2} = a + b_1 \log p_1 + b_2 \log p_2 \qquad (3.10)$$

In effect, our preference for Equations (3.9) and (3.10) represents a rejection of the elasticity of substitution on theoretical grounds. The elasticity of substitution requirement that $b_1 = -b_2$ in these relations imposes assumptions we do not regard as suitable for a priori imposition upon the data. However, empirical tests of relationships (3.9) and (3.10) may prove that the elasticity of substitution is a useful approximation in certain contexts.

MEASUREMENT

Let us now turn to the question of measurement of the elasticity of substitution. Assuming that (i) and (ii) just mentioned hold, we must inquire whether a least squares regression of the form (3.8) yields a good estimate of the true elasticity of substitution: $e = \alpha_1 - \beta_1 = \beta_2 - \alpha_2$. In the previous chapter we observed that the existence of a supply relationship biases toward zero any least squares estimate of a price elasticity of demand. This is due to the fact that the error term in the demand relationship has a positive correlation with the price term. Unfortunately, the identical simultaneity problem exists with regard to a regression of the form (3.8).

That is, a disturbance to (3.8) such as a temporary shift in demand in favor of q_1 will be associated with an accommodating movement of p_1/p_2 as

---

This makes the demand functions homogeneous of degree zero so that doubling all prices and money income will not change the quantities demanded. If we also assume as in (ii) in the text that

$$\alpha_y - \beta_y = \beta_n - \alpha_n = 0 \qquad (b)$$

we can subtract the two equations in (a) to get

$$\alpha_1 + \alpha_2 = \beta_1 + \beta_2 \qquad (c)$$

which is the same as Equation (3.6). Therefore (i) and (ii) in the text can be replaced by (a), the absence of money illusion, and (b), identical elasticities with respect to the other variables.

suppliers of q_1 raise prices to ration the available quantity, and suppliers of q_2 lower prices to eliminate accumulating stocks. Just as in the case of price elasticities, the estimate of the elasticity of substitution will be biased toward zero unless supply elasticities are infinite. The size of the bias will be large accordingly when the disturbances to (3.8) are large relative to the disturbances to the supply functions. There is a presumption, however, that the elasticity of substitution relation will be more stable than the corresponding demand relation. Disturbances to one of the demand functions in (3.3) are likely to have their counterparts in disturbances to the other demand function. Accordingly, when we divide these demand functions, the one disturbance will tend to cancel out the other and the elasticity-of-substitution relation may be quite stable on the demand side. On the supply side, on the other hand, the individual disturbances reflect events in two different countries and are therefore less likely to cancel each other out. The increased stability on the demand side in the absence of the same on the supply side may therefore reduce the bias in the estimate associated with the simultaneous interaction of demand and supply.

It appears from our discussion that there are many reservations, both theoretical and statistical, concerning the concept of the elasticity of substitution. It is only natural to ask then why so much effort has been devoted to estimating it. The most obvious answer that suggests itself is that the estimated elasticities of substitution are generally more negative and more significant statistically than the estimated demand elasticities. Such results are often considered to provide better evidence of the workings of the international price mechanism. This conclusion may not be warranted, however. That is, in contrast to the typical demand elasticity that is approximated by α_1 or β_2 (both negative), the elasticity of substitution approximates $\alpha_1 - \beta_1$ or $\beta_2 - \alpha_2$. These latter approximations are clearly more negative than α_1 or β_2.[10] Furthermore, when the assumption $\alpha_1 - \beta_1 = \beta_2 - \alpha_2$ is erroneous, large negative estimates may result simply due to the paths followed by p_1 and p_2.[11]

INTERPRETATION AND USE OF RESULTS

Let us now consider the question of interpreting and using the measured values of the elasticity of substitution. Since the theory of international monetary relations and the balance-of-payments adjustment process is traditionally

[10] We should also point out that ordinary demand studies that use the price of a close substitute as a deflator for own price typically obtain larger elasticities comparable to the estimates of the elasticities of substitution.

[11] See the Appendix to this chapter.

cast in terms of demand functions, it is natural enough that investigators have attempted to derive demand elasticities from the measured substitution elasticities. We have already mentioned that the elasticity of substitution can be thought of as the sum of direct and cross elasticities: $e = \alpha_1 - \beta_1 = \beta_2 - \alpha_2$. When one of the two factors is zero or negligible, e will approximate the other. Thus, for goods that do not substitute for one another, $\beta_1 \simeq \alpha_2 \simeq 0$, and $e \simeq \alpha_1 \simeq \beta_2$, which are the basic price elasticities. Note, however, that since the measurement of an elasticity of substitution can be justified only when the two goods in question are rather similar, we could hardly expect that $\beta_1 \simeq \alpha_2 \simeq 0$.

There is another approach that has been taken. Having estimated e, we have available two equations and four unknowns (α_1, β_1, α_2, β_2)

$$\alpha_1 - \beta_1 = e \qquad \beta_2 - \alpha_2 = e \tag{3.11}$$

If we could posit some other equations, we would then be able to estimate each of the four unknowns. One possible candidate is Hicks's [8] substitution effect, describing the reaction of demand to changes in relative prices *when choice is constrained to a single indifference curve* (level). Under such a situation the following is true:[12]

$$q_1 p_1 \left(\frac{dq_1}{dp_1}\frac{p_1}{q_1}\right) + q_2 p_2 \left(\frac{dq_2}{dp_1}\frac{p_1}{q_2}\right) + q_n p_n \left(\frac{dq_n}{dp_1}\frac{p_1}{q_n}\right) = 0 \tag{3.12}$$

Researchers have taken the liberty to alter this to

$$(q_1 p_1)\alpha_1 + (q_2 p_2)\beta_1 + (q_n p_n)\gamma_1 = 0 \tag{3.13}$$

where γ_1 is from the demand function

$$q_n = c p_1^{\gamma_1} p_2^{\gamma_2} y^{\gamma_y} p_n^{\gamma_n} \tag{3.14}$$

---

[12] Hicks's [8, pp. 308–11] proof of this is difficult. A simpler, less elegant proof of the two-good case is instructive.

The consumer chooses the quantity couple (q_1, q_2) from a single indifference curve

$$u(q_1, q_2) = k \tag{a}$$

such that total expenditure

$$y = p_1 q_1 + p_2 q_2 \tag{b}$$

is minimized.

Letting $\partial u/\partial q_i = u_i$, the minimization of (b) constrained to (a) yields the familiar tangency condition

$$\frac{u_1}{p_1} = \frac{u_2}{p_2} \tag{c}$$

Thus (a) and (c) can be solved to yield the optimum quantity couple.

To explore the effect of a change in p_1, we can differentiate (a) and (c) to yield

$$u_1 \, dq_1 + u_2 \, dq_2 = 0 \tag{d}$$

$$p_2(u_{11} \, dq_1 + u_{12} \, dq_2) = u_2 \, dp_1 + p_1(u_{21} \, dq_1 + u_{22} \, dq_2) \tag{e}$$

(Footnote continued on next page)

The transition from Equation (3.12) to (3.13) is not wholly acceptable. The parameters α_1, β_1, and γ_1 are total elasticities describing the effect of a price change inclusive of the income effect. In contrast to this, the elasticities in (3.12) describe only the substitution effect and require a compensating variation of money income y to constrain choice to the initial indifference level. This can be made clearer by referring to the indifference map in Figure 3.3.

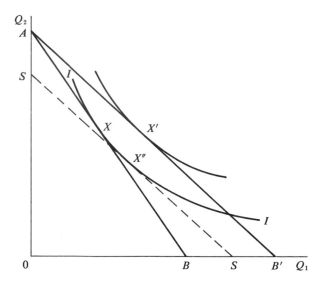

FIGURE 3.3

Income and Substitution Effects

where

$$u_{ij} = \frac{\partial^2 u}{\partial q_i \, \partial q_j} \qquad \text{and} \qquad dp_2 = 0$$

Solving (d) and (e) with (c) yields

$$dq_1 = Zp_2 u_2 \, dp_1 \tag{f}$$

$$dq_2 = -Zp_1 u_2 \, dp_1 \tag{g}$$

where

$$Z = (p_2^2 u_{11} - 2p_1 p_2 u_{21} + p_1^2 u_{22})^{-1}$$

Therefore

$$(p_1 q_1)\alpha_1 + (p_2 q_2)\beta_1 = (p_1 q_1)\frac{p_1}{q_1}\frac{dq_1}{dp_1} + (p_2 q_2)\frac{p_1}{q_2}\frac{dq_2}{dp_1}$$

$$= p_1^2 Z p_2 u_2 - p_1^2 Z p_2 u_2$$

$$= 0$$

The initial budget line is AB and quantity bundle X is selected. When the price of q_1 falls, the budget line moves to AB' and a new quantity bundle X' is selected. Hicks has shown that this reaction to a price change can be broken into two components. The first is the substitution effect, defined as holding real income (utility level) constant. This can be seen in Figure 3.3 as the movement from X to X'', where X'' is the tangency point between the initial indifference curve II and a budget line SS parallel to AB'. Thus the substitution effect describes the demand reaction to price changes when choice is constrained to the initial indifference level. The second component is the income effect, the movement from X'' to X', which is defined by holding prices constant but increasing money income so as to move SS to AB'.

In accordance with our earlier discussion, Equation (3.12) holds for the pure substitution effect, that is, for the movement from X to X'', while the price elasticities ($\alpha_1, \beta_1 \dots$) refer to the total adjustment X to X'. These will be approximately the same when the income effect is small, that is, when commodity q_1 requires a small portion of the total budget.

If we accept Equation (3.13), we can substitute Equations (3.11) into it, and solve for α_1, to yield [13]

$$\alpha_1 = \frac{q_2 p_2}{q_1 p_1 + q_2 p_2}\, e - \frac{q_n p_n}{q_1 p_1 + q_2 p_2}\, \gamma_1 \qquad (3.15)$$

If commodity q_n is a substitute for q_1, the value of γ_1 will be positive and

$$\tilde{\alpha}_1 - \frac{q_2 p_2}{q_1 p_1 + q_2 p_2}\, e \qquad (3.16)$$

will be less negative than α_1. Thus $\tilde{\alpha}_1$ will underestimate α_1 (in absolute value).

The foregoing approach to estimating the price elasticity of demand tends to impinge upon one's tolerance of statistical tricks. This is especially the case in view of the highly questionable nature of some of the steps involved. It may also be that the utility analysis itself is of dubious validity in this context.[14] We could no doubt introduce other equations for the purpose of refining or altering the estimates of the direct elasticities.[15] But the question is, why estimate these elasticities in such an indirect manner? If one is interested in the

---

[13] Zelder [24] used a more elaborate formula, which includes the elasticity of substitution between q_1 and q_n. There is, however, no essential difference between our formula and his.

[14] Smith [7] is not troubled by the concept of a community indifference function but does question the required tangency of the budget line and the indifference curve. This, he points out, requires that importers behave competitively, which is unlikely to be the case when the imports are capital goods (factors of production).

[15] One additional formulation, which is due to Ginsburg [5], is worth noting. The following identity can be written

$$q_1 \equiv \frac{q_1}{q_1 + q_2} \cdot \frac{q_1 + q_2}{q_{tot}} \cdot q_{tot}$$

(Footnote continued on next page)

price elasticity of demand, would it not be better to use the more direct techniques discussed in the preceding chapter? We have already indicated at some length the numerous difficulties that arise in estimating the elasticity of substitution. This, combined with the further assumptions necessary to calculate the price elasticity from it, certainly puts a great strain on the analysis and the interpretation of results.

In view of what has just been said, what is the case, if any, that can be made for estimating the elasticity of substitution in international trade? On purely theoretical and statistical grounds, we have argued in favor of computing price elasticities directly if this is the object of the analysis. It may be, however, that the measurement of direct elasticities yields poor results in comparison with the measurement of substitution elasticities due to the reduced simultaneity bias as discussed before. It is also true that with use of this analysis the need for data other than relative quantities and prices may be obviated, with concomitant economy of operation. But the validity of these points is primarily a question of fact, which ought to be investigated by estimating both types of elasticities in a given situation and comparing the results.

Nonetheless, there are situations in which it may be useful to pose hypotheses in terms of the elasticity of substitution, in particular when interest may not center entirely on the elasticity but as well on other influences that affect export sales. One such situation might be when we wanted to explain existing trade patterns of particular exporting countries vis-à-vis one another. Such knowledge could be useful in establishing an industry's export-price policy and in formulating government policies affecting exports. Ginsburg's work [5], which is based upon the pooling of time-series and cross-section data, is especially interesting in this regard and therefore worth discussing briefly. It should be noted, however, that his work is subject to our criticisms noted earlier concerning the choice of explanatory variables and the separation of the price variables.

---

where q_1 and q_2 are imports into a third country from Countries 1 and 2 and q_{tot} is total imports. The elasticity of q_1 with respect to p_1 can therefore be expressed as the sum of three terms: the elasticities of $q_1/(q_1 + q_2)$, of $(q_1 + q_2)/q_{tot}$ and of q_{tot} with respect to p_1. All three can be expected to be negative and therefore the first will be less negative than the number we are after, α_1, the elasticity of q_1 with respect to p_1. Thus another lower limit estimate of α_1 is

$$\tilde{\alpha}_1 = \frac{d[q_1/(q_1 + q_2)]}{dp_1} \frac{p_1}{q_1/(q_1 + q_2)} = \frac{d[(q_1/q_2)/(q_1/q_2 + 1)]}{dp_1} \frac{p_1}{[(q_1/q_2)/(q_1/q_2 + 1)]}$$

Substituting in Equation (3.2), $f = q_1/q_2$, yields

$$\tilde{\alpha}_1 = \frac{d[f/(f+1)]}{dp_1} \frac{p_1}{f/(f+1)} = (f+1)^{-1}e = \frac{q_2}{q_1 + q_2} e$$

where e is the elasticity of substitution. This estimate closely resembles the first one in Equation (3.16).

POOLED TIME–SERIES AND CROSS–SECTION ESTIMATION

We have been proceeding as if time-series data on relative quantities and relative prices were used to estimate the elasticity of substitution. Alternatively one could use cross-section data relating to some specified period of time. The difference in the regressions can be seen as follows

$$\log \left(\frac{q_1}{q_2}\right)_{it} = a_i + b_i \log \left(\frac{p_1}{p_2}\right)_{it} \quad \text{(fixed } i\text{)} \qquad (3.17)$$

$$\log \left(\frac{q_1}{q_2}\right)_{it} = a_t + b_t \log \left(\frac{p_1}{p_2}\right)_{it} \quad \text{(fixed } t\text{)} \qquad (3.18)$$

where $(i = 1, \ldots, N)$ and $(t = 1, \ldots, M)$. The subscripts 1 and 2 in the quantity and price ratios are now to be interpreted as referring to Country 1 and Country 2. Equation (3.17) thus represents the time-series approach across all years for a given commodity, $(q_1/q_2)_i$. Equation (3.18) is the cross-section approach across all commodities for a given year. In the case of Equation (3.17), there will be N separate regressions yielding an elasticity of substitution b_i for each of the commodities. For Equation (3.18) there will be M separate regressions yielding an elasticity of substitution b_t for all of the commodities in a given year. Implicit in the cross-section approach is the assumption that the behavior of the various commodities included in the analysis is commensurable, so that b_t can be interpreted as a kind of average elasticity of substitution for all the commodities. Since the cross section should comprise only reasonably close substitutes, it is evident that we need to make the same assumptions concerning elasticities that were mentioned earlier in connection with Equation (3.10).

These two separate approaches can be logically combined. This can be done by pooling data cross sections for different time periods into a single regression equation as follows

$$\begin{aligned}
\log \left(\frac{q_1}{q_2}\right)_{it} &= a_{it} + b_{it} \log \left(\frac{p_1}{p_2}\right)_{it} \\
&= (a + \alpha_i + \beta_t) + b_i \log \left(\frac{p_1}{p_2}\right)_{it}
\end{aligned} \qquad (3.19)$$

The elasticity b_i is assumed to vary between commodities but to be constant over time, and the level of the function $(a + \alpha_i + \beta_t)$ is assumed to vary among commodities and over time in such a way that β_t, the change from year to year, influences all commodities identically.[16]

---

[16] This formulation is due to Ginsburg and Stern [6]. It was suggested by an analysis-of-covariance technique developed originally by D. B. Suits.

When the regression indicated by Equation (3.19) is actually performed, the commodity and time characteristics, α_i and β_t, are represented by dummy variables. Thus in the regression a value of one or zero is given the commodity dummy corresponding to α_i depending on whether the particular price and quantity observation comes from the ith commodity or not, and the same is true for a particular year t. There will consequently be separate regression coefficients for each commodity dummy variable α_i and each year β_t.[17] Now if $(p_1/p_2)_{it} = 1$, which means that the relative prices of commodity i are equal, it follows from Equation (3.19) that

$$\log \left(\frac{q_1}{q_2} \right)_{it} = a + \alpha_i + \beta_t \qquad (3.20)$$

A value of $(a + \alpha_i + \beta_t)$ greater than zero signifies the extent of the "nonprice" preference of the importing country (i.e., the rest of the world) for Country 1 goods. A negative value of this sum measures the nonprice preference for Country 2 exports.

The constant term a measures the average preference of the importing country for all the commodities in all the time periods covered by the sample. Its value does not depend on a particular commodity or year. The value of the commodity variable α_i determines whether the preference for a particular commodity differs from the average preference a for all commodities. The α_i's will vary for particular commodities, depending on such factors as transport costs, quality differences, and the demand characteristics of particular import markets. The β_t's measure how relative preferences vary with the time periods due to such factors as changes in world or regional incomes or changes in commercial policy.

The b_i's in Equation (3.19) measure the price elasticities of substitution. These elasticities are constrained by the form of this equation to be constant for each commodity, but the elasticities are permitted to vary among commodities. Thus, if the b_i's are negative, as we would hypothesize, Country 1 will experience, when its price is lower, a greater export demand than Country 2.

It should be evident that the pooling of the cross-section and time-series approaches provides a much richer analysis than either approach individually. Combining the two approaches also makes possible the assessment of the importance of qualitative variables. It is noteworthy that further experimentation with Equation (3.19) by Ginsburg [5] has shown that the results can be improved upon considerably by disaggregating the quantity and price ratios according to individual importing regions and by segmenting the price ratio

---

[17] A full explanation of the use and interpretation of the dummy variables is given in Ginsburg [5].

into intervals in order to allow for complex curvilinearity in the relationship.[18] It would thus appear that a great deal of interesting work can be done using a combination of cross-section and time-series data in estimating the variety of factors, including prices, which determine export ratios and market shares.[19]

CONCLUSION

Our intention in this chapter has been to provide arguments for viewing with skepticism the often-measured elasticity of substitution in international trade. It was shown in particular that the commonly used estimation procedure was valid in the case of two commodities only when there was equality of the algebraic sum of cross and direct elasticities of demand and equality of the income and any other price elasticities of demand. A suggested way in principle to take these conditions into account was to regress relative quantities on separate price variables for the goods in question, income, and the prices of other goods. In case the coefficients on the latter two variables were believed to be small, a regression of relative quantities on the separate price variables (rather than on the price ratio) might be acceptable.

[18] Ginsburg's expanded version of Equation (3.19) is as follows

$$\left(\frac{q_1}{q_1 + q_2}\right)_{i,t,r} = (a + \alpha_i + \beta_t + \gamma_r) + [(b + \delta_i + Z_t + \theta_r) \log \left(\frac{p_1}{p_2}\right)_{i,t,r} + \sum_j \lambda_j (\text{INT}_j)]$$

This formulation expresses $[q_1/(q_1 + q_2)]_{i,t,r}$, Country 1's market share of combined 1 and 2 exports to region r, of commodity i, in year t as a regression on $\log (p_1/p_2)_{i,t,r}$, the relative price of the commodity in that region and year. It will be noted that the dependent variable here is expressed in terms of a market share. Observations were included only when both countries exported to a particular region, thus ruling out zero or 100 percent market shares. Ginsburg is now investigating methods for taking these extreme observations into account.

Both the intercept ($a + \alpha_i + \beta_t + \gamma_r$) and the slope ($b + \delta_i + Z_t + \theta_r$) vary among commodities, years, and regions. Since the slope determines the elasticity of market shares due to the factors just mentioned, this formulation permits detailed analysis of the determinants of elasticities. The intercept measures the influence of nonprice preferences on Country 1's market share. Since the $\log (p_1/p_2)_{i,t,r}$ is zero when both prices are identical, nonprice preferences are measured by the sum of the intercept coefficients. If this sum exceeds 0.5, then Country 1 goods are favored.

The remaining price coefficients λ_j measure nonlinearities in the relation between market shares and relative prices. Each λ_i determines how an importer's reactions occurring in a specified price range differ from the average within a central price range, as measured by b. Separate elasticities can thus be calculated for particular price intervals.

[19] Ginsburg is now engaged in the treatment of interaction effects in the explanatory variables used in the covariance analysis and in the extension of the model to cover more than two countries.

We sought next to question the basis for preferring the measurement of the elasticity of substitution over the measurement of direct demand elasticities as evidence of the international price mechanism. It was shown that the elasticity of substitution was bound to be more negative than the direct elasticity, and that such more negative estimates might result simply from the paths followed by the prices in question. There was some reason to believe, however, that the elasticity-of-substitution relation might be more stable than the separate demand functions.

We then investigated the manner in which the direct elasticity could be derived from the measured substitution elasticities. The question here, however, was why such an indirect procedure was necessary. It may be, as stated, that the indirect approach reduces simultaneity bias and is also more economical in terms of data requirements. These are factual considerations, however, which should be investigated in their own right.

It was suggested finally that there might be particular empirical circumstances involving the export behavior of individual countries when the elasticity of substitution could be measured in conjunction with other explanatory variables. Ginsburg's work on the pooling of time series and cross sections of export behavior was shown in this regard to be potentially very fruitful.

APPENDIX TO CHAPTER 3

In order to investigate the elasticity of substitution when Equation (3.6) is not satisfied, let us differentiate Equation (3.5) to yield

$$
\frac{d \log q_1/q_2}{d \log p_1/p_2} = (\alpha_1 - \beta_1)\left(1 - \frac{d \log p_2}{d \log p_1}\right)^{-1} + (\beta_2 - \alpha_2)\left(1 - \frac{d \log p_1}{d \log p_2}\right)^{-1}
$$
$$
+ (\alpha_y - \beta_y)\left(\frac{d \log p_1}{d \log y} - \frac{d \log p_2}{d \log y}\right)^{-1}
$$
$$
+ (\alpha_n - \beta_n)\left(\frac{d \log p_1}{d \log p_n} - \frac{d \log p_2}{d \log p_n}\right)^{-1}
$$

The last two terms should not affect our estimate of the elasticity of substitution since they reflect changes in q_1/q_2 due to causes other than price movements. If the y and p_n terms are included in the regression equation, the effects of changes in y and p_n on q_1/q_2 will be removed via the multiple correlation technique. If they are not included, the estimated elasticity will be biased unless

$$
\alpha_y = \beta_y \tag{a}
$$

or

$$\frac{d \log y}{(d \log p_1 - d \log p_2)} = \frac{d \log y}{d \log (p_1/p_2)} = 0 \qquad \text{(b)}$$

(that is, y does not respond to p_1/p_2). A similar statement applies to the last term.

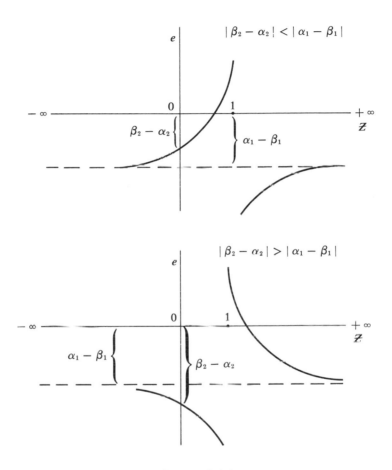

FIGURE 3.A.1

Range of Values of Elasticity of Substitution

Turning now to the first two terms, we see that the elasticity depends on $d \log p_1/d \log p_2$, the particular path followed by the price relative. However, the elasticity will be $\alpha_1 - \beta_1$ when $\beta_2 - \alpha_2 = \alpha_1 - \beta_1$.

Letting

$$Z = \frac{d \log p_1}{d \log p_2} = \frac{dp_1/p_1}{dp_2/p_2}$$

we can solve for e as

$$e = \frac{(\alpha_1 - \beta_1)Z + (\alpha_2 - \beta_2)}{Z - 1}$$

We have, then, the elasticity of substitution as a sort of weighted average of the direct and cross elasticities of demand, with the weights depending on Z, the path of the price relative. Two cases can occur and are graphed in Figure 3.A.1.

The value of e will approximate $\alpha_1 - \beta_1$ at the extreme values of Z, that is, when the variation of p_1 dominates the variation of p_2. When p_1 varies little, Z will be near zero and e will approximate $\beta_2 - \alpha_2$. The reader will note that there are very distinct regions where e is positive. These regions are characterized by movements of p_1 and p_2 that are similar in magnitude and identical in sign.

REFERENCES

1. Bannerji, H., "Elasticities of Substitution for India's Imports," *Artha Vijnana*, 1 (December 1959), 349–66.

2. Brown, A. J., "The Fundamental Elasticities in International Trade," in T. Wilson and P. W. S. Andrews, eds., *Oxford Studies in the Price Mechanism*. London: Oxford University Press, 1951.

3. DaCosta, G. C., "Elasticities of Demand for Indian Exports—An Econometric Investigation," *Indian Economic Journal*, 13 (July–September 1965), 41–54.

4. Fleming, J. M. and S. C. Tsiang, "Changes in Competitive Strength and Export Shares of Major Industrial Countries," International Monetary Fund, *Staff Papers*, V (August 1956), 218–48.

5. Ginsburg, A. L., *American and British Regional Export Determinants*. Amsterdam: North-Holland Publishing Company, 1969.

6. Ginsburg, A. L. and R. M. Stern, "The Determination of the Factors Affecting American and British Exports in the Inter-War and Post-War Periods," *Oxford Economic Papers*, 17 (July 1965), 263–78.

7. Harberger, A. C., "Some Evidence on the International Price Mechanism," *Journal of Political Economy*, LXV (December 1957), 506–21; W. L. Smith, "Comment," *Review of Economics and Statistics*, XL (February 1958, Supplement), 127–29.

8. Hicks, J. R., *Value and Capital*. Oxford: Clarendon, 1946.

9. Junz, H. B. and R. R. Rhomberg, "Prices and Export Performance of Industrial Countries, 1953–63," International Monetary Fund, *Staff Papers*, XII (July 1965), 224–69.

10. Kaliski, S. F., "A Comment on Dr. Zelder's Estimates," *Manchester School*, XXVI (September 1958), 241–46.

11. Kreinin, M. E., "Price Elasticities in International Trade," *Review of Economics and Statistics*, XLIV (November 1967), 510–16.

12. Kubinski, A., "The Elasticity of Substitution between Sources of British Imports, 1921–1938," *Yorkshire Bulletin of Economic and Social Research*, II (January 1950), 17–29.

13. Kubinski, Z. M., "The Effectiveness of Preferential Import Duties," *Economic Record*, XXXV (December 1959), 424–27.

14. MacDougall, G. D. A., "British and American Exports: A Study Suggested by the Theory of Comparative Costs," Part I, *Economic Journal*, LXI (December 1951), 697–724; Part II, LXII (September 1952), 487–521.

15. MacDougall, Sir D. et al., "British and American Productivity, Prices and Exports: An Addendum," *Oxford Economic Papers*, 14 (October 1962), 297–304.

16. Morgan, D. J. and W. J. Corlett, "The Influence of Price in International Trade: A Study in Method," *Journal of the Royal Statistical Society*, Series A, CXIV (Part III, 1951), 307–58.

17. Morrissett, I., "Some Recent Uses of Elasticity of Substitution—A Survey," *Econometrica*, 21 (January 1953), 41–62.

18. Nicholson, R. J., "Product-Elasticity of Substitution in International Trade," and "Rejoinder" by D. G. A. MacDougall, *Economic Journal*, LXV (September 1955), 441–49.

19. Ooms, V. D., "Models of Comparative Export Performance," *Yale Economic Essays*, 7 (Spring 1967), 103–41.

20. Polak, J. J., "Note on the Measurement of Elasticity of Substitution in International Trade," *Review of Economics and Statistics*, XXXII (February 1950), 16–20.

21. Shinkai, Y., "Price Elasticities of the Japanese Exports: A Cross Section Study," *Review of Economics and Statistics*, L (May 1962), 269–73.

22. Stern, R. M. and E. Zupnick, "The Theory and Measurement of Elasticity of Substitution in International Trade," *Kyklos*, XV (Fasc. 3, 1962), 580–93; E. H. Preeg, "Comment," *Kyklos*, XVI (Fasc. 4, 1963), 667–70.

23. Tinbergen, J., "Some Measurements of Elasticities of Substitution," *Review of Economics and Statistics*, XXVII (August 1946), 109–14.

24. Zelder, R. E., "Estimates of Elasticities of Demand for Exports of the United Kingdom and the United States, 1921–38," *Manchester School*, XXVI (January 1958), 33–47.

4

The Estimation of
International
Capital Movements

Chapter 2 provided a discussion of the demand relationships that determine the international flow of goods and services. In this chapter we shall complete our analysis of the determinants of the balance of payments by discussing the nature, causes, and measurement of international capital flows. The present state of econometric inquiry into the capital account is in sharp contrast with the current account. The theoretical aspects of the current account are comparatively well developed and the import/export demand relations involved are highly standardized. Moreover, there are numerous studies of the current account that provide generally good statistical results. In contrast, the theory of capital-account relationships is not well formalized and there exists considerable leeway in the choice of explanatory variables. Furthermore, there are but a handful of econometric studies of capital flows, most of which provide generally poor statistical results.

The explanation for the relative intractability of the capital account can be found in the fundamental differences in the relationships involving real and monetary phenomena. The flow of goods and services is subject to the very powerful economic forces governing supply and demand of tangible items. The relative stability of tastes will assure the relative stability of the demand for goods as a function of price. Significant instability in tastes is most unlikely to occur, so that tastes may ordinarily be neglected in the demand functions. Capital flows, on the other hand, will be influenced importantly by changes in tastes for the alternative securities. The desire to hold a security will be a function of the expected rate of return, not the market rate. This expected return is determined subjectively by the investor and involves a decision that may be quite short-lived. Capital flows consequently may result more from changes in tastes for securities (i.è., expected yields) than from changes in the observed market returns. Theoretical and empirical analysis of security holdings will need to deal with this fact accordingly by developing hypotheses on the formation of expectations. We can anticipate that the isolation of such psychological influences will be somewhat more difficult than the isolation of income and price effects in the analysis of the demand for real goods and services.

The principal role played by nonprice allocative variables forms a second source of difficulty for econometric study of the capital accounts. In our discussion of the demand for imports/exports, we mentioned the role of the capacity utilization variable in reflecting the use of queues to limit sales as an alternative to price increases. A similar phenomenon influences the flow of capital. The bank-lending rate may be set at some low figure while at the same time the bank turns away potential borrowers. Such borrowers may then look to foreign sources for funds. However, this cannot be thought of as a queue phenomenon, since waiting in line will not assure servicing. Rather, credit rationing reflects a suspension of the normal demand-and-supply mechanism. Markets are not cleared and the observed price-quantity point will not reflect the hypothesized ex ante demand.

A third source of difficulty is the important impact of institutions and institutional changes on capital flows. The impact of the institutional environment on the flow of real goods is likely to be minor when compared with its impact on capital flows. Restrictions on capital movements may be quite subtle and highly variable. A firm knowledge of the institutions surrounding the flow of capital will surely be an important element in any study of capital flows that is to be taken seriously.

Keeping the foregoing points in mind, let us now turn directly to the issues involved in measuring the determinants of the capital account. Our discussion will be divided into two sections. The first section provides a very general and comparatively lengthy theoretical description of international capital flows of all varieties, followed by presentation of a framework for analyzing particular capital flows. Our theoretical discussion is developed at some length because the lack of an explicit theory has led to improper specifications of the underlying behavioral relationships in many published empirical studies. In the second section we will discuss the empirical application of the theoretical model, dealing particularly with the concrete choice of explanatory variables.

THE THEORY OF INTERNATIONAL CAPITAL MOVEMENTS

The theory of international capital movements is currently in considerable turmoil. Traditionally, models of international capital transactions have been based upon a set of independent activities, typically trade, interest arbitrage, and forward market speculation. Capital movement, according to this view, is a flow phenomenon; that is, the flow of capital is related to levels of other variables such as interest-rate differentials. Flow models of capital movements have recently come under considerable attack. They imply, for instance, that in a static world, with fixed interest rates, investors will continue to accumulate claims on foreigners indefinitely. The inadequacy of such an assumption has led to the construction of stock models of capital movements, based upon portfolio-adjustment assumptions, according to which the stock of claims on foreigners is related to levels of variables such as interest-rate differentials and net worth.

Although the current stock models are clearly preferable to flow models of international capital movements, they are not wholly adequate either. Before discussing several shortcomings of these models, let us consider one in some detail. According to the stock models, the international flow of capital results from the decisions of individual investors who allocate their net worth among the alternative investment opportunities. This allocation is very similar to the allocation of income to various consumable commodities. In the case of the investor, net worth is allocated to investment opportunities to provide high yield and low risk.[1] The mixture of expected return and risk will depend on the investor's preferences. Assuming two alternative types of investments and one type of credit, we may write the following expression

$$K = K(\mu_k, \sigma_k, \mu_c, \sigma_c, \mu_b, \sigma_b, W) \qquad (4.1)$$

to indicate that the investment in asset K will depend on the expected return to K, μ_k; the risk associated with K, σ_k; the return μ_c and risk σ_c of the alternative investment; the expected cost and cost-variability (say, from default) of borrowing, μ_b and σ_b; and net worth W.[2] We can expect that increases in return μ_k and decreases in risk σ_k will be associated with increased holdings of K. Similarly, reductions in return and increments to risk of the substitute will induce increases in the allocation of funds to K. We would generally expect W to have a positive effect on the holdings of K just as income has a positive effect on the demand for real goods. However, in perverse cases, increases in net worth may be associated with reductions in the holdings of a security. This is analogous to the inferior good in real demand analysis.

In addition to the opportunity to purchase securities, the investor may be able to issue securities himself or equivalently obtain bank loans to secure additional funds. Increases in the rate and risk of borrowing, μ_b and σ_b, will stimulate reductions in the holdings of K. For example, increases in the rate at which credit can be obtained to finance inventories will result in the reduction of inventory holdings.

---

[1] The investor may dislike uncertainty or he may value losses of income much more highly than additions and therefore guard against such loss by avoiding risky investments.

[2] The risk variables may or may not be associated with the standard errors of subjective probability distributions. They are meant to be simply what the investor states about the risk quite apart from any sophisticated ideas concerning what risk is or should be.

We have already suggested by the use of the borrowing variables μ_b and σ_b that our hypothesized investor may issue securities (borrow) as well as purchase them. For example, banks may be characterized as borrowing short-term funds in order to finance long-term lending. The supply of securities or equivalently the demand for credit may also be described by Equation (4.1) with minor modifications of the explanatory variables. That is, the supply of security K will depend on the expected interest payment μ_k and the variability of that payment (say, from default) σ_k; similar variables for a substitute credit source, μ_c and σ_c; the return and risk that are expected when the funds are allocated to some investment opportunity, μ_b and σ_b; and net worth W.

Equation (4.1) has been used to describe the desired stock of assets and, with a slight modification, the desired stock of liabilities. The observed capital flow corresponds to a change in the stock of these assets/liabilities that is induced by a change in the explanatory variables on either the demand or supply side. A complete empirical examination of international capital movements will thus require estimated equations for both the demand and supply of securities. The theory we will discuss presently will concentrate primarily on the demand side. The supply of securities will result from conditions internal to each country and an examination of the supply side would require us to discuss internal monetary relations. We will therefore assume that internal conditions in each country determine the prevailing interest rates and that the flow of capital results from demanders seeking securities at the internally determined rates. But in any event, if desired, the general equation (4.1) may be applied to domestic monetary relations, and a full model of the international monetary system can be constructed within the same framework.

The foregoing very general description of the capital decision is meant to describe the demand and supply of funds embodied in all capital instruments, including short-term and long-term, portfolio, and direct investments. Before discussing the selection of the variables that appropriately reflect the risks and returns of specific types of instruments, let us consider two important shortcomings of the portfolio-adjustment view of capital movements. The first stems from the static conception of portfolio adjustment, in which net worth is taken as given. This may enable portfolio models to explain, say, the ratio of foreign to domestic assets, but this leaves undetermined the scale of portfolio holdings. In many cases, capital movements may be more the result of decisions that influence the size of net worth rather than the allocation of net worth among potential assets. To put this in another way, the portfolio-adjustment models provide only a partial explanation of capital movements.

The second drawback concerns the excessive simplicity of the model. In effect, it asserts the obvious: investments are chosen on the basis of risk and return. This tends to obscure the true complexity of the investment decision.

The formation of expectations regarding risks and returns is a very complicated phenomenon. In addition, short-term constraints on various transactors may be so severe that long-run portfolio-balance considerations are secondary in determining behavior. With these limitations in mind, let us resume our discussion of the portfolio-adjustment model.

The Stock-Flow Problem　We have already mentioned the fact that the traditional view of international capital movements is based upon a *flow* model in which the flow of capital (the change in the stock) is related to interest-rate variables. The portfolio-adjustment model we have just discussed relates the *stock* of capital to interest-rate and net worth variables. Still a third view would have us believe that some capital flows result from stock decisions and others from flow decisions.[3]

There should be no room for confusion on this point. Careful consideration of the behavior of the relevant transactors implies that the portfolio and credit decisions and direct investment are *stock* phenomena. The desired *stock* of claims against foreigners is related to the return, risk, and net worth variables. In a static world there would be no capital flow as portfolios would be fully adjusted to the desired levels.

Of course, a growing net worth will be allocated to the investment opportunities according to the levels of the yields. This is sometimes confusedly referred to as a flow, when in fact it is a stock adjustment to the change in net worth. We should also observe that if we neglect the net worth variable, then the data may be more amenable to a flow description. This can be taken to be the principal reason why such investigators as Kenen [18], Black [3], and Stein [29] have had considerable success with flow equations. Another possible explanation lies in the adjustment-lag structure.

Although the capital movements necessarily result from a stock decision, it is unlikely that actual stocks are instantaneously adjusted to the desired levels. The lag between a change in an independent variable and recognition of that change, the lag between recognition and action, the time spent in queues waiting to be serviced by creditors, and transactions costs will all tend to delay the adjustment of the actual stock of credit to the desired stocks.

There is a possibility that although the capital movement is actually a stock phenomenon, it may appear to be a flow due to the nature of the response lag.[4] This will be the case when the adjustment is spread evenly over a large number of periods. Thus, suppose that the actual stock Y_t is related to explanatory variables as follows

$$Y_t = k + \sum_{i=0}^{\infty} \alpha_i X_{t-i} \qquad (4.2)$$

---

[3] These issues pertain especially to the works of Bell [2], Kenen [18], and Stein [29].
[4] This point is made by Hendershott in [29].

Then the flow $Y_t - Y_{t-1}$ is given by

$$Y_t - Y_{t-1} = \alpha_0 X_t + \sum_{i=0}^{\infty} (\alpha_{i+1} - \alpha_i) X_{t-i-1} \qquad (4.3)$$

If the values of α are such that $\alpha_{i+1} \simeq \alpha_i$ for all i, then Equation (4.3) becomes

$$Y_t - Y_{t-1} \simeq \alpha_0 X_t \qquad (4.4)$$

that is, the *flow* is related to the *level* of the explanatory variable. Thus, we see that a stock phenomenon may appear to be a flow phenomenon when the adjustment to the desired stock is rather evenly spread over many periods.

Our general description of the capital decision will now need to be specified more precisely for certain subcategories of assets. In the remainder of this section we will discuss the selection of the variables that appropriately reflect the risks and returns of specific types of investments and their close substitutes.

Short-Term Portfolio Investment [5] We will discuss the theory of short-term capital movements in the context of a two-country world. For convenience, we will call the domestic country America and the foreign country England. An American investor seeking to purchase a foreign security for investment purposes would first buy pounds at the going rate and subsequently purchase the foreign security. At the maturity date of the security he would receive the principal and interest earnings in pounds, which would be redeemed for dollars through the foreign exchange market. If the exchange rate could not change during the maturity period, then the investor would be assured of earning the foreign interest rate in his own currency, dollars. If, however, the price of pounds were to fall substantially during the maturity period, the domestic investor would be left holding relatively cheap pounds and his investment may have yielded a net loss in terms of dollars. The need to insure against such a loss can be met by means of a transaction in the market for forward pounds. Thus, for example, when a 90-day English security is purchased, the American investor would simultaneously assume a contract to sell the pounds in 90 days at the currently quoted forward rate, thereby insuring against any loss (or gain) from a fluctuation in the exchange rate. Such a transaction is referred to as covered interest arbitrage to indicate that the underlying motive is interest earnings and that the possibility of exchange loss is "covered" by the forward contract.

[5] Several theoretical descriptions of short-term capital movements exist in the literature. The one presented here is essentially a modification of the work of Levin [23], which is based on a theoretical analysis of portfolio selection in the context of the foreign exchange market.

While there are quite naturally several markets for forward pounds of varying contract date, we will assume for the present that only 90-day forward foreign exchange is available. Similarly the domestic and foreign securities are assumed to have 90-day maturities. The following notation will be employed:

R_s = the current spot rate; the dollar price of one pound delivered today.

R_f = the current forward rate; the dollar price today of one pound to be delivered in 90 days.

i_a = the American 90-day interest rate.

i_e = the English 90-day interest rate.

p_e = the pound price of English goods.

p_a = the dollar price of American goods.

Three opportunities for investment are available to the domestic investor. He may purchase domestic securities; he may purchase foreign securities with the exchange risk covered in the forward market; or he may speculate in the forward market. Speculation in the forward market involves the acquisition of contracts to buy (sell) foreign exchange in 90 days in the hope that the future spot rate will be higher (lower) than the current forward rate. When the contract becomes due, the speculator sells (buys) pounds in the spot market to discharge (obtain) the foreign exchange obtained (necessitated) by his contract. An alternative investment opportunity, uncovered interest arbitrage, involves the purchase of a foreign security without a cover in the forward market. We will think of such a transaction as being covered interest arbitrage with a simultaneous and equal speculative purchase of a forward contract.[6] Accordingly, uncovered interest arbitrage will be implicitly examined by considering covered arbitrage and speculation.

The domestic investor will allocate his net worth W_a among the alternative investment opportunities in an effort to achieve high yield and low risk. The holding of English assets acquired by the covered interest-arbitrage transaction is given by

$$A_a = A_a(\overset{+}{\mu_e}, \overset{-}{\sigma_e}, \overset{-}{\mu_a}, \overset{+}{\sigma_a}, \overset{-}{\mu_s}, \overset{+-}{\sigma_s}, \overset{+}{W_a}) \qquad (4.5)$$

where μ_e and μ_a are the expected yields of the foreign and domestic securities and μ_s is the expected yield from speculation, while σ_e, σ_a, σ_s are the risks associated with these investments. The influences of these independent variables are given by the signs above them.

[6] Suppose for example that an investor transfers $1 through the spot market to obtain a foreign security worth $1/R_s$ pounds. This transaction is equivalent to a $1 transfer through the spot market covered in the forward market by a sale of forward pounds equal to $(1/R_s)(1 + i_e)$ combined with a forward speculative purchase of $(1/R_s)(1 + i_e)$ pounds. The investor who engages in uncovered arbitrage will do so only if both the covered arbitrage and the speculative position are expected to yield a return.

Increases in the covered return to foreign securities μ_e, and decreases in the risk of holding them σ_e will induce shifts out of the domestic securities and into the foreign securities, that is, increases in the arbitrage stock demand A_a. The domestic return μ_a and risk σ_a will have just the opposite effect on A_a. The signs on μ_s and σ_s are not so obvious since there is no monetary constraint on the speculative position similar to the portfolio-size constraint on purchases of domestic and foreign assets. However, an increase in the return on the speculative position will be accompanied by an increased speculative position and therefore increased total risk. To economize on risk elsewhere, the investor may shift out of the relatively risky foreign asset and into the domestic security, and consequently reduce A_a. The sign on σ_s is somewhat more ambiguous. Increases in the speculative risk will be associated with a reduction in the speculative position. Whether this will be translated into changes in the arbitrage demand is unclear. Except in the perverse case of the inferior security, the influence of the wealth variable W will be positive.

The expected return variables in Equation (4.5) may be defined somewhat more concretely. For the moment we will assume that the security is denominated in the foreign currency. The return on covered interest arbitrage μ_e can be calculated as follows. The domestic investor will use one dollar to purchase $1/R_s$ in pounds, buy a foreign security of that value, and assume a forward contract to sell $(1 + i_e)/R_s$ pounds in 90 days at the rate R_f. In 90 days the foreign security will yield $(1 + i_e)/R_s$ pounds, just enough to meet the contract assumed earlier. That contract will provide $(1 + i_e)R_f/R_s$ dollars, for a nominal rate of return of $(1 + i_e)R_f/R_s - 1$. But this is not an entirely riskless investment. In the first place, there is a possibility that exchange controls will be implemented by the foreign country. There is also the possibility that the security will have to be sold before maturity to finance domestic transactions. Finally, the security may be sold before maturity to switch funds to domestic securities to take advantage of increases in yields. These considerations imply:[7]

$$\mu_e = \frac{(1 + i_e)R_f}{R_s} - 1 + \bar{v}_e \qquad (4.6)$$

and

$$\sigma_e = \sigma_e(v_e) \qquad (4.7)$$

where $\bar{v}_e$ is the expected influence of the three considerations mentioned above on the rate of return, and $\sigma_e(v_e)$ reflects the variability or risk associated with that return.

The domestic security will yield an interest rate of i_a if held to maturity. As with the foreign asset, there is a possibility of switching into a higher-

---

[7] Balances for transactions purposes may be considered by adjusting these yields to include the convenience rendered by the liquid balance.

yielding asset, this time the foreign security. In addition, the domestic security may have to be liquidated to finance transactions. We have, therefore,

$$\mu_a = i_a + \bar{v}_a \tag{4.8}$$

and

$$\sigma_a = \sigma_a(v_a) \tag{4.9}$$

with $\bar{v}_a$ and $\sigma_a(v_a)$ defined to reflect the variability of the rate of return associated with the factors discussed above.

A speculative contract to sell one pound in 90 days at the current forward rate R_f will yield a profit of $(R_f - R_s^{90})$ dollars in 90 days, where R_s is the spot rate in 90 days. The expected return will not depend on the actual spot rate in 90 days, but rather on the expected future spot rate, $\overline{R}_s^{90}$. Thus we have

$$\mu_s = |R_f - \overline{R}_s^{90}| \tag{4.10}$$

and

$$\sigma_s = \sigma_s(R_s^{90}) \tag{4.11}$$

where $\overline{R}_s^{90}$ is the expected future spot rate and $\sigma_s(R_s^{90})$ reflects the investor's confidence that the future rate will actually conform with his expectations.

To this point the form of the function in Equation (4.2) has been left arbitrary. One form in particular has received considerable attention in both theoretical and empirical discussions of short-term capital flows. That is, the arbitrage demand A_a has been taken to depend on the expected yields only through the difference in those yields, the covered interest differential $\mu_e - \mu_a$

$$A_a = A_a(\mu_e - \mu_a, \sigma_e, \sigma_a, \mu_s, \sigma_s, W_a) \tag{4.12}$$

Furthermore, it has been assumed that American investors will hold English securities only when the expected yield on the English securities exceeds the expected yield on the competing American security; that is, $A_a = 0$ when $\mu_e - \mu_a \leq 0$.[8] This restriction just noted ignores the possibility of risk re-

---

[8] If slight increases in μ_e over μ_a bring forth a flood of American investors seeking English securities, and if English investors behave symmetrically, the forward and spot rates will adjust to maintain the equality of the yields, $\mu_e = \mu_a$. In the absence of the uncertainty terms, this becomes

$$\frac{(1 + i_e)R_f}{R_s} - (1 + i_a) = 0$$

which can be manipulated [neglecting $i_e(R_f - R_s)/R_s$], to yield the familiar "interest parity condition"

$$\frac{R_f - R_s}{R_s} = i_a - i_e$$

relating the forward premium to the interest rate differential.

duction through portfolio diversification, a principle that may induce the securing of a relatively low-yield asset. Moreover, a restriction such as this, being essentially empirical in character, should not be imposed upon the data unless there exists overwhelming support for it on a priori grounds.

The selection of yields in Equations (4.6) and (4.7) has been based on the assumption that the foreign security is denominated in the foreign currency. In some cases the security will be denominated in dollars, and the risk of exchange-rate fluctuation is transferred to the security seller. For example, American banks may issue dollar-denominated loans to foreign customers. In this case, the appropriate yield variable in the supply-of-funds equation will be the yield quoted in the contract, while the yield variable in the demand-for-funds equation (supply of securities) will include the adjustment necessary to cover in the forward exchange market.

It may be noted parenthetically that what we have just said departs from our earlier-stated intention of concentrating on the demand-for-securities equation rather than the supply. We do so because the roles of the two equations have been reversed. While before, the borrowing rate was thought to be essentially internally determined and the international capital movement resulted from investors' seeking out of foreign investment opportunities, we now have the lending rate being internally determined with borrowers seeking out loanable funds. The only theoretical or empirical difference is the question of who undertakes the international exchange of capital or who bears the exchange risk, and what the appropriate return variables to use in the demand and supply equations consequently are.

The equations just discussed describe the American demand for English securities, or equivalently the American supply of funds to English borrowers. With minor obvious modifications the same equations can describe the demand for American securities by English investors.

Speculation We have just described speculation as the acquisition of forward contracts to buy (sell) foreign exchange in anticipation that the future spot rate will be higher (lower) than the current forward rate. The expected yield from such a transaction is given by Equation (4.10) as the absolute difference between the current forward rate and the expected future spot rate.

It should be emphasized that speculation does not directly involve the flow of capital since no securities are transferred between countries by such a transaction. However, speculative activity may influence the movement of capital in three different ways. First of all, the holding of foreign securities by domestic investors described by Equation (4.5) is directly influenced by the return and risk associated with speculative transactions. Thus, for example, in periods when the expected return to speculation is high, investors may shift out of foreign securities and into domestic securities. Secondly, speculative activity will influence the forward rate and consequently the covered return on foreign securities. For example, a speculative attack on the pound will involve the sale of forward pounds in anticipation of a fall in the spot rate (a devaluation of the pound). The sale of forward pounds will depress the forward rate and consequently the covered return on English securities μ_e. This will make English securities less attractive to American investors and a capital flight from English securities will occur. Finally, the speculative activity may influence the expected return and risk variables. Periods of considerable speculative activity associated with large expected returns and low risk to speculation are likely to be accompanied by the fear of capital controls and therefore a reduction in the expected return and an increase in the risk associated with the foreign security. This will also serve to make the foreign security less attractive.

If our only concern were to estimate the demand-for-capital equation (4.5), then there would be no reason to discuss a speculative function. The considerations in the paragraph above could at most influence our choice of explanatory variables. However, a complete model of the balance of payments will properly include the forward exchange rate as an endogenous variable. Speculative activity will have an important impact on that forward rate and should be included in the model. Our discussion of speculation is thus included in this chapter not because it represents a capital movement directly, but rather because it is part of the general portfolio decision which includes the acquisition of foreign securities.

The speculative purchases or sales of forward pounds by American investors is given by

$$S_a = \operatorname{sign}(\overline{R}^{90} - R_f) \times S_a(\overset{+}{\mu_s}, \overset{-}{\sigma_s}, \overset{-}{\mu_e}, \overset{+}{\sigma_e}, \overset{-}{\mu_a}, \overset{+}{\sigma_a}, \overset{+}{W_a}) \qquad (4.13)$$

where the signs above the variables indicate their influence on S_a. The first term, $\operatorname{sign}(\overline{R}^{90} - R_f)$, indicates the sign of the difference between the expected future spot rate and the current forward rate and will determine whether the investor is buying or selling forward pounds. If the expected future spot rate exceeds the current forward rate, this first term will be positive, indicating a demand for forward pounds. If the reverse is true, the term will become negative and the speculative position will be composed of contracts to sell or supply pounds. The scale of the speculative position will be determined by the second term. The explanatory variables are defined by Equations (4.5) to (4.11), and the signs above them follow from the discussion of Equation (4.1).[9]

Parenthetically, we should note that we have implicitly assumed that forward contracts are available without cost. In fact, bankers and brokers

[9] This discussion will be amended somewhat when a "margin" is required to assume a forward contract, since the margin requirement reduces the effective rate of return on speculation and also introduces the speculative position into the portfolio-size constraint.

may either require a margin on the contract or deny the contract altogether. This considerably complicates our theory, particularly since the margin requirement and the extent of rationing may vary considerably, depending on the turbulence in the foreign exchange markets. When margins are required, both the return on covered interest arbitrage and the return on forward market speculation will be reduced by an amount depending on the extent and terms of the margin requirement. When forward market contracts are unavailable, only uncovered arbitrage will be possible and the foregoing theory will have to be appropriately amended.

Trade Credit and Trade Arbitrage The second main type of short-term capital movement consists of trade credit, loans issued ostensibly for the financing of international trade. In the course of their business dealings, traders will have an opportunity to borrow funds from one country and invest them in another. In some cases, funds are supplied by the exporter or the exporter's bank to allow the importer a temporary delay in payment for goods received. That is, funds are borrowed from the exporting country and invested in inventories in the importing country. This flow is appropriately called trade credit. In other cases, the funds may appear to be financing trade in this fashion when in fact they are invested in portfolio securities. This is a pure interest arbitrage transaction involving borrowing in one country at a relatively low interest rate and investing at a higher rate in another country. It is appropriately termed trade arbitrage. Other individuals may desire to undertake a similar transfer of funds, but will be unable to secure the foreign loans with the ease that traders can. We will consider the case of trade arbitrage first.

Let us assume that there is no time required for the shipment of goods between the countries and that the importers are able to forecast sales with perfect accuracy. In this case, there is no need for inventory since the importers will arrange to have the goods delivered on precisely the same day as they are sold. There is thus no need for commercial credit. The American importer may pay for the goods by purchasing pounds on the spot market. Alternatively he may have "hedged" earlier against the possibility of exchange-rate fluctuation through a forward contract to buy pounds assumed 90 days before the transfer of funds was required. Neither of these transactions involves the flow of capital. However, the importer may make a profit if he can obtain credit. He may delay payment for the goods by borrowing funds from an English bank at the rate i_e. In this case, the P_e pounds necessary to pay the English exporter are supplied by a bank in the foreign country. The American importer purchases a forward contract to buy $P_e(1 + i_e)$ pounds in 90 days at the rate R_f to meet his obligation with the bank. A total of $P_e(1 + i_e)R_f/(1 + i_a)$ dollars is used to purchase American securities, which in 90 days will yield $P_e(1 + i_e)R_f$ dollars, just enough to meet the forward contract to buy pounds. This transaction yields him a current savings of $P_e[R_s - (1 + i_e)R_f/(1 + i_a)]$ dollars.

This transaction consists of an immediate payment for the imports through the spot market and a simultaneous pure interest arbitrage transaction involving borrowing from the English bank and purchasing an American security. Funds that may appear to be financing trade are in fact going into American securities. According to our general model of the portfolio decision, the demand for such credit (supply of securities) will be given by

$$\text{Cr}_e^a = \text{Cr}_e^a(\mu_e, \ \sigma_e, \ \mu_c, \ \sigma_c, \ \mu_a, \ \sigma_a, \ W_a) \tag{4.14}$$

to denote that the demand for English credit (in dollars) by American importers depends on the cost and cost variability of that credit and alternative credit, μ_e, σ_e, μ_c, σ_c; the rate and variability of return to be gained from that credit, μ_a, σ_a; and the net worth of the American importer, W_a. The natural definitions for μ_e and μ_a are

$$\mu_e = \frac{(1 + i_e)R_f}{R_s} - 1 \qquad \text{(nominal cost of credit)} \tag{4.15}$$

$$\mu_a = i_a$$

The possibility of exchange control affecting capital flows associated with merchandise trade is very remote, and σ_e and σ_a may be taken therefore to be zero.

One may wonder whether Equation (4.14) is an accurate representation of the demand for trade arbitrage funds. When $\mu_e < \mu_a$, each dollar secured is expected to yield a net return. It would appear that traders would desire as much credit as there is available. On the other hand, Equation (4.14) suggests that traders may spend more time seeking out arbitrage funds when the spread between μ_e and μ_a is large. Similarly, the trader's net worth W_a may influence his search for arbitrage funds. Of course, both of these possibilities may prove to be unimportant empirically.

There will also be a flow of funds associated with American exports, or English imports. The English importer may anticipate the required payment and borrow from his bank $P_a/R_s(1 + i_a)$ pounds. These funds are used to purchase $P_a/(1 + i_a)$ dollars of American securities, which in 90 days would be worth just the amount required to purchase the American goods. As before, this is a combination of a trade decision and a portfolio decision. The portfolio decision can be described as

$$\text{Cr}_e^e = \text{Cr}_e^e(\mu_e, \ \sigma_e, \ \mu_c, \ \sigma_c, \ \mu_a, \ \sigma_a, \ W_e) \tag{4.16}$$

to denote that the demand for English credit (in pounds) by English importers depends on the factors already mentioned. The natural definitions in this case are

$$\mu_e = i_e$$

$$\mu_a = \frac{(1 + i_a)R_s}{R_f} - 1 \quad \text{(nominal cost of credit)} \quad (4.17)$$

$$\mu_c = \mu_a$$

$$\sigma_c = \sigma_a = \sigma_e \simeq 0$$

We have stated that trade arbitrage may be thought to involve jointly the trade flow and the pure interest arbitrage financed by the credit source. Now any investor, regardless of whether he is an importer or not, has the opportunity of engaging in the pure interest-arbitrage transaction. He needs no funds of his own as banks (or other creditors) extend credit to finance the interest arbitrage. The profit to be made is limited only by the amount of credit available. There are, however, two important distinctions between the trader and the nontrader. The first has already been mentioned and concerns the risk variable. Trade arbitrage is appropriately thought to be a riskless investment opportunity. Exchange control is unlikely to affect capital flows associated with export and import trade. Accordingly both the trader and his credit sources will be much more willing to engage in pure interest arbitrage than a nontrader and his creditors. Moreover, the credit source may not realize that he is supporting pure interest arbitrage. The second distinction applies only to the case when funds are being sought by a nonresident. The trader will have close contacts with foreign sources of credit not available to other nonresidents. Accordingly, we will assume that credit is available only to traders.

If as suggested above, traders seek all the credit that is available for trade arbitrage, the flow of funds will be completely determined by the willingness of creditors to supply funds. According to our portfolio selection theory, the supply of credit by English creditors to American importers is given by

$$\text{Cr}_e^a = \text{Cr}_e^a(\mu_k, \sigma_k, \mu_c, \sigma_c, \mu_b, \sigma_b, W_e) \quad (4.18)$$

where μ_k, σ_k reflect the return from the credit; μ_c, σ_c reflect returns to alternative investments; μ_b, σ_b reflect the cost of borrowing; and W_e is the net worth of the English creditor. In the event that the credit source is also an exporter, the return from that credit should include the profit rate on the exports induced by the credit extension. The risk that capital controls will affect the return can be thought to be zero up to some level of credit that increments with the level of English exports. Accordingly, English exports may be an explanatory variable.

An equation identical to (4.18) will describe the extension of credit by English banks to English importers. In this case the return μ_k will necessarily not include any profit rate. In addition the risk term should include English imports and not exports.

Finally, let us consider the case when the capital flow is used to finance inventories of the traded good, that is, when it is trade credit. We must discard the assumption that there is no time required for shipment and no uncertainty with regard to sales. Both of these considerations will lead to the holding of inventory. The former requires inventories in the holds of ships in transit and the latter requires inventories on hand. Such inventories will be financed by commercial credit. The source of that credit will depend on the nominal interest rates. American importers will look to English banks when

$$\frac{(1 + i_e)R_f}{R_s} - 1 < i_a \tag{4.19}$$

that is, when the nominal interest rate is lower in England than in America or when the covered interest differential exceeds zero. The demand for such credit will increment with the return to inventory holdings.

Domestic industries will also have need for funds to finance inventories. If those funds are most cheaply secured abroad, then there will be a natural desire on the part of all domestic industries to seek foreign sources of credit. However, the same considerations that deter nontraders from pure interest arbitrage financed by commercial banks will also deter domestic industries from using foreign funds to finance inventories. These considerations are the risk associated with capital controls and the lack of close business contacts with foreign creditors. Nonetheless, some short-term credit may be extended to finance trade strictly external to the lending country, and a variable reflecting returns to such inventories might be taken into account.

Only minor adjustments are needed to include the inventory factor. The amount of credit demanded by American importers from English sources [Equation (4.14)] will have to include a return-to-inventory variable. This simply reflects the fact that the return from the investment of the loan will be the return to inventory when that loan is used to finance inventories rather than arbitrage. The supply-of-credit equation (4.18) may also be affected by the inventory factor. Credit extended to finance inventories of exported goods is likely to generate significantly more exports and hence more profit than similar extensions of credit for arbitrage.[10] Accordingly the return to credit extended for inventory purposes will far exceed the return to arbitrage credit.

[10] This point will also apply to the flow of real goods. The extension of credit for inventories is likely to have a prime impact on the value of the international flow of goods, since presumably without credit no flow could occur. A rather small extension of credit for inventories may beget large increases in trade flows. The extension of credit for trade abritrage, on the other hand, is likely to have a marginal impact on the international flow of goods. Such arbitrage credit will provide a source of additional profit to the trader, which may be passed on to the consumer in the form of lower prices, thereby inducing a greater volume of sales and a larger flow of goods. The import/export functions used by Levin [23] in his model of the foreign exchange market include this influence.

Long-Term Portfolio Investment   Credit instruments are divided in practice somewhat arbitrarily into long-term and short-term categories with a maturity date of one year as the borderline. For our purposes, however, the distinction between short- and long-term capital flows is not to be sharply drawn, although of course the explanatory variables may have to be adjusted to apply specifically to the long-term instruments.

One important distinction between long- and short-term capital that deserves emphasis concerns liquidity and risk. Long-term securities will be somewhat less liquid than short-term securities. But this amounts to little more than observing that long-term securities are not close substitutes for transactions balances. Related to this is the added risk associated with exchange controls, since as the maturity date moves into the future, the investor becomes less and less certain concerning the possibility of exchange control.

Another important feature of long-term investment may be the absence of a well-organized forward market. Although the investor may be able to obtain a forward cover for his investment, the cost of that cover may possibly be prohibitive. Long-term investment may therefore be conveniently thought to include an important speculative element.

The appropriate return variables to explain long-term bonds will be obvious since they have certain stated yields associated with them. The appropriate return variables to use with equities will not be obvious, however. The returns to equities are dividends and capital gains. In order to explain the acquisition of equities, we will have to understand the formation of expectations about dividends and capital gains. The appropriate choice of variables is discussed further in the next section.

It should be noted that the short-term interest rate may have an effect on long-term security acquisitions. The substitution between short- and long-term securities on the demand side may not be important, but the ability to borrow short-term funds at low interest rates may well induce significant additional long-term acquisitions. In terms of our general model described by Equation (4.1), this consideration is reflected in the borrowing variables, μ_b and σ_b.

Direct Investment   Direct investment is distinguished from portfolio investment by the extent of control over the firm's decisions exercised by the investor. The returns to direct investment include a return for that decision making as well as a normal return for capital. Kindleberger [19, pp. 389–93] points out that direct investment will be preferred to portfolio investment only when the return for decision making or entrepreneurial wisdom is "abnormally" high. Otherwise the investor will prefer to allocate his entrepreneurial abilities elsewhere. He would then invest in either bonds or equity and sell or rent any patents the industry might need in addition to the capital funds.

Abnormal returns to entrepreneurial control will occur especially in industries that are monopolized and in cases where disequilibrium profits can be earned. Accordingly, we shall expect to find relatively large corporations with significant monopoly power and/or aggressive management engaging in direct investments. This description is consistent with Vernon's [34] theory of the product cycle. According to that theory, heavy expenditures for research and development occur in the United States and consequently new products are first marketed there. As the product matures, firms become more responsive to least-cost locations. One firm makes the decision to locate a subsidiary abroad. Other firms may follow not so much out of real economic incentives as from simple fear of the possibility of losing their competitive position due to competition from the foreign production. Such a fear need not and often does not have a basis in economic facts.

One point that should be clear is that a portfolio-adjustment view of direct investment is not particularly illuminating. The location of facilities abroad is one of a large number of intertwined decisions made by international corporations. The simplicity of the portfolio-adjustment model barely begins to explain such a process. Although adequate models of direct investment do not exist, there is a rather large literature on domestic investment that should form a useful starting point. It should be mentioned, however, that the empirical support of investment theories is notoriously weak. When we add the location factor required to explain direct investment, we should expect still weaker evidence.

This completes our theoretical discussion of the investment decision. We have considered a whole spectrum of investment opportunities ranging from short-term securities to equities and direct investment. As we move through this spectrum, expectations of future events become more and more important, and the specification of the proper explanatory variables becomes more and more difficult. In the next section, we will provide a discussion of the empirical application of our model, in which we will be forced to deal with the formation of expectations. Our theoretical discussion suggests that we will obtain the best fits for short-term capital and the worst fits for direct investment.

THE MEASUREMENT OF INTERNATIONAL CAPITAL MOVEMENTS [11]

There remain a fairly large number of problems that must be solved before our general model of international capital movements can be esti-

---

[11] The following discussion is based in large part on Leamer and Stern [21].

mated. These problems are concerned generally with how best to represent the behavioral characteristics as yet unspecified and how to handle some purely statistical problems. We shall deal in particular with the following: (1) choice of net worth variable; (2) measuring expected returns and risk; (3) choice of trade variables; (4) handling of speculative activity; (5) capital controls and credit rationing; (6) disaggregation schemes; (7) lag structure; (8) functional form; and (9) simultaneity.

Choice of Net Worth Variable   Net worth and other scale variables are presumably very important in determining capital movements, and their omission in many published empirical papers is a very serious shortcoming. This is analogous to excluding an income term in an import-demand equation. From the point of view of the private sector, net worth is private capital stock, plus net claims on foreigners, plus government debt. GNP may be an appropriate proxy. However, disaggregated equations should use a net worth item specific to the institutions and individuals who are undertaking the particular capital transaction. Furthermore, it seems very doubtful that corporations are behaving as implied by the portfolio-adjustment model and, therefore, aggregation that includes the corporate sector should be avoided.

Measuring Expected Returns and Risk   Since the expected returns and risk variables used in most theoretical descriptions of asset accumulation are ordinarily unobservable, it is necessary to adopt some procedure to make these concepts operational. We can either seek proxy variables to represent expected returns and risk or else construct models of expectations formation concerning these phenomena. It may be possible in addition to identify time periods separately on the basis of important changes in expectations that affect behavior.

Uncertainty over returns stemming from the holding of foreign debt instruments is associated primarily with the possibility of devaluation and/or capital controls. The proxy variables sought should therefore reflect pressure on the authorities induced by balance-of-payments difficulties. Expected returns and risks of equities and direct investments may also be affected by such balance-of-payments considerations, but in addition expectations will depend upon business-climate variables.[12]

An alternative to using proxy variables is to construct a model of expectations formation. Ordinarily, this involves the assumption that the expected future returns/risk are a constant function of current and historical

[12] See Miller and Whitman [24] for a more extensive discussion of proxy variables for returns/risk that relate to portfolio investment. Their model includes the lagged value of the U.S. balance-of-payments liquidity deficit and deviations of U.S. GNP from trend. They have also experimented unsuccessfully with changes in aggregate exchange reserves of selected foreign countries, the ratio of forward and spot rates, and a ratio of the spot rate in period $t+1$ to the spot rate in period t.

values of the rates in question. This assumption is clearly inapplicable to the spot rate in a pegged exchange-rate system, although it may be acceptable in this system when applied to the forward rate and to returns to equities and direct investment.[13]

A further alternative is to identify turbulent periods in which changes in expectations had an important effect upon behavior. This may be done by exploring the regression residuals in an interest-parity model, as Stein did [29], by assuming that large residuals from interest parity reflect a suspension of the normal behavior pattern in favor of speculation. In place of concentration on the residuals, however, a preferable approach, discussed more fully below, might be to separate the data on an a priori basis into "normal" and "speculative" periods and perform regression analysis separately on each data set.

On occasion researchers have used the domestic counterpart of the foreign investment as an explanatory variable, particularly in the case of direct investment.[14] The rationale is that the level of domestic investment reflects the appropriate yield variable. However, the comparatively good fits that are obtained should not be construed as an empirical solution to the problem since there still remains domestic investment to "explain." More important, this represents a confusion in the appropriate causal sequence that determines both foreign investment and domestic investment simultaneously. The impact of such a causal reordering on the implications of an estimated model has not as yet been analyzed.

Choice of Trade Variables Our theoretical analysis has indicated that credit extended to commercial traders is related to the profitability of the transaction from the points of view of both borrower and lender. Traditionally trade credit is related not to profit variables, but rather to imports or exports, i.e., sales. It is important to decide just what trade variables should be used to explain trade credit and to link those variables with the underlying profitability motivations.

Banks and corporations are, of course, the two main sources of credit for the financing of private commercial trade. As far as banks are concerned, the link between trade flows and the volume of credit supplied seems tenuous. Banks will be accumulating claims on foreigners on the basis of returns to such claims. It is by no means clear how aggregative trade flows are linked with returns from the standpoint of banks, although such flows may have some bearing upon how banks evaluate risk factors such as capital controls.

A much clearer link exists between trade flows and corporate willingness to lend. Extensions of credit will be made by corporations to foreign cus-

---

[13] Branson's work [6] is especially noteworthy for his attempt to incorporate expectations into his model.

[14] For examples, see Prachowny [26] and Rhomberg [27].

tomers primarily as an enticement for sales. Increases in exports will therefore tend to be associated with increases in the credit outstanding. However, assuming that the corporation has profit objectives, credit extensions are properly linked with the profits from the sale, not the sale itself. Higher profit sales are likely to be associated with much greater credit extensions than lower profit sales of the same volume. Furthermore, there may be a strong causal relationship going the other way, with credit extension influencing sales.[15]

Just as there is no clear-cut link from exports to credit extensions to foreigners, credit demand by foreigners is not straightforwardly related to exports. A firm engaged in importing will have certain inventory needs. Credit to finance those inventories may be obtained from domestic sources or foreign sources, or through internal cash flows. It is probably the case that smaller, less well-established importing firms are likely to rely more on external sources of funds than larger, well-established firms. We might expect therefore to observe relatively large credit extensions when new markets are being opened up, as in the case of Japan in the late 1950's and early 1960's. In contrast, increases in exports to more mature markets may engender somewhat less credit demand since importing firms in such circumstances may have greater resort to internal financing. Pinches on internal funds will of course reestablish the link between imports and credit demands. However, just as in the case of credit supply, credit demand is properly linked to profits, not sales. One further point of interest is that the link between credit demand and sales may be broken if the credit extension is used to finance additional real investment or portfolio accumulation. The desire to obtain credit for these purposes naturally depends on the return involved.

While we have discussed the well-known but questionable link between short-term claims on foreigners and exports, it should be noted that there is a possible link between such claims and imports. That is, importers and/or the banks with whom they deal may hold balances in the foreign currency for transactions purposes. Import increases will therefore stimulate larger transactions balances and thus larger claims on foreigners. In the case of the U.S., importers will not need such balances since imports are commonly financed in terms of dollars. Firms and banks in other countries who undertake trade denominated in dollars will maintain transactions balances in U.S. banks both for trade with the U.S. and for extra-U.S. trade.

Our discussion suggests that merchandise trade variables are not well suited to explain credit extensions because they may only indirectly reflect the profitability motivations of the transactors on both the supply and demand sides and because the direction of causation is unclear. However, with

---

[15] In such a case, an ordinary least squares regression of credit extensions on sales will be subject to simultaneity bias. More will be said about this below.

lack of information relating to profitability, it may be necessary to rely on some measure of sales for explanatory purposes. It seems, however, that the primary variable for explaining trade financing should be expressed in terms of *changes* in sales rather than levels. The reason for this is that rapid growth in sales that reflects favorable profit opportunities will engender increases in trade credit. When sales and profit opportunities level off, there will be a tendency for firms to rely more on internal financing and domestic credit sources. The result will be a leveling off and perhaps even a decline in the use of foreign credits.

Speculative Activity   It is well known that, in a pegged exchange-rate system, speculative activity may fundamentally alter the nature of the foreign exchange markets. During periods of substantial speculative activity, the forward market may dry up, existing credit lines may be curtailed and new ones denied, credit rationing may become more prevalent, inventory speculation may become pronounced, and so forth. In such circumstances, expectations may increase so much in importance that they dominate behavior. This means that the behavioral relations applicable during a "normal" period may be effectively suspended since responses will be swamped by expectational forces that are not fully incorporated in the usual empirical models of capital movements. What is suggested therefore is that we separate "normal" from "speculative" periods according to the absence or presence of expectations concerning exchange-rate changes outside of the official limits.

If the normal periods dominated the sample, the speculative periods could be treated as outliers and discarded. There is no sound statistical way of doing this, however, without a great deal of effort. But this does not justify resorting to ad hoc procedures that are potentially dangerous from the standpoint of data interpretation. In this regard, we have already taken note of Stein's construction [29] of a speculative pressure variable based on the residuals of a regression of the forward premium on the uncovered interest-rate differential. This procedure has been criticized in separate comments on Stein's work by Heckerman and Laffer [29], who contend that the residuals may reflect other things besides speculative pressure.[16]

An alternative to Stein's approach would be to identify periods of exchange-market turbulence on some a priori basis. One such possibility is to consult expert opinion with regard to the periods when currencies are believed to have been especially affected by substantial speculative transactions. A preferable substitution for relying on informed judgment, however, might be the use of data on forward exchange rates. Theoretical considerations sug-

---

[16] Stein's procedure may be all the more questionable since, as Jay H. Levin has pointed out in private discussion, Stein's model of the foreign exchange market makes inadequate provision for hedging by traders in the forward market and does not clearly distinguish the stock of investor short-term capital that represents covered interest arbitrage.

gest that speculative confidence in the spot exchange-rate limits in the pegged rate system will be reflected by infinitely elastic speculative activity in the forward market at these limits. The forward rate may move outside the limits only if speculators lack confidence in the government's willingness and ability to maintain the spot rate and if there is no official counterspeculation to peg the forward rate.[17] A reasonably objective method for separating speculative from normal periods might then be founded on the basis of whether the forward rate for a given period lay inside or outside the official support limits designated for the spot rate.[18]

Capital Controls and Credit Rationing   We have already mentioned that controls and credit rationing will have an impact on capital movements. When controls result in the reduction of effective returns, a suitable variable may be added to the equation without difficulty. However, when capital controls take the form of quotas, it may be better to discard the equation altogether. Consider, for example, Figure 4.1, with demand *DD* and supply *SS* of securi-

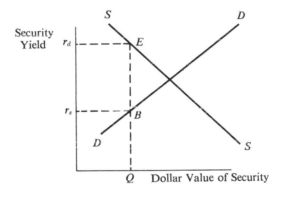

FIGURE 4.1

The Effect of Capital Controls

[17] Note that Stein's analysis implicitly assumes the forward rate to be determined by interest arbitrage considerations. We, however, regard the forward rate to be determined primarily by speculative activity, at least outside the support points.

[18] See Leamer and Stern [21] for a graph in which the 90-day forward rates for the pound, mark, and French franc are plotted as a percent of the official spot peg on an end-of-month basis for the period 1960–69 (September). The graph suggests that the pound was under speculative pressure to devalue periodically throughout the period. The speculative attack on the pound in 1961 was accompanied by opposite pressure on the mark. The years 1968 and 1969 were very turbulent, with pressure on all three currencies. It would thus appear that empirical studies that include U.K. assets will necessarily have to deal with the speculation problems more or less throughout the 1960's. Analysis of the mark and the franc will have to deal with speculation particularly in 1968 and 1969. As suggested above, these data points might best be analyzed separately.

ties as a function of the security yield. The negative slope of *SS* expresses the
relation that the supply of securities will vary inversely with the yield (i.e.,
cost) and that the demand for securities will vary directly with the yield (i.e.,
return). The imposition of a quota *Q* on security buyers (in the absence of
credit rationing) will result in an equilibrium at *E*. The observed point will
not fall on the demand-for-securities curve *DD* and thus will yield no information about that schedule. Capital controls may also be imposed by the
capital-importing country. In this case the equilibrium point in Figure 4.1
will be at *B* on the *DD* curve, and no information about the *SS* schedule is
disclosed.

A symmetric situation exists when credit rationing occurs. This is depicted in Figure 4.2. Credit suppliers (i.e., security buyers) may establish an

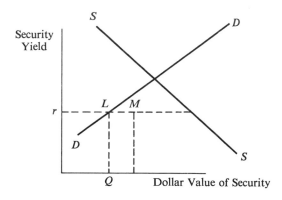

FIGURE 4.2

The Effect of Credit Rationing

arbitrarily low rate *r* and ration the forthcoming supply. The observed point
L would lie on the demand-for-security schedule *DD* but not on the supply-
of-security schedule *SS*. Worse yet, the existence of unsatisfied and complain-
ing customers may induce credit suppliers to grant loans in excess of that
indicated by *DD*, which is drawn on the assumption of equilibrium in the
market. An equilibrium point *M* that lies on neither *DD* nor *SS* may thus
result.

The statistical examination of economic relationships is predicated on the
assumption that the observations may properly be thought to reflect those
relationships. When such things as legal restrictions or rationing interfere

with these relationships, statistical fits that result may be meaningless. In the case of capital movements, such interferences may well be the rule and not the exception. An excellent study by Bryant and Hendershott [7] deals with the problem of capital controls by assuming that their effect is to reduce the observed quantity by a proportion dependent on the existing controls. They argue that the controls relevant to their study of U.S.–Japanese capital flows were voluntary in nature, and that the imposition of the controls reduced the observed responses to other stimuli but did not eliminate them. To proceed in this way requires of course much detailed knowledge of the controls and their effects, and there may not be any straightforward way to allow quantitatively for the reductions in responses.

Level of Aggregation The problem of aggregation stems from the inherent complexity of the real world. There will be many different countries and in each there will be security offerings of many different maturities. Correspondingly, there will be interest rates and forward exchange rates of

TABLE 4.1

International Investment Position of the
United States at Year-End 1967
(Billions of Dollars) †

	Western Europe	Canada	Latin American Republics	Other Foreign Countries	Total [a]
U.S. assets and investments abroad, total	35.4	29.4	20.7	31.7	122.3
Private investments	25.3	29.3	16.2	19.0	93.3
Long-term	22.6	28.1	13.1	14.2	81.4
Direct	17.9	18.1	10.2	10.8	59.3
Foreign dollar bonds	0.7	5.5	0.6	1.7	9.7
Other foreign bonds	0.1	0.7	0.2	0.1	1.1
Foreign corporate stocks	2.1	2.8	0.1	0.2	5.2
Banking claims	0.8	0.2	1.5	1.2	3.7
Other	1.0	0.8	0.5	0.2	2.4
Short-term assets and claims	2.7	1.2	3.1	4.8	11.8
Reported to banks	1.2	0.6	2.6	4.2	8.6
Other	1.5	0.6	0.5	0.6	3.2
U.S. Government credit and claims	10.1	— [b]	4.6	12.7	29.0

TABLE 4.1 (Cont.)

	Western Europe	Canada	Latin American Republics	Other Foreign Countries	Total [a]
Foreign assets and investments in the U.S., total	41.0	9.3	6.5	10.3	69.6
Long-term	20.2	5.3	2.5	3.0	32.0
Direct	7.0	2.6	0.2	0.2	9.9
Corporate stocks	10.5	2.5	1.3	1.1	15.5
Corporate and other bonds	1.4	— [b]	0.1	0.2	2.2
Other	1.3	0.2	1.0	1.5	4.4
Short-term assets and U.S. Government obligations	20.7	4.0	4.0	7.3	37.7
Private obligations	10.8	2.7	3.8	5.3	22.9
Reported by banks	9.8	2.4	3.7	5.0	21.2
Other	1.0	0.3	0.1	0.3	1.7
U.S. Government obligations	9.9	1.3	0.2	2.0	14.8
Marketable or convertible bonds or notes	1.3	0.7	— [b]	0.1	2.4
Bills and certificates	6.3	0.3	0.1	1.7	9.3
Other	2.3	0.3	— [b]	0.2	3.1

[a] Total includes international organizations and unallocated.
[b] Less than $500,000.
† Adapted from U.S. Department of Commerce, *Survey of Current Business*, 48 (October 1968), 20.

varying maturities. A significant problem thus confronts the researcher in selecting the appropriate level of aggregation. In making such a selection, one should apply the general principle that micro-response functions should be aggregated when the responses are similar. Returns from disaggregation will be greater when categories of distinctly different responses can be isolated. This suggests that some disaggregation by region will be profitable. Ideally one would disaggregate by motivation as well, thus distinguishing short-term portfolio, trade credit, and trade-arbitrage capital movements. In fact, however, it will be impossible ordinarily to obtain data disaggregated by motivation. The choice of explanatory variables should thus include variables associated with each motivation.

Some idea as to the nature and importance of various capital items for the United States can be gathered from Table 4.1. Many of the categories in the table may be further disaggregated. For example, short-term banking claims on foreigners may be classified as in Table 4.2. Further disaggregation is possible by region, as well. It should be abundantly clear that a primary decision is required on the choice of aggregation. Unfortunately, the currently available studies provide relatively little insight into the problem.

TABLE 4.2

Short-Term Claims on Foreigners Reported by
Banks in the United States at Year-End, 1967

(Billions of Dollars) ‡

Dollar loans		3.2
Official institutions	0.3	
Banks	1.6	
Others	1.2	
Dollar collections outstanding		1.5
Dollar acceptances		3.0
Other dollar claims		0.5
Foreign currency deposits and other		
claims		0.4
Total		8.6

‡ Adapted from Board of Governors of the Federal Reserve System, *Federal Reserve Bulletin*, 54 (July 1968) A–81.

A problem related to aggregation is the construction of index numbers. A given semidisaggregated class of securities may require interest rates and forward exchange rates of varying maturities and regions. Collinearity in the movements of these rates is likely to impede estimation. Although this is a difficult problem, it is not a unique one. In trying in Chapter 2 to explain imports and exports, we were confronted with a similar phenomenon that involved many different countries and many different commodities. In that situation, we saw fit to construct index numbers, which we hoped would capture the essential features of the phenomenon.[19] Although the construction of index numbers is an appealing solution to this problem, it should be pointed out that no such index numbers exist in fact. This is the case especially since the requisite data for weighting purposes are just not available on a systematic basis. In the absence of such indexes, we will be forced to make an in-

[19] In the Appendix to Chapter 2, we saw that a weighting scheme for the price indexes depended fundamentally on small cross elasticities of demand for import goods. A similar situation exists with regard to capital flows. If changes in foreign rates of return are accompanied by substantial shifts among foreign securities, then it will be impossible to select useful weights for the construction of an interest-rate index.

formed judgment in choosing the appropriate explanatory variables for each capital item.[20]

Lag Structure   Lagged variables will be required to reflect both the adjustment mechanism and also the formation of expectations. As discussed extensively in Chapter 2, it is a common procedure to attempt to capture these effects simply by adding lagged explanatory or dependent variables to the basic model. Implicitly this involves the assumption of a fixed but unknown response pattern. In the case of capital movements, this procedure may be found lacking in at least two respects. One is that it makes little or no distinction between the two types of lags. Such a distinction could be important from a policy standpoint since, for example, expectations could be altered significantly by virtue of the announcement effects stemming from policy changes. It might be desirable therefore to employ explicit models of adjustment and expectations in order to be able to distinguish these influences from one another.[21]

Mechanical use of lagged variables also ignores potentially useful information on the determinants of the response pattern. An important shortcoming of the portfolio-adjustment models is that they tend to ignore short-run constraints upon behavior that determine methods and speeds of adjustment. In some cases, these constraints may become so important that the long-run portfolio-balance considerations are barely reflected in behavior.

In the construction of a model of expectations formation, it is possible of course to allow for adaptations in the expectations. Such a model leads to a set of fixed weights on past observations.[22] This is not a completely acceptable procedure since the extent to which future projections are adjusted in the light of the discrepancy between current projection and current observation is not a fixed fraction but rather depends upon current and past information. Also, risk factors as well as expectations will be adjusted in response to current evidence. To the extent that his projections come to fruition, an investor may justifiably gain confidence in his ability to project and shift his portfolio to more risky assets. Clearly the problem of expectations formation is in need of further study.

Choice of Functional Form   We saw in Chapter 2 that the use of simple regression techniques requires that the hypothetical relationship be linear in

[20] At this point we would like to emphasize the illegitimacy of the often-used methodology of trying several different interest-rate variables, selecting the one that yields the best fit, and reporting only that one. Though the end product of such a procedure is not clear, what is clear is that the standard errors and R^2 that are reported tend to lose their meaning with each additional experiment.

[21] Waud [35] has pointed out that in simple models of partial adjustment and adaptive expectations, it may be impossible to identify the two elements separately. Feige [10] has shown, however, that more complex models allow such an identification.

[22] See Waud [35] or Feige [10] for a discussion of adaptive expectations models.

its parameters. Within that linear class, there is an infinite variety of functional forms from which to choose. Economic theory often provides little if any basis for choice and researchers commonly select linear or log-linear forms, perhaps regarding the problem as unimportant for the inferences and decisions to follow. However, in the case of asset accumulation, economic theory does suggest a more restrictive class of functional forms.

A general asset-demand function relates the stock of assets A to a set of scale variables W (that determine the portfolio size) and a set of preference variables r (that determine the allocation of the portfolio among competing assets), $A = f(r, W)$. The associated capital flow at a fixed interest rate is

$$F = \frac{dA}{dt} = \frac{\partial f}{\partial W} \frac{dW}{dt}$$

Policy analysis will of course be concerned with the flow induced by a change in interest rates

$$\frac{dF}{dr} = \frac{\partial^2 f}{\partial W \partial r} \frac{dW}{dt}$$

Functional forms such as $A = g(r) + h(W)$, which constrain $\partial^2 f / \partial W \partial r$ to zero, also constrain the flow induced by interest-rate policy to zero and thus presuppose the answer to an important policy question.[23] Since portfolio increases are almost certainly allocated among assets according to the constellation of interest rates, such forms should be avoided. The very popular form $A = f(r)W$ of course remains acceptable.

Simultaneity   The existence of another relationship affecting the variables in the capital equation was first pointed out by Stein [29]. The reader may recall that one of the conditions for unbiased least squares estimation is the independence of the explanatory variables and the disturbance term in the relationship. It is not difficult to show that an explanatory variable in the arbitrage function A is related to a disturbance to that relationship. Suppose that there is an increased desire by Americans to hold English securities unrelated to the levels of the explanatory variables.[24] Such a disturbance would be accompanied by a spot purchase of pounds and a forward sale to effect the purchase of the English security. These purchases will tend to raise the spot rate (if it is not at the upper limit of its allowable fluctuation) and lower the forward rate. But both these rates are explanatory variables and any disturbance to the relationship will cause the estimates of the coefficients in the arbitrage function to be biased. The bias will be small when the disturbances

[23] Branson's work [6] is a case in point.
[24] If one wishes, he may think of this disturbance as associated with some variable that has been inadvertently excluded from the least squares equation.

are small or when the spot and forward rates are influenced only slightly by the disturbances to the arbitrage function.[25]

Another element of simultaneity is exactly the same as the existence of a supply relationship in the analysis of import demand. That is to say, we have been discussing the demand for foreign securities as an increasing function of the return. There will also be a supply of foreign securities, which is a decreasing function of the return. The usual conclusions regarding bias in the estimates apply. The reader may consult Chapter 2 on this point.

While one should of course be concerned with the problem of simultaneity, as such authors as Stein [29], Black [3], and Branson [6] have been, there is some question as to whether this concern may be a bit premature given that the underlying structural relationships have been far from being appropriately specified. As a consequence, recent contributors such as Bryant and Hendershott [7], who use ordinary least squares and take great pains in setting forth their framework for analysis, are laying the groundwork for future work more effectively than authors of works relying on simultaneous models. The latter models will perhaps bear practical fruit at some later date, when the problem of simultaneity may be of greater relevance.

CONCLUSION

The explanation of international capital movements will be subject to a large number of difficulties. These include the impact of psychological variables, the subtle role played by institutions, the complexity of the financial markets, and some fairly common statistical problems. While these difficulties were evident in a number of the early studies of capital movements, they were perhaps of a lesser significance in comparison with the inadequate theoretical framework in many of these studies that resulted in improper specifications.

Although there are clear signs that the most recent work in this field is attempting to cope with some of the difficulties mentioned,[26] there is a large range of possible research activity still open. This includes in particular the

---

[25] There are a large number of other estimating methods which are available when a simultaneity problem such as this one occurs. The reader may consult, for example, Johnston [17] or Goldberger [12] for discussion of simultaneous equations methods. Stein [29] used reduced-form estimation via ordinary least squares. He did not present structural coefficients. That is, the coefficient on his interest rate reflects the total impact that an increase in the interest rate has on the capital flow, including implicitly the feedback effects of the increased arbitrage demand on spot and forward rates and consequently on the arbitrage demand.

[26] See Leamer and Stern [21] for a review of the empirical literature on capital movements.

generation of proxy variables, the selection of the net worth term and other appropriate constraints, and the role of the forward market. It is hoped that future research efforts will be brought fruitfully to bear on the vitally important subject of the capital account.

REFERENCES

1. Arndt, S. W., "International Short Term Capital Movements: A Distributed Lag Model of Speculation in Foreign Exchange," *Econometrica*, 36 (January 1968), 59–70.

2. Bell, P. W., "Private Capital Movements and the U.S. Balance of Payments Position," in *Factors Affecting the U.S. Balance of Payments*. Joint Economic Committee Compendium of Papers. Washington: U.S. Government Printing Office, 1962.

3. Black, S. W., "Theory and Policy Analysis of Short-term Movements in the Balance of Payments," *Yale Economic Essays*, 8 (Spring 1968), 5–78.

4. Board of Governors of the Federal Reserve System, *Federal Reserve Bulletin*, 54 (July 1968).

5. Borts, G. H., "A Theory of Long-Run International Capital Movements," *Journal of Political Economy*, LXXII (August 1964), 341–59.

6. Branson, W. H., *Financial Capital Flows in the United States Balance of Payments*. Amsterdam: North-Holland Publishing Company, 1968.

7. Bryant, R. C. and P. H. Hendershott, "Capital Flows in the U.S. Balance of Payments: The Japanese Experience, 1959–1967" (in process).

8. Canterbery, E. R., "Exchange Rates, Capital Flows, and Monetary Policy," *American Economic Review*, LIX (June 1969), 426–32.

9. Cohen, B. J., "A Survey of Capital Movements and Findings Regarding Their Interest Sensitivity," in *The United States Balance of Payments*. Hearings Before the Joint Economic Committee. Washington: U.S. Government Printing Office, 1963.

10. Feige, E. L., "Expectations and Adjustments in the Monetary Sector," *American Economic Review*, Papers and Proceedings, LVII (May 1967), 462–73.

11. Floyd, J. E., "International Capital Movements and Monetary Equilibrium," *American Economic Review*, LIX (September 1969), 472–92.

12. Goldberger, A. S., *Econometric Theory*. New York: John Wiley and Sons, 1964.

13. Grubel, H. G., "Internationally Diversified Portfolios," *American Economic Review*, LVIII (December 1968), 1299–1314.

14. Gruber, W., et al., "The R & D Factor in International Trade and International Investment of United States Industries," *Journal of Political Economy*, LXXV (February 1967), 20–37.

15. Helliwell, J., "A Structural Model of the Foreign Exchange Market," *Canadian Journal of Economics*, II (February 1969), 90–105.

16. Ingram, J. C., "Growth in Capacity and Canada's Balance of Payments," *American Economic Review*, XLVII (March 1957), 93–104.

17. Johnston, J., *Econometric Methods*. New York: McGraw-Hill Book Company, 1963.

18. Kenen, P. B., "Short-Term Capital Movements and the U.S. Balance of Payments," in *The United States Balance of Payments*. Hearings before the Joint Economic Committee. Washington: U.S. Government Printing Office, 1963.

19. Kindleberger, C. P., *International Economics*. Fourth Edition. Homewood: Richard D. Irwin, 1968.

20. Laffer, A. B., "Short-Term Capital Movements and the Voluntary Foreign Credit Restraint Program" (in process).

21. Leamer, E. E. and R. M. Stern, "Problems in the Theory and Empirical Estimation of International Capital Movements," presented at the Universities–National Bureau of Economic Research Conference on International Mobility and Movement of Capital, January 1970. New York: Columbia University Press (forthcoming).

22. Lee, C. H., "A Stock-Adjustment Analysis of Capital Movements: The United States–Canadian Case," *Journal of Political Economy*, 77 (July/August 1969), 512–23.

23. Levin, J. H., *Forward Exchange and Internal-External Equilibrium*. Michigan International Business Studies. Ann Arbor (forthcoming).

24. Miller, N. C. and Marina v. N. Whitman, "A Mean-Variance Analysis of U.S. Portfolio Foreign Investment," *Quarterly Journal of Economics* (forthcoming).

25. Nurkse, R., *Problems of Capital Formation in Underdeveloped Countries*. New York: Oxford University Press, 1967, Chap. VI.

26. Prachowny, M. F. J., *A Structural Model of the U.S. Balance of Payments*. Amsterdam: North-Holland Publishing Company, 1969.

27. Rhomberg, R. R., "A Model of the Canadian Economy Under Fixed and Fluctuating Exchange Rates," *Journal of Political Economy*, LXXII (February 1964), 1–31.

28. Scaperlanda, A. E. and L. J. Mauer, "The Determinants of U.S. Direct Investment in the EEC," *American Economic Review*, LIX (September 1969), 558–68.

29. Stein, J. L., "International Short-Term Capital Movements," *American Economic Review*, LV (March 1965), 40–60, with "Comments" and a "Reply" by H. P. Gray, D. G. Heckerman, A. B. Laffer, P. H. Hendershott, T. D. Willett, and J. L. Stein, *American Economic Review*, LVII (June 1967), 548–69.

30. Stein, J. L. and E. Tower, "The Short Run Stability of the Foreign Exchange Market," *Review of Economics and Statistics*, XLIX (May 1967), 173–85.

31. Stevens, G. V. G., "Fixed Investment Expenditures of Foreign Manufacturing Affiliates of U.S. Firms: Theoretical Models and Empirical Evidence," *Yale Economic Essays*, IX (Spring 1969).

32. Stoll, H., "An Empirical Study of the Foreign Exchange Market Under Fixed and Flexible Exchange Rate Systems," *The Canadian Journal of Economics*, I (February 1968), 55–66.

33. U.S. Department of Commerce, *Survey of Current Business*, 48 (October 1968).

34. Vernon, R., "International Investment and International Trade in the Product Cycle," *Quarterly Journal of Economics*, LXXX (May 1966), 191–207.

35. Waud, R. N., "Misspecification in the 'Partial Adjustment' and 'Adaptive Expectations' Models," *International Economic Review*, 9 (1968), 204–17.

36. Willett, T. D., "The Influence of the Trade Balance and Export Financing on International Short-Term Capital Movements: A Theoretical Analysis," *Kyklos*, XXII (Fasc. 2, 1969), 314–27.

37. Willett, T. D. and F. Forte, "Interest Rate Policy and External Balance," *Quarterly Journal of Economics*, LXXXIII (May 1969), 242–62.

Forecasting
and Policy Analysis
with Econometric Models

In the previous chapters we have discussed in detail the estimation of the individual economic relationships that directly determine the balance of payments. The next step is the integration of these relationships into a comprehensive quantitative model designed to provide understanding and, ultimately, control of the economic environment. We shall see in this chapter that the problems of constructing a multi-equation econometric model are very much more difficult than the problems inherent in estimating individual relationships. In practice, these difficult problems have been largely ignored and consequently only meager evidence exists concerning what should or should not be done when a model is constructed. For this reason this chapter should be taken to be tentative and suggestive.

Historically, the quantitative analysis of the balance of payments began with the estimation of individual import and export demand equations. Considerable effort was expended in the 1940's and early 1950's in the measurement of income and price elasticities. There was a preoccupation during this time with the importance of the price variable, and it was common for researchers to subject their price variables to tests of significance in an effort to credit or discredit the hypothesis that price changes had little or no effect on the flow of goods and services.

In the 1950's, quantitative inquiry concerning the determinants of the balance of payments turned to multi-equation models. This shift in emphasis required, of course, the concurrent evolution of large-scale electronic computing facilities. It is now possible to build upon the many studies that have been made of particular relationships and to construct relatively large and complex econometric models. Our concern in the present chapter will be with the structure of such models, using as building blocks the relationships developed in the preceding chapters that dealt with the flow of goods and services, and of capital.

ECONOMIC FORECASTING

We may begin our discussion of forecasting with a justification for allocating resources to such efforts. It may be noted first that an econometric model of economic phenomena is designed to enhance our understanding of the interplay of forces behind the phenomena being studied. It is safe to say that no amount of *a priori* theorizing will disclose the quantitative impact of one variable on another. Moreover, the very preciseness of specification required in econometric model building should necessitate very careful and logical thought on the part of the analyst. Such thinking may often greatly enhance the analyst's theoretical view of the phenomena being studied, even before any empirical fits are obtained.

Nonetheless, greater understanding of economic events should not be viewed necessarily as a goal unto itself. Rather, understanding should be looked upon as a tool for optimal decision making designed to attain the economic objectives of the society. The making of both public and private economic decisions is measurably improved when there is a fundamental understanding of the consequences of such decisions. Thus, for example, government policymakers will be interested in the impact of various monetary and fiscal policies on the domestic economy and balance of payments, while private investors will want to know something about future profit rates in the industries of immediate concern to them.

This suggests that an econometric model and an associated forecast should be deemed successful insofar as decisions are made more effectively. The discussion to follow will therefore be cast in a decision-making context. Let us for the moment concern ourselves with some general considerations of model building.

General Concepts of Econometric Model Building An econometric model is a set of equations, including statistically estimated relations, that seeks to explain in quantitative terms some observed economic phenomena. Besides the econometric relations, the model may also include both identities and noneconometric behavioral relations (e.g., a tax relationship specifying some legally determined percentage of income).

In order to focus on concepts and problems pertaining to econometric models in general, let us consider a model of the following form

$$Y_1 = f_1(Y_2, Y_3, \ldots, Y_n, \quad X_1, X_2, \ldots, X_m)$$
$$Y_2 = f_2(Y_1, Y_3, \ldots, Y_n, \quad X_1, X_2, \ldots, X_m)$$
$$\ldots$$
$$Y_n = f_n(Y_1, Y_2, \ldots, Y_{n-1}, \quad X_1, X_2, \ldots, X_m)$$

$$(5.1)$$

This model includes n equations, econometric or otherwise, each of which describes a particular variable Y_k as a function of the $(n - 1)$ remaining Y_i and m other variables, X_j, $(j = 1, \ldots, m)$. The Y_i variables are called *endogenous variables* since these variables are explained by or, equivalently, are endogenous to the model. Correspondingly, the X_i variables are called *exogenous variables* to indicate that no attempt is made to explain or forecast their values, or perhaps more accurately, that none of the endogenous variables influences the exogenous variables.

Before proceeding, we should perhaps caution the reader that this general representation of an econometric model does not imply that all the explanatory variables noted need be used in each equation. Rather, the explanatory variables in each equation are potential choices, not necessary ones. Consequently, we should take the functions f_i to be general enough to exclude any of the potential explanatory variables. Thus, for example, the case when Y_1 depends on X_3 and X_7 alone is implicitly considered by the very general function f_1. In addition, one or more of the equations may be identities or behavioral relationships that are arrived at by other than statistical methods.

Ordinarily the functions f_i used in economic research will permit the "solution" of the equation system (5.1). That is, we may express the endogenous variables as functions of the exogenous variables alone, as follows

$$
\begin{aligned}
Y_1 &= g_1(X_1, X_2, \ldots, X_m) \\
Y_2 &= g_2(X_1, X_2, \ldots, X_m) \\
&\quad \ldots \\
Y_n &= g_n(X_1, X_2, \ldots, X_m)
\end{aligned}
\tag{5.2}
$$

This of course requires that all of the relationships hold simultaneously, which implies rapid adjustment to disequilibria. This assumption is not so strong when adjustment lags are included in individual relations.

When the model is expressed in the form of the first system (5.1), we will call it a *structural model*. That is to say, System (5.1) represents the structure of the economic phenomena. It is meant to indicate how any particular variable directly influences any endogenous variable. System (5.2), on the other hand, is referred to as the *reduced form*. We may think of it as being an equilibrium system. To illustrate this point, we might consider the first equation of the structural model (5.1). A change in X_1 will induce a change in Y_1, but this change in Y_1 will induce changes in $Y_2, \ldots, Y_n$, which in turn alter Y_1 once more. Eventually, assuming stability, the system will settle down to an equilibrium again. This equilibrium influence of X_1 on Y_1 is expressed by the first equation of the reduced form system (5.2). Hence to repeat, the structural model indicates the initial impact of one variable on another, while the reduced form indicates the final equilibrium.[1]

The reduced form system (5.2) will play the central role in both forecasting and policy analysis. *Forecasting* will require the selection of a particular set of values for the exogenous variables X_j, which will be inserted into the reduced form equations to calculate forecast values for the endogenous variables Y_i. *Policy analysis* will involve such a question as: "If the value of a policy instrument X_i is altered, what will be the effect on variable Y_k?" The answer to such a question may be read directly from the kth reduced form equation.

Conditional and Unconditional Forecasts   We have just described forecasting as requiring the selection of a particular set of values for the exogenous variables, which together with the reduced form system will imply values of the endogenous variables. This suggests that a forecaster may make either a conditional or an unconditional forecast. A *conditional forecast* will be of the form: "If the values of the exogenous variables turn out to be this, then the values of the endogenous variables will be that." In other words, the forecast is conditioned on the future values of the exogenous variables. An *unconditional forecast* may be represented as: "The values of the endogenous variables will be this." That is, the forecast is not conditioned on any future events. The difference between a conditional and an unconditional forecast should be clear. In the case of the conditional forecast, the forecaster in effect is admitting that he is unable or unwilling to project the values of the exogenous variables X_i. With an unconditional forecast, however, the forecaster will in effect provide the projected values of the exogenous variables.

---

[1] We can illustrate these points with a simple demand and supply model

$$Q = \alpha + \beta P + \gamma D \tag{i}$$
$$P = a + bQ + cS \tag{ii}$$

Equation (i) is the demand equation indicating quantity demanded Q as a linear function of the price P and some demand factor D. Equation (ii) is the supply equation indicating the supply price P as a linear function of the quantity sold Q and a supply factor S. This is a structural model with endogenous variables Q and P, and exogenous variables D and S. The corresponding reduced form is

$$Q = (1 - \beta b)^{-1}(\alpha + \gamma D + \beta a + \beta c S) \tag{i$'$}$$
$$P = (1 - \beta b)^{-1}(b\alpha + b\gamma D + a + cS) \tag{ii$'$}$$

We see from Equation (i) that a one-unit increase in D will have an impact on the quantity demanded equal to γ units. This "shift" in the demand curve will tend to induce a rise in the price due to the upward sloping supply function. Such a price increase will dampen the impact of the change in D on the market-clearing quantity. The equilibrium result can be read from the reduced form equation (i$'$), which indicates that the initial impact of size γ will be damped by the factor $(1 - \beta b)^{-1}$.

A pure conditional forecast is represented by the reduced form system alone. This implicitly contains all of the conditional statements that can be made. A pure unconditional forecast will report only the forecast values of endogenous variables. The reduced form would not be required here inasmuch as the values for the exogenous variables will have been specified. Most econometric forecasts fall between the pure conditional and unconditional cases. The reduced form or the structural model is therefore ordinarily reported. In addition, most likely values of the X_i are used to calculate the forecast Y_j. The user of the forecast is thus provided with both the most likely forecast as the forecaster sees it, and a means to alter that forecast in the event that the user disagrees with the forecaster's opinions about the future values of X_i. Thus, this hybrid forecast is preferred, since it provides the maximum of information.

Informative and Decision Forecasts   A forecast will ultimately lead to decisions on the part of the forecast user. The forecaster may play one of two roles in this process. He may provide information about future events which will be analyzed by some decision maker, or he may use the information to make decisions himself. In the first instance, a forecast will provide probability statements about future events, while in the second the forecaster provides his view of what will occur without appending any probability statements. In the latter event, the forecast user is implicitly denied those decision making powers that relate to the weighing of the likelihood of various outcomes.

A concrete example of the difference between these two types of forecasts may be useful. If a forecaster predicts sales of one million units, production will be geared to that level of sales. If, however, the forecast specifies the probability of other levels of sales, management may decide on a production level best suited to its goals. For example, there may be a reasonably good chance of sales of two million units, and management may decide to have the excess capacity available in that event.

Let us consider first the *informative forecast*, which involves the forecaster as information provider but not as decision maker. An informative forecast seeks to provide useful information about the future. This information takes on the form of a probability distribution, indicating the forecaster's opinions regarding the likelihood of the possible values of the forecast variable. A useful way of summarizing this distribution is in terms of the most likely value and a 95 percent confidence interval. A *point forecast* (without the confidence interval) cannot be an informative forecast since it does not provide the required probability distribution.

It is of considerable importance to be able to evaluate the quality of a forecast after the event has occurred. A forecast may not be judged alone, but must be compared with other competing forecasts. Figure 5.1 depicts two probability distributions, *A* and *B*, which represent competing informative forecasts. Forecast *A* reflects relatively weak opinions about the event. If y_1 occurs, we will tend to favor forecast *A*, since y_1 is more likely under that forecast; conversely, if y_2 occurs, forecast *B* would be preferred.

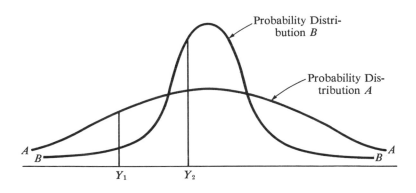

FIGURE 5.1

Probability Forecasts

This concludes our discussion of informative forecasts. Let us now turn to *decision forecasts*. We will view the process of decision making as deciding upon an act *a* that depends upon the future value of an endogenous variable *Y*. Since *Y* is unknown, there is the possibility of making a nonoptimal decision. The penalty for such a decision will be described by a loss function *L*(*a*, *y*), which describes the penalty for choosing act *a*, when *y* turns out to be the true value of *Y*. A reasonable decision rule is to select *a* that minimizes the expected loss

$$E(L) = \sum_{y} L(a, y) P(Y = y) \qquad (5.3)$$

where $P(Y = y)$ is the probability that the future value of *Y* will be *y*. This probability distribution is implicitly provided by the informative forecast.

For any act *a* that is chosen, there will be a value of *Y* for which *L*(*a*, *y*) is minimal. A decision forecast will provide only this value of *Y*. This will lead the forecast user necessarily to one particular act *a*. The forecaster will decide on the value of the point estimate of *Y* in the same way that any other decision maker would select an act given the probability distribution of *Y*, *P*(*Y*), that is, on the basis of some loss function, explicit or otherwise. He therefore usurps the forecast user's decision-making powers.

The evaluation of decision forecasts will necessarily be different from the evaluation of informative forecasts. Since a decision forecast purports to minimize the loss we will incur from incorrect decision making, we will quite naturally give the best grades to those forecasts that truly minimize the loss. This will necessitate a comparison of two or more alternative forecasts. In the event that only one model is available, we may generate a dummy forecast for purposes of comparison. Suitable dummy forecasts may, for example, be the naive "no change" forecast or the projection of past trends.

This discussion of the difference between informative and decision forecasts is meant to emphasize that the form a forecast assumes will depend on the forecaster's role in the decision process. In our judgment, the proper form of the forecast will most often be *informative* and *unconditional*, with the reduced form system included to allow the forecast user some adjustment of the forecast according to his own judgment about the future values of the exogenous variables. However, most forecasts have in fact been of the decision variety.[2]

Forecast Error   There are three sources of forecast error. In the first place, there are natural disturbances to the true relationships. Secondly, we are using estimates to represent the true relationships. The discrepancy between the estimates and the true relationships will result in forecast error. Finally, the discrepancy between the true levels of the exogenous variables and their estimated levels will induce additional forecast error. A conditional forecast will involve only the first two sources of error. An unconditional forecast will involve all three, although the last may swamp the other two. For this reason, practicing forecasters tend to neglect the first two sources of error.

This concludes the essentially mechanistic aspects of forecasting. As yet, the two most fundamental questions remain unanswered: What variables should be endogenous and what variables should be exogenous? Which explanatory variables should be used in each structural equation? Answers to these questions are about one part mechanical and nine parts intuitive, as we shall see. This is an area in which experience weighs very heavily.

Exogenous and Endogenous Variables   Let us consider the first question: which variables to have exogenous. Suits [22] provides in this regard a useful catalog of exogenous variables. The first type consists of those that are historically given. These variables measure events that have occurred before the forecast period. A problem can arise, however, when a forecast for a particular period has to be made in the course of a period still in progress and/or when the relevant data may not be fully collected. In such an event, some method of extrapolating the data already collected or some projection scheme

---

[2] In some cases it may prove difficult to classify results as being informative or decision forecasts. For instance, when the reduced form is reported, we will somewhat arbitrarily classify the forecast as informative since confidence intervals may be generated on the basis of the forecast user's opinions about the future values of the exogenous variables.

must be used to arrive at particular values for the historically given variables. Experience suggests that reasonably good accuracy can be obtained in such circumstances.

Slowly changing variables make up a second set of exogenous influences. The appropriate values to assign to these variables will presumably be easily calculated by projecting the historical paths. Examples would be population and the labor force.

The third class of exogenous variables involves the set of government policy instruments, such as tariff levels and taxes. From the point of view of the government forecaster, the levels of these variables can be forecast with great accuracy. Although there may be considerable difficulty in projecting these policy instruments when one is not privy to such information, it is not possible to include them endogenously in an econometric model since the government policymakers are unlikely to display a consistent pattern that could be well approximated by an econometric equation. Accordingly, the projection of government policy will play a principal role in introducing error into an unconditional forecast.

The three sets of variables just mentioned are exogenous both from the point of view of the particular model and from the point of view of the economic system generally. That is to say, they are inputs into the economic system and do not to any significant degree respond to events that occur within that system. For this reason they are necessarily exogenous variables in any econometric model.

The fourth set of exogenous variables is composed of variables that are in fact endogenous to the economic system in general, but that for some particular econometric model are selected to be exogenous. For example, a one-equation model of imports might express imports as a function of GNP and prices. In such a model both GNP and prices are exogenous. To our mind, the decision of what to include in this fourth set of exogenous variables and what to include endogenously is the most troublesome problem that faces an econometric model builder. A model builder must ask himself if moving a variable from the fourth class of exogenous variables to the set of endogenous variables will improve the forecast. There is unfortunately often little information he can bring to bear on this question. A related problem is the optimal level of disaggregation. It is safe to say that a disaggregated model will yield more detail than an aggregated model, but it does not follow that the aggregates will be better forecast.

The development of econometric models quite naturally began with relatively small models with relatively few variables and equations. These gradually evolved into larger and more complex models, predicated on the assumption that the more variables endogenously determined, the better the model. In recent years, however, the pendulum has tended to swing the other way in response to arguments that the very large models are so complex that no one can fully grasp their fundamentals and that their relationship to the actual phenomena under study becomes more and more coincidental as they increase in size. According to this line of argument, a small manageable model may thus be preferable.

The fifth and final set of exogenous influences in an econometric model will consist of variables that represent rare events expected to influence the phenomena under study. For example, a commercial trade agreement soon to be ratified may be expected to increase the flow of trade. Since the effect of such an agreement could not be estimated from historical data, we may want to adjust our historically estimated relationships to allow for increased trade. This may be effected by putting exogenous variables that will reflect the likely magnitude of the event into one or more of the structural equations. The choice of the values of these variables will rest entirely on good judgment.

Explanatory Variables   Let us now turn to the other question raised earlier concerning the choice of explanatory variables for each structural equation. In the preceding chapters we have discussed the estimation of individual equations and have argued that the appropriate explanatory variables should be suggested by theoretical considerations. This is not necessarily a preferred procedure for multi-equation systems, since when we combine these individual relationships, we will want to avoid the possibility of relatively small estimation errors being transmitted and amplified from equation to equation in such a way that the estimation error of the system as a whole far exceeds the sum of its parts. To put the problem precisely, ordinary least squares applied individually to the structural equations of a large model is not the optimal estimating procedure when the goal is an accurate reduced form.

Although multi-equation estimation methods are available, they are difficult to apply and have not been used to any great extent. In practice, most econometric model builders have used single-equation least squares methods of estimation with an experimental approach designed to reduce the danger of an inaccurately estimated model. For instance, several regressions may be fitted and the "best" one selected. It is important here to emphasize that the summary statistics that indicate good fits, for the individual structural equations, do not insure that the reduced form system is in itself very reliable. These summary statistics are calculated on the assumption that the explanatory variables are given. In fact, many of the equations will include endogenous variables whose values are not given to the forecaster, but rather are calculated from the reduced form.

To express this differently, we observe that when the reduced form is calculated from the structural form, we will have to divide by the structural coefficients on any of the endogenous variables that are also used as explanatory variables. If such a structural coefficient is small and unreliable, this division will greatly amplify the inaccuracy of the reduced form. Accordingly, we should put a premium on large reliable structural coefficients for any endogenous explanatory variables. Whereas experimentation is to be avoided when inference on parameter values of structural equations is desired, such experimentation may be an absolute must in order to arrive at a reasonably reliable reduced form.

The accuracy of the equation system as a whole may be assessed by using the historical values of the exogenous variables together with the reduced form to calculate estimates of the endogenous variables that may be compared with the actual historical values. Unfortunately, a discrepancy between the estimated and the historical values may not lead directly to the particular equation that is the source of that error, since errors will be transmitted in a very complex fashion from equation to equation.

POLICY ANALYSIS

Some separate comments may be in order on the subject of policy analysis. We have already indicated that policy analysis is no more than seeking an answer to a question of the form: "If the government does this, what will be the result?" The answer to such a question can be read directly from the reduced form system (5.2) when the other exogenous variables are given their fixed forecast levels. We should observe that policy analysis and conditional forecasts are essentially the same thing and may be distinguished only by the emphasis placed on a particular set of the exogenous variables by policy analysis.

Another form of policy analysis is *impact analysis*, which deals with the question: "If the government alters this policy instrument by this amount, by how much will that endogenous variable change?" Again the answer is contained in the reduced form system, but this time may be expressed in terms of a *policy multiplier*

$$\frac{dY_j}{dX_k} = \frac{\partial g_j}{\partial X_k} \tag{5.4}$$

where g_j is the jth reduced form equation. Such a multiplier indicates the marginal response of the jth endogenous variable to a variation in the policy instrument X_k. A model designed for impact analysis alone will be significantly easier to construct than other models, since the choice of endogenous variables will be more or less straightforward. That is, an impact model may have many exogenous variables and only a few endogenous ones. This will be undesirable in a forecasting model since in order to construct a forecast, the levels of all the exogenous variables would have to be selected. The model it-self would play a minor role in the forecast and might be better discarded altogether.

However, the impact analysis will be useful only when the policymakers are able to react rapidly to economic events. Ordinarily the policy will be selected at some time before the actual event, in which case the policymaker must know both the policy multiplier and by how much the endogenous vari-able will differ from its optimal level. A forecast would therefore be required.

ECONOMETRIC MODELS OF THE BALANCE OF PAYMENTS

Having reviewed in general the main issues in the use of econometric models for forecasting and policy analysis, let us turn next to consider specifically the question of the structure of econometric models that are designed to in-vestigate the balance of payments and its components. That is, we will ex-amine in more detail the selection of endogenous and exogenous variables. As we have already implied, this question has not been and perhaps never will be satisfactorily answered. Indeed, the issues involved are at the very heart of economic science insofar as they relate to one's view of the world in general and economic phenomena in particular and to the choice of simpli-fying assumptions that will help to order these phenomena in ways that will improve our comprehension of and ultimately our control over them.

In earlier chapters, we have seen that there is considerable choice for competing selections of explanatory variables in individual equations. When we wish to combine equations into a comprehensive structural model, the problems of choice become manifold. Ultimately, competing models will have to be judged by performance. When a particular model performs poorly, it may be appropriately modified to improve performance. We nevertheless need some basis for departure in constructing a model. What should it be? What, in other words, is the appropriate structure for the model? We cannot hope to give a definitive and unambiguous answer to this question. But we can at least propose a framework that will help the researcher in making his own decisions and serve also as a means by which we can analyze certain specific models that have in fact been used for forecasting and policy analysis.

The process of model building should be attuned essentially to the tasks which the model is expected to perform. Our discussion here is meant to illustrate how a model may be constructed to perform a particular task, namely forecasting the balance of payments. A more relevant model would include domestic effects as well; but the process of model construction is essentially the same in both cases.

A Model of the World Economy The basis of our discussion will be a ten-market model of the world economy. More complex models as well as simpler ones could of course be constructed by disaggregating or aggregating the various markets we shall identify. Given the fact that most models that have been constructed to date are much simpler than the one we shall describe, we shall lean in our discussion more towards simplicity than complexity.

We will view the universe of economic events as the set of all economic exchanges, each exchange involving one supplier and one demander. Exchanges that may be considered to be essentially the same are classed together and called a market. The world economy is then a huge and complex set of interrelated markets. The number of markets we might discuss is limited only by the total number of exchanges, each exchange being at least in some respect different from all others. What we wish to accomplish in terms of theory is to combine, condense, or drop most of these markets in order to simplify and to bring order to the seemingly chaotic events, and yet at the same time to maintain the essential features of the exchange phenomenon. Many of the issues that arise in the process of simplification are essentially empirical. It is therefore important that the model we use at the initial stages of empirical analysis be general enough to include many of the competing views of the world economy. We may then allow the data to suggest the appropriate simplifications that are empirically relevant.

However, generality in specification combined with the usual data limitations will ordinarily leave the researcher with little results of any use. Accordingly, he will be forced to impose his own theoretical views upon the data. The point where theory should end and the data should take over in the process is by its nature difficult to determine. The theoretical view we will present is a comparatively weak one, and we shall discuss at some length a number of additional assumptions that will make the theoretical base stronger, but less general, as well.

The construction of our model of the world economy will require, first, a classification of exchanges into a set of markets. Each market is meant to include all of but only those exchanges that for our purposes may be considered to be essentially the same. Furthermore, every exchange may be easily classified into one of the markets. We shall abstract in particular, however, from imported capital goods.

Let us then divide the world into two hypothetical countries, domestic and foreign, to be denoted by America and England. The balance of payments between these two countries will result from the complex interaction of ten markets. These are the markets for: (1) American importables (English exportables); (2) American exportables (English importables); (3) American securities; (4) English securities; (5) American home goods (not tradeable);

(6) English home goods; (7) American capital goods; (8) English capital goods; (9) American labor; and (10) English labor.

It is not difficult to see how events in each of these markets may influence the balance of payments. The first four markets will determine directly the international flows of goods and services and securities. The next four markets for home goods and capital goods will compete with the exportables and importables markets for the existing resources. For example, price increases for American home goods or American capital goods will tend to lower the American supplies of importables and exportables as real resources are shifted from those industries to the home or capital goods industries in response to the price increase. Similarly, American demand will shift from the home or capital good onto the importables and exportables. All of these consequences of price increases in the home or capital goods markets will tend to increase American imports and decrease American exports.

The capital goods markets will also play the highly important role of determining the level of investment in each of the industries. Of course, events in the goods markets will have an important impact on this decision also. In addition, the securities markets will play a role in determining the interest rate and hence the demand for capital goods. Finally the labor markets will determine the wage rates, which will in turn influence supply functions in all the goods markets and the demand function in the capital goods market.

This description is not meant to include all possible interactions, but rather is meant to indicate that each of the markets may play an important role in influencing the balance of payments. Nor is this model meant to be the only possible model of an open economy. As we have mentioned, more complicated models as well as simpler ones could surely be constructed by varying the level of commodity or regional disaggregation or aggregation. The present model is meant to be a sort of middle ground from which to view all balance-of-payments models. It will provide a foundation for the construction of both simpler and more complex models as well as serve as a useful reference from which to evaluate other models.

For example, let us consider a simple two-country Keynesian model

$$Y_i^D = C_i + I_i + X_i - M_i \qquad i = 1, 2 \qquad (5.5)$$

$$C_i = a_i + b_i Y_i \qquad i = 1, 2 \qquad (5.6)$$

$$M_i = X_j = e_i + m_i Y_i \qquad i \neq j = 1, 2 \qquad (5.7)$$

$$Y_i^S = Y_i^D \qquad i = 1, 2 \qquad (5.8)$$

where Y_i^D, Y_i^S, C_i, M_i, X_i, and I_i are aggregate demand, aggregate supply, consumption, imports, exports, and (autonomous) investment. The model has only two markets—the markets for Country 1's and Country 2's goods. Home goods, capital goods, and exports are considered to be essentially the same in each country. Events in the securities market and the labor market are assumed to have an insignificant impact on the goods markets and are thus neglected. Although this Keynesian model represents a much simpler view of the world economy than our ten-market model, it may nevertheless capture the essential features of the important phenomena, such as the international transmission of the business cycle. As we shall see, most of the models which have in fact been constructed have this simple Keynesian structure.

Let us now explore in more detail for our broader model possible arguments for its simplification that are analogous to those arguments implicit in the Keynesian model above. We will want to consider each market's impact on the balance of payments to try to make some judgment as to whether that market may be excluded from the model or aggregated with another market. The decision to exclude a market may be based on one of two propositions. We may feel that the impact of a market on the balance of payments is relatively slight. Alternatively we may observe the complexity of a market and conclude that only very great research efforts could make any quantitative sense out of the observed events. Accordingly, an educated guess as to the future values of the variables controlled by this market will be as accurate as any model forecast. In other words, the cost of an improved forecast in terms of research effort may not be worth the amount of improvement so afforded. In what follows we will argue only on the basis of the first proposition: remoteness.

Considering our model from the United States' point of view, the first step of simplification may be to discard the foreign markets: English home goods, English capital goods, and English labor. The impact of these markets on the U.S. balance of payments may be very remote. Nonetheless, they will influence the English supplies and demands of American importables and American exportables. We may want to decide how these functions will enter our model before we make a decision about discarding any of the three foreign markets. For instance, if we should decide that the price of imports (English exports) is to be forecast exogenously, then the link between this price and the events in the three English markets may be neglected, and these three markets may be discarded.

If the international flow of capital forms a small stable entry in the balance of payments, the securities markets may also be neglected. However, if investment demand (capital goods demand) is responsive to interest rates or other events in the securities markets, we may need to include the securities markets endogenously in order to predict investment.

The first two markets—importables and exportables—are certainly required in any balance-of-payments model. Each of these markets includes two demand functions and two supply functions. The American importables market is made up of American demand and supply and British demand and supply. If we like, we may think of the American demand for British exports as being the difference between the American demand for importables and the American supply, that is, an excess demand function. Nonetheless, we will have to realize that the American demand for British exports will be influenced by American supply factors, in particular the capital stock employed by the American suppliers of import-competing goods. Of course, in the short run the capital stock is fixed and we may ignore its impact on the flow of goods. We have, therefore, justified the severing of one link between the consumable goods markets and the capital goods markets, at least in short-run models. However, in models designed to forecast several years into the future, it may be quite important to maintain this link between investment and the supply capacity of the various industries.

This discussion could in principle be pursued at much greater length. We will nevertheless terminate it here since there is no end of variation in the models that might be constructed to fit particular empirical circumstances. The construction of an econometric model is an exceedingly difficult task if done in a reasonable fashion. Since our discussion has been centered not on "what to do" but rather on "how one might decide what to do," we will have succeeded in our goal if the reader has a flavor of the complexity of the issues and a feeling about how one might seek solutions.

EVALUATION OF ECONOMETRIC MODELS OF THE U.S. BALANCE OF PAYMENTS

We have already stressed the point that the only norm with which to judge a model is performance. Let us consider then for illustrative purposes some models that have been used for prediction or policy analysis with regard to the United States. Using our ten-market model as a guide, we will first explore these models to deduce the implicit answers to the questions we have posed. We will then ask how well the model performs. In the event that the model performs well, we will have a reason to favor the kind of structure employed. If the model performs poorly, we may wish to avoid such a structure in the future.

The Brookings Report   The first model we will examine was constructed by the staff and associates of the Brookings Institution in 1962 under contract with the Council of Economic Advisors [21]. At that time there was growing concern over large balance-of-payments deficits and the resulting gold outflow from the United States. Government policymakers accordingly sought answers to two important questions: was the situation likely to continue, and, if so, what policy measures would be appropriate to remedy it?

An econometric model was used to forecast the level of the components of the U.S. current account in 1968. The capital account was projected exogenously on the basis of several assumptions about such things as growth, profit, and depreciation rates. The econometric model of the current account divided the world into three regions: the U.S., Western Europe, and the Rest of the World. For our purposes, we need consider only the U.S. and Western European regions of the model. In this case the structure of the model may be represented by two equations: U.S. demand for Western European goods and Western Europe's demand for U.S. goods.

It should be clear that this model is extremely simple. If we use our ten-market model as a guide, we will be able to find only the markets for international goods. In addition, these markets consist of a demand side only. The real problem of forecasting is left to the selection of the exogenous variables, and the projection of the many balance-of-payment items that are excluded from the model. The bulk of the Brookings Report in fact discusses these problems and the econometric model is hidden in an appendix. One cannot help wondering if the model had a significant impact on the projection or whether it was merely window-dressing for a basically noneconometric forecast.

The Rhomberg and Boissonneault Model A model which provides an interesting contrast to the Brookings model has been presented by Rhomberg and Boissonneault (R & B) [19]. The R & B model is essentially an expanded version of the Brookings model. The R & B forecast is more heavily dependent on the nature of their model. As in the Brookings work, the world is divided into three regions. The features of the model that interest us are best illustrated by examining only the equations for the U.S. and Western Europe. The structure may then be reduced to six equations, three for each region: a consumption function, an import-demand function, and an export-supply price equation. This contrasts with the Brookings model, which contains only the import functions. Thus, the R & B model includes the supply side in the importables and exportables markets and also the demand side of the two home-goods markets (U.S. and Western Europe). Four of our ten markets are included, but with only the demand side for two of them. There are no interest rates; no concept of capacity; no mechanism for generating domestic prices; and so forth.

As it has been repeatedly emphasized, the absence of certain relationships from a model does not constitute grounds for criticism. Performance is what counts. Since both the Brookings and R & B models were used to generate a forecast for 1968 under two sets of similar assumptions, we will be able to assess their accuracy. The forecast changes are given in Table 5.1 together with the actual values for 1968. It is evident that the two models substantially underestimated the changes that occurred on both the export and import sides. The initial assumptions for the increases in real GNP turned out, interestingly enough, to be almost exact. While the increase in GNP prices was in fact greater than that which had been projected for both regions, it is noteworthy that inflation proceeded substantially faster in Western Europe, as had been hypothesized. The projected increase in U.S. export prices was in fact too low, whereas the increase in Western Europe's export prices was between the initial and alternative assumptions.

TABLE 5.1

Changes from 1961 to 1968 in U.S. Current Account
(In Billions of Current U.S. Dollars) †

	Initial Assumptions [a]		Alternative Assumptions [b]		
	Brookings	R & B	Brookings	R & B	Actual [c]
Exports of goods and services					
Merchandise	+11.2	+ 9.3	+ 7.6	+ 7.5	+13.5
Service	+ 3.0	+ 3.8	+ 3.0	+ 3.3	+ 8.3
TOTAL [d]	+14.3	+13.1	+10.6	+10.8	+21.8
Imports of goods and services					
Merchandise	+ 8.9	+ 8.1	+ 7.9	+ 7.1	+18.5
Service	+ 1.6	+ 3.1	+ 1.5	+ 2.7	+ 6.5
TOTAL [d]	+10.5	+11.2	+ 9.4	+ 9.7	+25.0
Current account balance	+ 3.8	+ 1.8	+ 1.2	+ 1.0	− 3.2
Allowance for E.E.C. discrimination	− 0.6	—	− 0.6	—	
Current account with E.E.C. allowance	+ 4.4	+ 1.8	+ 1.8	+ 1.0	

[a] Based on the following assumed percentage increases for the U.S. and Western Europe, respectively: real GNP, 43 and 33; GNP prices, 11 and 20; and export prices, 4 and 11.

[b] Based on the following assumed percentage increases for the U.S. and Western Europe, respectively: real GNP, 36 and 29; GNP prices, 11 and 11; and export prices, 4 and 7.

[c] The actual percentage increases from 1961 to 1968 for the U.S. and Western Europe, respectively, were: real GNP, 42.3 and 31.9 (partly estimated); GNP prices, 16.9 and 27.2 (partly estimated); and export prices, 9.8 and 9.8.

[d] May not be precise due to rounding.

† Adapted from R. R. Rhomberg and L. Boissonneault, "Effects of Income and Price Changes on the U.S. Balance of Payments," International Monetary Fund, *Staff Papers*, XI (March 1964), 82; U.S. Department of Commerce [29, p. 27]; and Organization for Economic Co-operation and Development [14].

The actual deterioration in the current account balance from 1961 to 1968 was $3.2 billion. This was in sharp contrast to the current account surplus that had been projected on the two assumptions noted. It is of course too much to expect that all the events that occurred between these years could have been foreseen. This is particularly true with regard to the impact of defense expenditures for Vietnam and the sharp rise in U.S. income and prices in 1967–68 that resulted in large increases in imports. It is nevertheless the case that the models did not yield very accurate projections. The moral is thus twofold: we need better models for forecasting purposes; and medium-term forecasting is a risky business indeed.

The Prachowny Model A substantially more disaggregated model of the U.S. foreign sector than either of the foregoing has been constructed by Prachowny [18] on a quarterly basis for the period 1953–64. As noted in Table 5.2, his foreign sector contained 23 equations, including identities. Some flavor of the degree of complexity or lack thereof in the various foreign sector equations is evident from the variables that are listed. The domestic sector of the model is relatively small and highly simplified, yet it permitted Prachowny to build in some of the domestic and foreign sector interrelationships.

A very important point to recognize with regard to this model is the fact that although a great number of equations have been added, the structure of the goods markets remains the same as in the simple Keynesian model. That is to say, the various demand components are added together into a single demand term, "aggregate demand," and supply is assumed to be forthcoming to meet any demand that arises. In other words, there is a single domestic goods market with the simple Keynesian supply response of providing all that is demanded. The problem of capacity limitations on production is ignored, as is the related problem of price determination. Such a Keynesian model should thus be applied only to short-run periods with ample excess capacity. When demand begins to impinge on productive capacity the Keynesian supply response is quite unlikely to be an adequate description of reality. Longer-run models will of course need to deal with both the determinants of prices and the determinants of domestic capacity. These considerations are dealt with to some extent in the other models of the U.S. economy to be examined below.

After estimating the various equations,[3] Prachowny was able to calculate impact multipliers to analyze the effects of changes in various exogenous variables on the balance of payments and GNP. In particular he considered the impact on the balance of payments of the imposition of the Interest

---

[3] In general, his statistical fits were distinctly better for the current account than for the capital account equations.

TABLE 5.2

Prachowny's Quarterly Model of the Foreign Sector
of the U.S. Economy, 1953–64 †

Equation	Dependent Variable	Major Explanatory Variables
Foreign Sector		
1	Imports of consumer goods	Real disposable personal income; relative prices; lagged imports.
2	Imports of investment goods	Real expenditures on producers' durable equipment; relative prices; lagged imports.
3	Imports of raw materials	Manufacturing production; real change in nonfarm business inventories; relative prices; lagged imports.
4	Merchandise exports	Real world exports (minus U.S. exports); relative prices; U.S. direct investment; trade credit; lagged exports.
5	U.S. payments for foreign travel	Current disposable personal income.
6	U.S. receipts for foreign travel from Canada	Canadian disposable personal income; Canada–U.S. exchange rate.
7	U.S. receipts for foreign travel from rest of world	Sum of consumer expenditures in France, Germany, Italy, and the U.K.
8	Transportation, private remittances, and other services	Imports; travel expenditures abroad.
9	Transportation receipts	Exports; travel receipts.
10	Private remittances	Lagged remittances.
11	Miscellaneous service payments	Lagged payments.
12	Private miscellaneous service receipts	Canadian GNP; GNP in the European OECD countries.
13	U.S. direct investment abroad [a]	Differential between U.S. long-term interest rate on government bonds and average of Canadian and U.K. rates; lagged investment.
14	Foreign direct investment in the U.S.	Same interest differential as Equation 13.
15	U.S. purchases of foreign long-term securities	Same interest differential as Equation 13; dummy variable for Interest Equalization Tax; lagged purchases.

† Adapted from M. F. J. Prachowny, *A Structural Model of the U.S. Balance of Payments.* Amsterdam: North-Holland Publishing Company, 1969.

TABLE 5.2 (Cont.)

Equation	Dependent Variable	Major Explanatory Variables
16	Foreign purchases of U.S. private long-term securities [c]	Same interest differential as Equation 13; lagged purchases.
17	Repatriation of dividends and interest earned in the U.S.	Sum of foreign direct investment and other private assets owned by foreigners times U.S. long-term interest rate; differential growth rate of GNP in other OECD countries and U.S.
18	Repatriation of dividends earned abroad [b]	Same interest differential as Equation 13; lagged investment times average of Canadian and U.K. long-term interest rates.
19	Repatriation of interest earned abroad [b]	Same interest differential as Equation 13; lagged private assets times average Canadian and U.K. long-term rates.
20	U.S. short-term capital movements [c]	Covered interest differential between U.K. and U.S. Treasury bill rates; exports; dummy variable for Voluntary Restraint Program.
21	U.S. long-term claims against foreigners [d]	U.S. Treasury bill rate; exports; dummy variables for Interest Equalization Tax.
22	Import identity	
23	Balance-of-payments identity	

Domestic Sector

24	Consumption expenditures	Real disposable personal income; lagged consumption.
25	Nonresidential construction	Based on Liu [11].
26	Producers' durable equipment	Based on Liu [11].
27	Residential construction	Based on Liu [11].
28	Investment in nonfarm business inventories	Real GNP; lagged stock.
29	Disposable personal income	Real GNP.
30	Industrial production	Real GNP.
31	U.S. long-term interest rate	Average quarterly yield on U.S. Treasury bills; lagged rate.
32	GNP identity	

[a] Excludes second and third quarters of 1957.
[b] Beginning first quarter of 1959.
[c] Beginning first quarter of 1959 through 1965.
[d] Through 1965.

Equalization Tax and the Voluntary Restraint Program during 1963–65. He presented in addition the results of some simple simulation experiments on the balance-of-payments and GNP impacts of a 1 percent increase in the Treasury bill rate coupled with some continuing changes in government expenditures.

While Prachowny's results are of considerable interest, they cannot of course be taken literally in view of the comparative simplicity of the model. That is, while the model is explicit in its treatment of the demand side for international transactions in goods, services, and financial instruments, it abstracts almost completely as we have noted from supply considerations in the relevant markets. Moreover, the absence of a mechanism generating domestic prices and interest rates in the model is an important limitation. If the model is to prove useful for purposes of forecasting and policy analysis, the measurement of the capital account relationships especially must be improved and a linkage accomplished with a comprehensive model of the real and financial relationships of the domestic economy. Despite these reservations, Prachowny's work represents an important step in the construction of a fairly detailed model of the U.S. balance of payments.

Other Models   There are a number of models of the U.S. economy now in existence that deal almost exclusively with the domestic sector. This reflects in part the orientation of the Keynesian system towards relationships involved in a closed economy, an assumption which until recent years at least has been plausible for the U.S. in view of the relatively small size of its foreign sector. There is some question now, however, about the appropriateness of these models in view of the increased importance of the balance-of-payments constraint and the consequent increased sensitivity of U.S. economic policy to international economic influences. It may be instructive to look briefly at how the foreign sector is handled in a number of these models in order to obtain some impression of the work yet to be done.

Let us consider first the Michigan econometric model of the U.S. economy [30], which is an annual model in which equations are estimated for components of aggregate demand; productive capacity and employment; income, labor costs, and prices; taxes and social insurance; and the financial sector. The change in imports, which is included as a part of aggregate demand, is held to be dependent mainly on a composite relation between the change in nonfarm GNP and capacity utilization and on the change in relative prices. Exports are taken to be exogenously determined and to change at some specified rate. A forecast is thus made of net exports as one of the components of aggregate demand.[4] No forecast is made of any of the financial items in the capital account.

---

[4] For example, in November 1966 according to [30, p. 4], it was forecast that the 1967 increase over 1966 (in 1958 prices) would amount to $3.8 billion for exports and

The Wharton quarterly model [7] of the U.S. economy consists of 47 equations with unknown parameters and 29 identities. It covers in its published version an estimation period from 1948 to 1964. Like the Michigan model, it is Keynesian in nature with respect to the determination of aggregate output and employment but includes equations for the determination of prices, wage rates, aggregate supply, and factor shares. It contains in addition a small monetary subsector dealing with the determination of interest rates. Imports are divided into three categories in the model: crude and processed food, crude materials and semimanufactured products, and all other imports (including services). There is a single equation for exports.

The import equation for crude and processed food is estimated in per capita form with real per capita personal disposable income and relative prices as the explanatory variables. Imports of crude materials and semi-manufactured products are assumed to depend on sales originating in the manufacturing sector, the change in manufacturing inventories, and relative prices. All other imports are assumed to depend on real personal disposable income, relative prices, and lagged imports. Exports are assumed to depend upon an index of world trade (proxy for world income), relative prices, and lagged exports. U.S. export prices are endogenously determined in the model while the world trade and price variables are exogenous. In the use of the model to generate *ex ante* forecasts and for purposes of policy simulation, values for imports and exports can be obtained as a component of aggregate demand [7, pp. 50–69].

The quarterly model of the U.S. economy developed by the Office of Business Economics [29] consists of 36 equations and 13 identities covering components of GNP, prices and wage rates, labor force and employment-related magnitudes, income components, monetary variables, and miscellaneous variables introduced to close the model. The model contains two equations for imports. Imports other than crude materials and foodstuffs are dependent on real disposable income and the ratio of nonwage to wage income. Imports of crude materials and foodstuffs are dependent on the real value of lagged private GNP. Neither equation contains a relative price term, it is interesting to note. Exports are treated exogenously in the model. None of the financial items in the balance of payments is included. The model is thus able to make a forecast of net exports as a component of aggregate demand.[5]

$3.4 billion for imports. The observed preliminary changes were $1.9 billion for exports and $2.1 billion for imports. The change in the balance of trade thus turned out to be − $0.2 billion rather than the $0.4 billion that had been forecast.

A separate quarterly model is now being developed at Michigan and forecasts based on it were first presented at the Annual Conference on the Economic Outlook in November 1968. Net exports were treated in this version of the model as completely exogenous.

[5] The forecast for 1965 in billions of current dollars seasonally adjusted at annual rates was as follows [29, pp. 26–27]:

(*Footnote continued on next page*)

The Federal Reserve–MIT econometric model [2] is a quarterly model of the U.S. economy that focuses mainly on the financial sector and on the links between this sector and those for goods and services. Its primary purpose is to quantify monetary policy and the effects this policy has on the economy. The model consists of three principal blocks of equations: a financial block; a fixed investment block; and a consumption-inventory block, which includes as well income shares, imports, and federal personal taxes. There is a single equation for imports that are assumed to depend on real GNP and a measure of capacity utilization. Dummy variables are included to capture the effects of the 1959 steel strike and the 1965 dock strike. Relative prices were omitted because they were found to be unimportant statistically. Exports are treated exogenously. None of the financial items in the balance of payments are considered. Thus, we again can obtain a model forecast of net exports as a part of aggregate demand.[6] The model was also used to analyze by means of simulation the effects of a $1 billion increase in unborrowed reserves, a $5 billion increase in defense spending, and a 10 percent increase in the personal tax rate.

The Brookings econometric model of the U.S. economy [9] is a gigantic affair compared with the other models we have mentioned. It contains more than 300 equations and has involved data collection for over 2000 variables.

	1Q		2Q		3Q		4Q		Year	
	P	A	P	A	P	A	P	A	P	A
Exports (exogenous)	34.7	34.7	40.4	40.4	40.1	40.1	40.8	40.8	39.0	39.0
Imports	28.2	28.6	30.3	32.4	30.7	32.7	32.0	33.9	30.3	31.9
Net Exports	6.5	6.1	10.1	8.0	9.4	7.4	8.8	6.9	8.7	7.1

Predicted (P) imports apparently fell short of actual (A) imports in each quarter. This was due mainly to the underestimation of imports other than crude materials and foodstuffs. Predicted net exports were thus $1.6 billion below actual net exports.

  [6] In the published version of the model [2, p. 22] predictions were given only for total imports (in billions of dollars at annual rates) in the context of the complete consumption-inventory block:

	1965		1966			
	3Q	4Q	1Q	2Q	3Q	4Q
Predicted imports	33.6	35.1	36.5	37.3	38.0	38.6
Actual imports	32.9	34.4	36.0	37.1	39.0	39.7
Difference	0.7	0.7	0.5	0.2	−1.0	−1.1

Allowing for data adjustments in the actual value of imports, predicted imports for the last two quarters of 1965 were closer to actual imports in the FED–MIT model than in the OBE model noted in the preceding footnote.

It consists of the following principal sectors: consumption; residential construction; inventories; orders; investment realizations; investment intentions; foreign sector; government revenues and expenditures; production functions and factor income payments; wages and prices; agriculture; labor force; monetary sector; and the automotive industry. The purpose of having such a large model is to capture the workings of the economy as an interrelated system and to be able to make forecasts and analyze the effects of policy in great detail.

Despite the size of the Brookings model, it contains a relatively simple foreign sector. There are two equations for imports and one for exports. The imports of finished goods and services are assumed to depend on real disposable personal income, relative prices, and lagged imports. Imports of crude materials, crude foodstuffs, and semimanufactures are assumed to depend on the change in real nonfarm business inventories, real gross product originating, relative prices, and lagged imports. Exports of goods and services are assumed to depend on real world exports excluding U.S. exports, relative prices, and lagged exports. Import prices are apparently taken to be exogenous in the model, whereas export prices are generated in a rather complex manner from the price deflators for five producing sectors. The model was estimated for 1948–60 and furnished the basis for some forecasts for 1961–62 as well as a number of different simulation experiments involving changes in government expenditures, government employment, personal income taxes with and without changes in monetary policy, and changes in monetary policy. The detailed results of the forecast as well as the policy simulations thus include estimated values of net exports in constant dollars [9, pp. 20 and 41].

Although the equation specifications differ somewhat, it should be clear from our discussion that the foreign sector is treated on a relatively very simple basis in the most noteworthy of the econometric models of the U.S. economy. This is in part a holdover from the period in which the foreign sector played only a minor role in the economy. It also reflects the fact that the construction of a comprehensive model of the foreign sector that includes international capital transactions is a very difficult task. It is obvious that the foreign sector has to be treated comprehensively in countries that are much more dependent on international trade and foreign capital markets than may be the case for the U.S.[7] But given the increased importance of balance-of-payments policy considerations in the U.S. especially since the early 1960's, much remains to be done to integrate the foreign and domestic sectors in econometric models of the U.S. economy.

---

[7] See [10] for a quarterly econometric model of Canada, in which relationships describing foreign trade and international capital movements are of central importance. Work is now in progress at the Bank of Canada to link the foregoing model with the FED-MIT model of the U.S. economy.

CONCLUSION

Econometric model building is properly viewed as a tool for optimal decision making. A model builder may assume one of two roles in the decision-making process. He may provide information about future events in the form of probability statements, in which case a forecast consumer can make his own choice of actions by weighing the likelihood of the various outcomes. Alternatively, the forecaster may usurp these decision-making powers and provide only a point estimate, in which case the forecast consumer is driven necessarily to a particular action. We have argued that the former (information-provider) role is the appropriate one.

The construction of an econometric model is much more an art than a science. The choice of variables and model structure is exceedingly difficult and has often been made more by chance than by design. While the only norm with which to assess a model is performance, this unfortunately provides little or no insight into the problem of model building. But what this norm does suggest is that a model ought to evolve by annual adjustments, rather than be created at a single point in time. However, any model must begin sometime, and its initial form may greatly influence its evolutionary path. How, then, should the model begin?

We have tried to provide a thought-structure within which the decisions involved in model building could be made. We first divided the universe of economic exchanges into a set of mutually exclusive markets, in such a way that all exchanges within a market are essentially the same and that any two exchanges from different markets are fundamentally different. Keeping in mind just what our model is meant to do, we examined each of the markets to determine whether it could be discarded with little or no impact on the performance of the model. Through this process an appropriate structure may be selected.

Finally, we have considered some examples of econometric models that have actually been used in balance-of-payments forecasting and policy analysis in the case of the United States. Except for Prachowny's model, these models have employed a fairly simple structure for the foreign sector. We have been afforded therefore relatively little experience that would suggest the most appropriate structure for balance-of-payments models. Hopefully, important advances in this area may be realized in the near future.

APPENDIX TO CHAPTER 5

"TWO–GAP" MODELS

A separate species of model worth considering is the so-called two-gap model, which has been used to forecast the foreign aid requirements of developing countries. The genesis of two-gap models stems from the supposed rigidities and lack of resources in less developed countries (LDC's) that may hamper the effectiveness of traditional policy instruments in these countries in achieving their stated economic goals. In such circumstances, foreign resources in the form of grants and loans will help in the achievement of their goals.

The goals typically involve high levels of employment, balance in foreign payments, and rapid economic growth. We know from the theory of economic policy that at least the same number of policy instruments is required if the aforementioned goals are to be achieved. Thus, the policy instruments in question will commonly involve fiscal, exchange-rate, and monetary policies. In effect then if these policies do not work well in the LDC's, by making foreign aid available, we are providing these countries with an additional instrument of policy. What we shall be concerned with in our discussion therefore is estimating the foreign resources required to meet a reasonable set of goals established by an individual LDC subject to the help and cooperation of a high-income, industrialized donor country.

The issues involved in forecasting foreign resource requirements are especially complex because it is impossible to know what is required from foreign sources over a period of five or ten years unless we have a fairly accurate idea of what determines economic growth. Since our knowledge of the determinants of growth is unfortunately still rather limited, researchers interested in constructing economic models for forecasting foreign needs have had to make numerous simplifying assumptions. While the range of possible assumptions combined with the diversity of intellectual temperament of individual researchers might have resulted in a fairly wide variety of models, the two-gap models to be discussed presently are all quite similar. There may accordingly be considerable room for alternative specifications of these models.

The models in question are highly aggregative and look upon economic growth as stemming exclusively from gross capital formation. Output capacity is most typically given by the Harrod–Domar function, the product of the constant output-capital ratio and the total capital stock

$$Q = \frac{1}{k} K \qquad (5.A.1)$$

where Q is the quantity of aggregate output, k is the capital-output ratio, and K is the capital stock.

In these models there are two limits to the amount of capital formation. The first is simply the lack of adequate resources. The economy in question may not have the capacity both to supply the consumption needs of its population and to produce or trade for the capital goods required for growth. To estimate the resource needs, it is necessary to calculate full employment output and subtract from that the level of required real consumption. The figure obtained represents the supply of savings, or the real output available for capital formation, after consumption needs are satisfied. In the event that the desired level of investment exceeds this figure, foreign resources will be required to fulfill the investment objective. This inadequacy of domestic productive capacity is usually referred to as the savings-investment gap, reflecting the fact that the gap is the difference between full employment real savings and the desired level of investment.

The second constraint on capital formation is the foreign exchange or export-import gap. Accelerated growth is supposed typically to be associated with rapidly expanding imports of goods and services. Exports, on the other hand, will tend to grow as the product of the developed countries' growth rate and their income elasticity of demand for LDC exports. Growth in exports may be relatively low due to the preponderance of primary products in total LDC exports. The consequence of this disparity in the rates of growth of imports and exports is that many LDC's will experience chronic balance-of-payments deficits. Foreign resources will thus be required to finance these deficits if the growth of GNP is to be sustained.

Although there is no *ex ante* relationship between the two gaps, they are observed to be the same due to the following *ex post* identity

$$Q - (C + I) = S - I = X - M = I_F \qquad (5.A.2)$$

Thus, according to this identity, if the domestic purchases of goods $(C + I)$ exceed aggregate output Q, this will be equivalent to the excess of investment I over savings S, which will in turn be equivalent to the excess of imports M over exports X, which finally is equal to foreign investment or the quantity of foreign resources made available for domestic use I_F.

If we consider these relationships in an *ex ante* or *desired* sense, the gaps need not be the same. In the event that the *ex ante* full employment levels do not conform to the equilibrium relationship (5.A.2), either government policy must adjust the *ex ante* values or the amount of income/expenditure will diverge from the full employment level to induce a change in the actual values of expenditure to conform with the equilibrium equation (5.A.2).[1]

---

[1] This can be illuminated with the aid of an example. Suppose that savings and imports are given by

$$Q - C = S = -10 + 0.2Q \qquad (a)$$

In the *ex ante* sense, one gap will ordinarily be larger than the other. If the investment plan is to be realized, foreign resources will be required to fill the larger of these two gaps. The smaller gap can then be widened to conform with the *ex post* identity (5.A.2). For instance, if the export-import gap is the *ex ante* constraint and if foreign resources are available to fill that gap, then either savings may be decreased or investment increased in order to bring about the *ex post* equality of the gaps.

It should be noted that the foregoing considerations are applicable to developed as well as developing countries. The very important distinction, however, is that the developed countries typically have greater mobility of resources, which will make their policies aimed at eliminating trade imbalances more effective. Many LDC's, in contrast, are forced to rely heavily on imports especially of capital goods for investment purposes. Once a level of investment is selected, the level of imports may be more or less fixed. Given the level of exports, a trade imbalance may thus be a necessary consequence of the investment program.

It will be evident from our discussion that there are three fundamental relationships used in two-gap models: the production function, savings function, and import function. Exports are typically thought to grow exogenously, and investment is calculated from the production function once a target growth rate is selected. This is of course an exceedingly simple description.

---

and

$$M = 10 + 0.3Q \tag{b}$$

where Q is the real value of GNP. If full employment Q [calculated from the capital stock by relationship (5.A.1)] is at the level of 100, then savings and imports can be calculated as $S = 10$ and $M = 40$. Consider now the following cases with investment I and exports X given in the parentheses.

Case I: ($I = 10$, $X = 40$). The desired level of investment and the exogenous level of exports are such that neither gap is operative. The equilibrium relationship (5.A.2) is satisfied.

Case II: ($I = 20$, $X = 40$). Investment exceeds the available savings, but the export–import gap is not operative. An inflow of 10 from foreign sources is required to support this investment. The country uses the inflow to increase its imports from 40 to 50, thereby creating a balance-of-payments deficit of 10. The *ex post* identity (5.A.2) is thus seen to hold.

Case III: ($I = 10$, $X = 30$). Savings supply is sufficient, but there is a balance-of-payments deficit of 10. An inflow of 10 to finance the deficit can be used either to increase investment or to reduce savings (increase consumption). This change is such that the *ex post* relationship (5.A.2) holds.

In the event that the inflow from abroad is not forthcoming, the country's growth objectives will not be fulfilled. But whatever occurs, the *ex post* relationship (5.A.2) must hold. Thus, in Case II, the actual level of investment may be reduced to 10 or an additional 10 in real savings may be forced upon the economy. Case III will require the restriction of imports, perhaps through slower growth of GNP.

The foregoing examples should indicate clearly the difference between the *ex ante* gaps and also the necessary equality of the *ex post* gaps. The examples also imply that when both gaps are operative, foreign resources will be needed to fill the larger of the two gaps.

It may be useful in any event to evaluate the model's relationships in more detail.

The Production Function   As indicated earlier, the production function is typically of the Harrod–Domar type

$$Q = \frac{1}{k} K$$

This involves the assumption that the available labor is not a significant constraint on output, and that even if substitution between capital and labor is possible in production, no substitution in fact occurs. Furthermore, the constant k rules out any possibility of shifting investment from less productive to more productive activities.

The constant k may be estimated in a number of ways, the most straightforward of which is a regression of ΔQ_t on I_{t-1}

$$\Delta Q_t = \frac{1}{k} I_{t-1} \tag{5.A.3}$$

where I_{t-1} is the gross domestic capital formation in the previous period. A similar approach, suggested by the United Nations group [27], specifies

$$Q_t = \alpha + \frac{1}{k} \sum_{T=0}^{t} I_T \tag{5.A.4}$$

where I_T refers to gross capital formation.[2]

These various estimates of the capital-output ratio are based on historical data, and it is taken for granted in this regard that the productivity of investment is immutably fixed. This is a rather restrictive assumption, for it may well be that historical performance is of limited relevance in the development context. In fact, a most significant aspect of a development plan may

---

[2] A slightly different formulation by Chenery and Eckstein [4] is based on the proposition that a part of the gross investment which occurs is allocated to replacement and social overhead capital. The amount thus allocated is a constant share z of current production. The capacity-creating investment is reduced to that extent

$$\Delta Q_t = \frac{1}{k} [I_{t-1} - zQ_{t-1}] \tag{c}$$

or

$$\frac{I_{t-1}}{\Delta Q_t} = k - z \left(\frac{\Delta Q_t}{Q_{t-1}} \right)^{-1} \tag{d}$$

The constant term k in a regression of the form in Equation (d), which relates the ratio of investment to the change in output to the inverse of the rate of growth of output, is seen to be the incremental capital-output ratio.

It may be noted further that Chenery and Bruno [3] in the case of Israel estimated k from input–output tables.

be an improvement in the capital-output ratio. That the capital-output ratio varies substantially in fact among countries at different levels of development attests to the significance of this point.

The Savings Function   Savings are typically related to output as

$$S = \alpha + \beta Q \tag{5.A.5}$$

This is of course an extreme simplification. Furthermore, the use of historical data to determine the marginal savings rate is questionable. Offhand, there would seem to be a presumption that a developing economy would experience rather wide shifts in the marginal savings rate over the time period for which a projection is being made. This would be particularly true when the government made a conscious effort to increase the savings rate. In addition, the data observations which are available may not accurately describe the savings function. When domestic investment opportunities are absent, full employment will be sustainable only at low or zero savings. Government policy aimed at maintaining demand for full employment would accordingly reduce savings below the theoretically possible savings rate, which is to be estimated.[3]

The Import Function   As before, by means of historical data, a simple regression of imports on GNP is often used to explain imports

$$M = a + bQ \tag{5.A.6}$$

The objections to such a procedure made with regard to the savings function could be repeated here almost verbatim. An import function such as Equation (5.A.6) is excessively simple and is doubtfully stable. The use of historical data ignores the very significant performance aspects of imports. That is, to the extent that relatively poor performance in the past is reflected in historically high levels of imports, should such performance be rewarded by larger inflows of foreign assistance? Also, to what extent should we expect a lowering of the import propensity due to import substitution? Are historically low levels of imports the result of excessive government interference causing various inefficiencies? If so, development objectives should allow for somewhat higher levels of imports to promote efficiency. These various considerations suggest that the historical data on imports in the form of Equation (5.A.6) are of doubtful relevance to a development projection.

[3] On this point Chenery and Eckstein [4] argue that investment opportunities are directly related to exports. They argue further that foreign capital inflow can substitute for domestic savings, and that savings will be depressed by such capital flows. Their arguments are supported by a regression of savings on GNP, inflow of foreign capital, and the export/GNP ratio. As one would expect, they find the marginal propensity to save to be higher than that calculated by simple regressions of savings on output.

TABLE 5.A.1

Estimates of the Trade and Savings Gaps
(Annual Basis) †

I. Estimates Based on LDC Foreign Exchange Requirements

Source	Period Covered	Growth Target (percent)	Import Require-ments	Export Earnings	Trade Gap	Service Gap	Foreign Exchange Gap
					($ billions)		
GATT	1956/60–1975	5	28–32	17	11	—	11
UN	1959–1970	5	41	29	12	8	20
FAO	1959–1970	5	42	31	10	8	18
Balassa 1.	1960–1970	4.5	38	33	5	6	11
Balassa 2.	1960–1975	4.7	49	42	7	7	14
Chenery/Strout 1.	1962–1970	5.2	58	45	13		13
Chenery/Strout 2.	1962–1975	5.2	76	57	19		19

II. Estimates of Savings Gap

Source	Period Covered	Per Capita Growth Target (percent)	Capital-Output Ratio	Capital Requirement (annual) ($ billions)
Millikan/Rostow	1953	2.0	3.0	$6.5
Hoffman	1960–1969	2.0	3.0	7.0
Tinbergen	1959	2.0	3.0	7.5
Rosenstein–Rodan	1962–1966	1.8	2.8	6.4
	1967–1971	2.2	2.8	6.4
	1971–1976	2.5	2.8	5.0

† J. Pincus, *Trade, Aid and Development*. New York: McGraw-Hill Book Company for the Council on Foreign Relations, 1967, pp. 298–99.

A somewhat more reasonable description of imports is to disaggregate into imports of consumption goods M_c and capital goods M_I

$$M_c = a_c + b_c Q \qquad\qquad (5.A.7)$$

$$M_I = a_I + b_I I \qquad\qquad (5.A.8)$$

indicating that imports for consumption are a function of gross output while capital goods imports depend on investment alone. The use of historical data to describe the import content of investment is more justifiable than its use in describing the required consumption-goods imports. In addition to these variables, Chenery and Eckstein [4] use reserves and export earnings to reflect the scarcity of foreign exchange.

Exports   Exports X are typically assumed to grow exogenously through time t

$$X_t = X_0(1 + \lambda)^t \qquad\qquad (5.A.9)$$

where λ refers to the rate of growth. An alternative approach is to make exports to developed countries a function of demand conditions there, usually with output as the explanatory variable. Unfortunately, such a procedure cannot insure improved forecasting unless the value of output in the developed economies can be reasonably well forecast.

Some Estimates of the Two Gaps   Some indications of the orders of magnitude of the two gaps are given in Table 5.A.1. Estimates of the savings gap are about $6 billion to $7 billion annually for 1970, while estimates of the foreign exchange gap, including both goods and services, run on the order of $12 billion to $20 billion. These estimates are subject of course to all the problems we have mentioned. That is, the projections assume that there are fixed and stable relationships involving the capital-output ratio, the behavior of savings, and changes in foreign trade, and that despite their simplicity these relationships capture the essence of economic growth in the LDC's.

Conclusion   The two-gap model is evidently subject to many criticisms.[4] Nonetheless, the model will prove or fail to prove itself only in performance. Unfortunately, however, there is almost no way to assess its performance. The implied forecasts are based on the assumption that the foreign aid required to fill the two gaps is in fact forthcoming. Inasmuch as none of the

---

[4] Many of the same considerations we have discussed are relevant also to projections of debt servicing in which estimates are made, under various assumptions concerning the volume and terms of aid and the growth of current account receipts, of the net financial flows from the industrialized countries to the LDC's and the proportions of current account receipts that may be preempted by debt servicing.

forecasts was actually accompanied by the "required" aid, the model cannot be said to have been tested. But even in the absence of such tests, all of the objections we have outlined will properly make us skeptical of the results based upon two-gap models.[5]

REFERENCES

1. Balassa, B., *Trade Prospects for Developing Countries*. Homewood: Richard D. Irwin for the Yale University Economic Growth Center, 1964.

2. Board of Governors of the Federal Reserve System, *Federal Reserve Bulletin*, Vol. 54 (January 1968).

3. Chenery, H. B. and M. Bruno, "Development Alternatives in an Open Economy," *Economic Journal*, LXXII (March 1962), 79–103.

4. Chenery, H. B. and P. Eckstein, "Development Alternatives for Latin America," *Journal of Political Economy* (forthcoming).

5. Chenery, H. B. and A. M. Strout, "Foreign Assistance and Economic Development," *American Economic Review*, LVI (September 1966), 679–733.

6. Chenery, H. B. and A. M. Strout, "Foreign Assistance and Economic Development: Reply," *American Economic Review*, LVIII (September 1968), 897–911.

7. Evans, M. K. and L. R. Klein, *The Wharton Econometric Forecasting Model*. University of Pennsylvania, Department of Economics, Studies in Quantitative Economics, No. 2. Philadelphia, 1967.

8. Fei, J. C. H. and G. Ranis, "Foreign Assistance and Economic Development: Comment," *American Economic Review*, LVIII (September 1968), 897–911.

9. Fromm, G. and P. Taubman, *Policy Simulations with an Econometric Model*. Washington: The Brookings Institution, 1968.

[5] Indeed, some writers on foreign aid question the whole exercise of calculating the two gaps. For example, Pincus [17, pp. 301 and 304] has stated:

The underlying issue is ethical, not technical. There is no way to estimate the appropriate aid total except in light of agreed standards. But the agreement about aid levels implies an agreement about goals and methods of reaching them. . . .

All econometric or impressionistic estimates of trade and savings gaps are in effect techniques of quantifying discontent according to a certain set of standards. They put the seal of rationality on [LDC] aspirations. Because it is a safe bet that many LDC's could grow faster if they could get more aid, the inaccuracy of such measures does no great harm. In the eyes of those who support increases in foreign aid, some gap is better than none.

10. Helliwell, J. F., et al., "Econometric Analysis of Policy Choices for an Open Economy," *Review of Economics and Statistics*, LI (November 1969), 383–99.

11. Liu, T. C., "An Exploratory Quarterly Econometric Model of Effective Demand in the Postwar U.S. Economy," *Econometrica*, XXXI (July 1963), 301–48.

12. Maizels, A., *Exports and Economic Growth of Developing Countries*. Cambridge: Cambridge University Press, 1968.

13. Organization for Economic Co-operation and Development, M. K. Evans, *An Econometric Model of the French Economy*. Paris: OECD, 1969.

14. Organization for Economic Co-operation and Development, *National Accounts of OECD Countries, 1958–1967*. Paris: OECD, 1969.

15. Organization for Economic Co-operation and Development, *Quantitative Models as an Aid to Development Assistance Policy*. Paris: OECD, 1967.

16. Organization for Economic Co-operation and Development, *Techniques of Economic Forecasting*. Paris: OECD, 1965.

17. Pincus, J., *Trade, Aid and Development*. New York: McGraw-Hill Book Company for the Council on Foreign Relations, 1967.

18. Prachowny, M. F. J., *A Structural Model of the U.S. Balance of Payments*. Amsterdam: North-Holland Publishing Company, 1969.

19. Rhomberg, R. R. and L. Boissonneault, "Effects of Income and Price Changes on the U.S. Balance of Payments," International Monetary Fund, *Staff Papers*, XI (March 1964), 59–124.

20. Rhomberg, R. R. and P. Fortucci, "Projection of U.S. Current Account Balance for 1964 from a World Trade Model," International Monetary Fund, *Staff Papers*, XI (November 1964), 414–33.

21. Salant, W. S., et al., *The United States Balance of Payments in 1968*. Washington: The Brookings Institution, 1963.

22. Suits, D. B., "Applied Econometric Forecasting and Policy Analysis," in *Forecasting on a Scientific Basis*, Proceedings of an International Summer Institute held in Curia, Portugal, September 1966. Lisbon: Centro de Economia e Financas, 1967.

23. Suits, D. B., "Forecasting and Analysis with an Econometric Model," *American Economic Review*, LII (March 1962), reprinted in R. A. Gordon and L. R. Klein, *Readings in Business Cycles*. Homewood: Richard D. Irwin, Inc., 1965, pp. 597–625.

24. Suits, D. B., *The Theory and Application of Econometric Models*. Center of Economic Research, Training Seminar Series. Athens, 1963.

25. Theil, H., *Economic Forecasts and Policy*. Amsterdam: North-Holland Publishing Company, 1961.

26. United Nations, *Macro-Economic Models for Planning and Policy-Making.* New York, 1967.

27. United Nations, *Studies in Long Term Economic Projections for the World Economy.* New York, 1964.

28. U.S. Congress, Joint Economic Committee, *The United States Balance of Payments.* Washington: U.S. Government Printing Office, 1963.

29. U.S. Department of Commerce, Office of Business Economics, *Survey of Current Business,* 46 (May 1966); 49 (June 1969).

30. University of Michigan, *The Economic Outlook for 1968.* Papers Presented to the Fifteenth Annual Conference on the Economic Outlook. Ann Arbor, 1967.

31. Vanek, J., *Estimating Foreign Resource Needs for Economic Development.* New York: McGraw-Hill Book Company, 1967.

PART II

International Trade and Welfare

Theory and Measurement
of Trade Dependence
and Interdependence

In Chapter 2, we discussed the analysis of time-series data of a *single country's* imports or exports with the object in mind of assessing quantitatively the separate influences of supply and demand on foreign trade. The present chapter, in contrast, employs a *cross-section* approach to the analysis of import or export data for many countries at a single point in time. Our discussion here will be cast in a *general-equilibrium* setting, in which it is of little consequence to identify the separate influences of demand and supply.

The cross-sectional nature of the data that compose the analysis will necessitate somewhat different interpretations of the results as compared with those in Chapter 2. In that chapter, the questions that were posed were specific to the country being analyzed. For example, we implicitly asked what would happen to Country A's imports if it suffered a 10 percent inflation. The questions to be discussed in the present chapter are, in contrast, comparative inquiries. That is, we will discuss why Country A imports *more than* Country B at a specific point in time, and why the flow of goods from A to B exceeds the flow from C to D. Nonetheless, it will be of some importance to know whether the cross-section conclusions have implications for specific countries. For instance, if we know why A imports more than B, we might be able to say that if B becomes more like A, then B's imports will diminish. We will thus be discussing issues such as this later in the chapter.

While our previous treatment of partial-equilibrium demand functions was most relevant for international monetary relations, the cross-section general-equilibrium functions of the present chapter will be discussed in the context of the pure theory of international trade. Those familiar with the pure theory have no doubt already recognized the theoretical issues at stake in trying to answer the question of why A imports (exports) more than B. That is, are the composition and quantity of a country's imports (exports) explained by technological differences as suggested by the Ricardian comparative advantage theory, by factor endowments as suggested by the Heckscher–Ohlin theory, by differences in tastes, or by a technological gap? The recent proliferation of theories purporting to explain the central forces behind the international flow of goods and services will necessarily require empirical efforts if economists are to settle on a generally acceptable theory.[1] Although the empirical work to be described in this chapter is still in the embryonic stage, we can expect additional analysis of this kind, which is likely to be of considerable use in supporting or rejecting these various competing hypotheses.

The second part of this chapter dealing with multicountry trade flows poses a question that has been largely ignored by the trade theorists who have generally labored in a two-country world. In such a world the determinants of trade flows are the same as the determinants of imports. Trade theorists have consequently offered few suggestions as to why pairs of countries become trading partners. Investigators of trade flows therefore have had to construct and test their own theories.

Three characteristics of the data distinguish this chapter from the preceding ones: (1) the use of cross-section data already mentioned; (2) the exclusion of price variables; and (3) the inclusion of static variables such as distance and trade preferences. The exclusion of price variables stems directly from the general-equilibrium nature of this analysis. In such a setting prices are endogenous and merely adjust to equate supply and demand.[2] We will not be satisfied with a tautological statement such as that A exports relatively little because her prices are high. Rather we will wish to know *why* A's prices are high. It should be strongly emphasized that the exclusion of price variables in no way implies that prices are not effective in allocating resources. On the contrary, prices are assumed to adjust quickly, and supply and demand are

---

[1] Hufbauer [9] presents a useful summary and interesting tests of these theories. He identifies seven competing theories purporting to explain comparative advantage in manufactured goods: (1) factor proportions; (2) human skills; (3) economies of scale and trade barriers; (4) stage of production; (5) technological gap; (6) product cycle; and (7) preference similarity. The relevant references can be found in the notes to Table 1 of Hufbauer's paper.

[2] This point can be clarified by considering demand and supply schedules as follows

$$q^D = f(p, D_1, D_2, \ldots, D_n)$$
$$q^S = g(p, S_1, S_2, \ldots, S_m)$$

which indicate that the quantity demanded depends on the price and a set of demand factors D_i, and that supply behaves similarly. We can solve these equations for the market-clearing quantity

$$q = q^S = q^D = h(D_1, D_2, \ldots D_n, S_1, S_2, \ldots, S_m)$$

That is, the observed quantity depends on the demand and supply factors but not on the price variable.

Those readers familiar with simultaneous equations methods (see, for example, Johnston [11]) will recognize this as reduced-form estimation, which is free of the simultaneity problems associated with the more traditional demand analysis such as that discussed in Chapter 2.

assumed to be responsive enough to price changes to bring about an equilibrium rapidly. This point concerning prices is of great importance and should be borne continually in mind in what follows.

Although prices are an improper explanatory variable in a general-equilibrium setting, it may be that prices are *temporarily* high due to a *disequilibrium* situation. In this case high prices as a proxy for disequilibrium may be a proper explanation for low exports. This suggests the use of data averaged over several years in order to assure the relevance of the results. The possibility of disequilibrium is discussed more completely later in this chapter. On the practical level, however, prices must be omitted due to the cross-section sample. Thus, it does not make sense to compare U.S. and U.K. prices in a particular year and pronounce one high and one low, since the U.S. and U.K. goods may not be identical.

The third distinguishing characteristic is the presence of static variables such as distance and trade preferences. Such variables cannot ordinarily be used in time-series analysis insofar as they may not change greatly over time. As we will see, both the total amount of trade and the particular flow from one country to another are significantly affected by such variables at any point in time.

The discussion that follows is divided into three sections. The first deals with the theory and measurement of the total value of imports (exports), the second with the theory and measurement of trade flows, and the third discusses the research implications of this analysis.

THE THEORY AND MEASUREMENT OF GENERAL-EQUILIBRIUM TRADE SECTORS

In this section we will be concerned with the determinants of the level of a country's imports and exports in a general-equilibrium setting. We will rely on the opportunity-cost theory of international trade to suggest explanatory variables and their probable effects on the dependent variable, imports (exports). The points to be discussed will be best illuminated in the context of a three-good world. There will be one home good that cannot be traded in the foreign market due, say, to transport costs or perhaps to the nature of the good, services being an example. In addition, there will be two foreign goods. A typical country will have resources suited to the production of only one of the foreign goods and will accordingly export that good and import the other. Such a situation is depicted in Figures 6.1 and 6.2.

Figure 6.1 depicts the consumption possibilities of the country in the absence of trade. The production possibilities curve AB indicates the maxi-

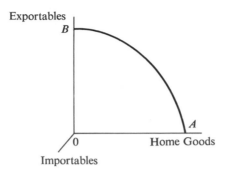

FIGURE 6.1

Consumption Possibilities in the Absence of Trade

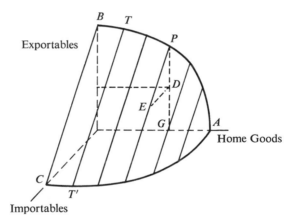

FIGURE 6.2

Consumption Possibilities with Trade

mum quantities of home goods and exportables that can be produced. Since no trade can occur, the country is restricted to consuming only what it can produce, the combinations that lie on *AB*. No consumption of importables is possible. The situation is different in Figure 6.2, where trading is allowed along international price lines such as *T'T*. Such a line is drawn parallel to the exportables–importables plane, that is, with a fixed level of home goods. It reflects the possibility of trading exportables for importables at the appropriate international-trading ratio. Consumption possibilities are therefore extended toward importables along such lines. A possible consumption point is indicated by E requiring production at P, imports of ED, and exports of PD.

Consider now a second country identical in all respects to the first country except that it has a smaller resource endowment and therefore a production possibilities curve somewhat closer to the origin. Such a country is sure to have a smaller foreign sector, that is, a smaller value of exports or imports. This suggests that we write

$$V_i^X = V_i^M = F_i = f(Y_i) \tag{6.1}$$

indicating that, in equilibrium, the value of exports of Country i, V_i^X, and the value of imports, V_i^M, equal the value of the foreign sector F_i, which is a function of the GNP of Country i, Y_i.

There are of course many reasons why Equation (6.1) will not hold. On the supply side, all countries are not endowed with roughly the same distribution of resources. Those countries with resource endowments especially

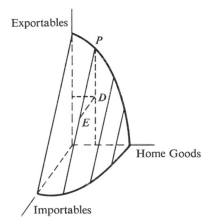

FIGURE 6.3

Resource Endowment Skewed Towards Export Production

suited to the production of exports will have a correspondingly larger foreign sector. Such a situation is depicted in Figures 6.3 and 6.4. The country with relatively more resources suited to the production of exportables is indicated in Figure 6.3. Exports are DP and imports ED, which are clearly larger than the corresponding values in Figure 6.4, $D'P'$ and $E'D'$. Yet both countries

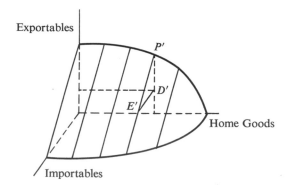

FIGURE 6.4

Resource Endowment Skewed Towards Home Goods Production

may have the same level of GNP, depending of course on the prices chosen to measure the value of the output bundles.[3]

Similarly, a country with a great diversity of resources allowing the production of all goods will have a reduced foreign sector. This situation is depicted in Figure 6.5 with a production possibilities *surface ABC*. A consump-

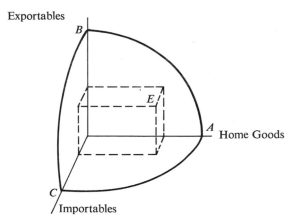

FIGURE 6.5

Balanced Resource Endowment

[3] This brings up another source of difficulty. Home goods are relatively expensive in Figure 6.3. How are we to calculate GNP figures for countries with different price structures? See Balassa [1] and Linnemann [16, p. 69] for comments on this problem.

tion point such as E may require no foreign trading at all if it falls on the production surface ABC.

These supply-side considerations lead to the following amendment to Equation (6.1). Resource endowments will have an increasing effect on the size of the foreign sector according to the following classification: balanced endowment, skewed toward the production of domestic goods, skewed toward the production of international goods.[4] A similar statement can be made for the demand side. That is, the demand characteristics can be ranked in the order of increasing stimulus to the size of the foreign sector: heavy demand for home goods, heavy demand for own international goods, heavy demand for importables.

A third influence that will disturb Equation (6.1) is the cost of international trade. Clearly a country that must incur unusually heavy costs to engage in international trade will have a correspondingly reduced foreign sector. Transport costs and tariffs are natural candidates to be included. More subtle trade obstacles such as language and cultural differences and political hostilities should also be included. The economic costs may be thought of as rotating downward the trading lines TT' in Figure 6.2, thereby making importables more expensive relative to exportables and reducing the ability of the country to consume the foreign goods. The psychic costs such as cultural barriers may be thought of as shifting the utility surface in favor of home goods and own international goods.

Finally we must admit that the data we have available will not have been generated under general-equilibrium conditions. Countries that were experiencing inflation would experience greater imports and reduced exports. Prices may lag behind the demand shifts that naturally occur in a growing world economy. A related factor completely ignored in our theoretical discussion is the presence of autonomous capital flows. For instance, a short-term capital inflow would substitute for the price adjustment needed to cure a balance-of-trade deficit. Furthermore, we ought to allow for capital flows that are long-term in nature. This suggests that those countries that import capital either due to autonomous transactions or due to accommodating adjustments of reserves in a disequilibrium period will have greater imports and reduced exports. The converse is true for capital exporters.

With the foregoing factors taken into account, our theoretical model may be summarized as:

B = a variable which reflects disequilibrium and capital flows. The letter B stands for balance.

E = resource endowment.

F = general-equilibrium value of the foreign sector.

---

[4] It will be noted that we have abstracted from the existence of economies of scale. Such economies can be thought of as affecting the shape of the production possibilities surface. However, in the absence of market imperfections they will not necessarily alter the level of trade in one direction or the other.

i = subscript indicating Country i.

R = general resistance to trade (transport costs, tariffs, etc.)

U = utility or demand structure.

V^X, V^M = value of exports and imports

Y = gross national product.

$$F_i = f(Y_i, E_i, U_i, R_i) \tag{6.2}$$

$$V_i^X = g(F_i, B_i) \qquad V_i^M = h(F_i, B_i) \tag{6.3}$$

Equation (6.2) indicates that the size of the foreign sector in a general-equilibrium context will be determined by GNP, resource endowment, utility structure, and resistance factors. The actual value of imports V^M and exports V^X will depend on this general-equilibrium foreign sector and the nature of the current disequilibrium B. This same description, it may be noted, is appropriate for disaggregated commodity groups.

Such a model is much too general for statistical application. Three variables (resource endowment, utility, and resistance) represent collections of influences and must be more precisely and more narrowly defined within the constraint of data availability. One possible approach is to use variables that directly measure these influences. For instance, in the case of resource endowment we might be able to use such variables as capital stock, expenditures on research and development, geographic area, average temperature, and average rainfall. To date, this has not been the procedure followed. Rather, it has been argued that all countries have roughly the same resource endowments and demand structures except as the countries differ in population and income. Accordingly, population and income are used as proxies for resource endowment and utility structure. In addition, the problem of disequilibrium has been ignored, and V_i^X and V_i^M have been set equal to F_i.

An empirical example of what we have been discussing can be found in work by Chenery [3, p. 634] (although his work is not particularly aimed at the subject matter of this chapter). Taking a cross section of the value of imports V_i^M, gross national product Y_i, and population size N_i for 62 countries in 1952–54, Chenery reached the following result

$$\log V_i^M = 20.4 + 0.987 \log Y_i - 0.281 \log N_i \tag{6.4}$$
$$(0.69) \qquad\qquad (0.045)$$

The reported R^2 adjusted for degrees of freedom was 0.81, a respectable figure. He also presented similar results for disaggregated commodity groups.

The population variable N may be associated with both the utility structure U and the resource endowment E. On the demand side, countries with greater populations will have heavy demands for home goods since foreign goods are dispensed with in order to feed, clothe, and shelter the inhabitants. On the supply side, countries with very small populations will have production possibilities skewed toward exportables (Figure 6.3), will therefore specialize, and will have sizable exports. Countries with somewhat larger populations will be able to diversify production (Figure 6.5) and will have somewhat fewer exports. Finally, countries with very large populations will have production possibilities skewed toward domestic goods and will have correspondingly reduced foreign sectors. We see, therefore, that both demand and supply considerations suggest that countries with large populations will have correspondingly small foreign sectors.

Now it may be objected that this explanation of the coefficient on N is contrived, at best. However, if we consider that our objective is to tie such empirical results to the traditional opportunity-cost theory of international trade, it seems plausible to argue that the negative influence of population is not inconsistent with that theory. In contrast to our view, it may be of interest to point out that some of the empirical studies bearing on this and related issues have all too often demonstrated a willingness to discard the existing theory. Linnemann [16, p. 15], for example, has suggested that the negative influence of N may be explained by economies of scale in production and significant barriers (tariff, transport, etc.) to international trade.[5]

It is perhaps worth emphasizing at this point that Chenery's model using income and population as the only explanatory variables is based on the proposition that individual countries follow generally the same path of development and consequently have similar resources/tastes at any point along that path. This raises the question of the extent to which an individual country can use the foregoing statistical results as an indication of its own future

---

[5] That is, he suggested that the negative influence of N may be explained by noting that in the relationship

$$\frac{F}{Y} = \alpha \left(\frac{Y}{N}\right)^{\beta} N^{\gamma}$$

we should expect β to be zero and γ negative. His argument is that in a world in which economies of scale and significant barriers to trade exist, industries would prefer to locate only in the largest markets to avoid the greatest transport costs. The smaller markets would not be able to support their own industries because of the economies of scale. A large local market is thus looked on as a source of comparative advantage. With a constant per capita income Y/N, an increase in N will increase the market size, thus allowing more industries to locate in the market in question and thereby reducing the dependence on trade. Accordingly the constant γ will be negative. Increases in per capita income with constant population, on the other hand, will increase the market size, thereby resulting in additional domestic industries but at the same time creating a demand for other (new?) products that cannot be economically produced in the country. The net effect, and consequently β, may be zero. Thus, the influence of N on F would be simply γ, which is negative.

Inasmuch as both our interpretation and Linnemann's are consistent with the observations, we are unable to establish any presumption as to which is to be preferred. It may be that the depressing effect of population on the foreign sector reflects a shift of demand and productive ability away from international goods as indicated by the opportunity cost theory. On the other hand, it is also possible that increases in population allow for greater diversification of home production and reduce dependence on international trade. This is a matter accordingly that remains open theoretically.

growth over time.[6] Or to put this in another way, are the cross-section results consistent with what we would expect from time-series?[7]

One can think of situations in which time-series and cross-section data would provide significantly different implications. For instance, the arrows in Figure 6.6 relating to V_i^M and Y_i can be interpreted as hypothetical indi-

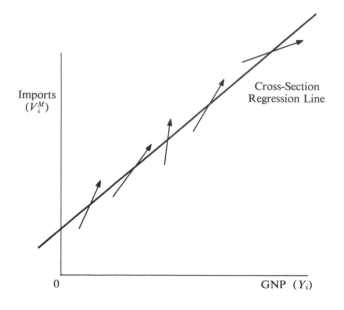

FIGURE 6.6

Hypothetical Growth Paths of Imports in Relation to GNP

[6] Chenery [3, p. 633] argues on this matter that his statistical results can be interpreted as short-run growth paths:

Historically, the growth of a country takes place in an environment in which trading possibilities and technology are constantly changing. The growth functions derived from cross section analysis, on the other hand, represent the adaptation of countries at different levels of income to conditions of technology and trade existing at one time. Ideally, they may be thought of as indicating the path that a typical country would follow if its income increased so rapidly that conditions of trade and technology were relatively constant.

[7] It is noteworthy that a question similar to this one is being asked on a theoretical level in the literature dealing with the effects of growth on international trade. This literature is much less restrictive, however, than the empirical work being cited. Thus, for example, in Johnson's model [10], allowance is made for intercountry differences in factor endowments, factor intensities in production, and propensities to consume the different goods. With reference to our discussion in the preceding footnote, population growth is shown by Johnson to be "ultra-anti-trade-biased" in the manufacturing country and to range from being "ultra-pro-trade-biased" to "anti-trade-biased" in the agricultural country.

cations of the recent growth history of several countries. The cross-section regression line shown would not capture the growth path of any of the individual countries. Some empirical support for the divergence of time-series as compared with cross-section results has been provided by Steuer and Voivodas [22], who subjected Chenery's results to a rather severe test. On the other hand, the annual cross-section results calculated by Pulliainen [20] for 1948–60 in his model of world-trade flows were relatively stable. A similarly stable pattern was found by Glejser [6] for 1954, 1958, and 1961 for imports, but there were differences in the parameter estimates for exports.

In the most extensive examination of this issue in a related context, Chenery and Taylor [4] explored the stability of cross-section estimates over time, compared cross-section with time-series estimates for individual countries, and attempted to project the time-series on the basis of the cross-section results. They concluded that the cross-section estimates captured the impact of the universal factors affecting all countries. The variation of characteristics among countries may nevertheless still cause substantial discrepancy between the cross-section and time-series implications, although we might expect that additional explanatory variables would narrow this discrepancy. A fully specified cross-section study might be able to capture the medium-run growth paths of individual economies. But such a study would probably not capture short-run cyclical patterns, nor would it capture the long-run patterns when technology/tastes may change considerably.[8] On the whole, therefore, this question of the applicability of cross-section results to time-series considerations must be approached with caution from the standpoint of individual countries.

A second empirical example that may help to elucidate our discussion can be taken from the work by Glejser [6], which has just been cited. For 61 countries for the year 1961, his results were:[9]

$$\log V_i^M = -0.3 + 0.87 \log Y_i - 0.14 \log N_i \\ + 0.24 \log D_i + 0.05 \log P_i \tag{6.5}$$

$$\log V_i^X = -0.8 + 1.03 \log Y_i - 0.26 \log N_i \\ + 0.20 \log D_i + 0.05 \log P_i \tag{6.6}$$

where D_i measures the closeness of other markets and P_i reflects membership in a preference group. Both these variables fall into the class of resistance variables, which we have associated above with the symbol R_i. The actual definition used for the vicinity variable is

$$D_i = \sum_{j \neq i} \frac{V_j^X}{D_{ij}} \tag{6.7}$$

---

[8] Kuznets [15, p. 2] has also expressed skepticism about using cross-section findings for inferring growth trends.

[9] Glejser actually used log V_i/Y_i as a dependent variable. The coefficients reported in the text are adjusted for consistency with the Chenery study.

where D_{ij} is the distance from Country i to Country j. Thus, D_i will be large when Country i is close to large markets and, correspondingly, the foreign sector will be large.[10]

Attention should be drawn to the fact that the coefficients for exports and imports in Equations (6.5) and (6.6) are not the same. This suggests that the equation of V_i^X and V_i^M to F_i in (6.2) and (6.3) is not appropriate. Examination of the coefficients in Equations (6.5) and (6.6) indicates that increases in GNP and reductions in population will add more to exports than to imports, and consequently improve the trade balance.[11]

The result just noted should be interpreted with considerable care. Our earlier discussion has indicated that a difference between V_i^X and V_i^M can occur either because of an autonomous capital flow or because of a short-run disequilibrium in the balance of payments. The autonomous capital flow offers the easiest way out. The richer countries may experience an autonomous and willing capital outflow in favor of the poorer countries either in the form of development aid or as private capital transactions. However, the same result has been found [2] for trade in manufactured products among the industrialized countries. This rules out the development aid argument, but leaves open the possibility of private capital flows.[12]

If, instead, we turn to the short-run imbalance explanation, we are led to the conclusion that the wealthier countries enjoy payments surpluses while their less fortunate neighbors suffer payments deficits. The general-equilibrium opportunity-cost theory offers no insights into the nature of such disequilibria. Rather, we must rely on a partial equilibrium explanation to the effect that short-run deficits result from excessive price inflation and/or rapid growth, the former phenomenon especially associated with the poorer nations.

Our discussion to this point has concentrated on aggregate imports and exports. Nonetheless, almost all that has been mentioned applies equally well to individual commodity groups. An analysis of this kind applied to disaggregated commodity classes would be intended to disclose the nature of comparative advantage. That is, it would be designed to disclose the determinants of the commodity composition of imports (exports). As might be expected, income and population turn out not to be particularly powerful explanatory variables for the trade in many commodity classes, particularly those requir-

[10] For example, Glejser's results indicate that Belgium, which is relatively closest to large markets, would enjoy twice as much trade, ceteris paribus, as, say Australia, which suffers the most from distance. Pulliainen's results [20] for 1948–60 referred to above also call attention to the importance of distance; these results show a slight reduction in the effects of distance during this period.

[11] This also suggests, as Glejser [6, p. 52] has pointed out, that the so-called (Sombart) law of declining foreign trade does not hold for the export side. For further critical discussion and empirical testing of this law, see Kuznets [15, esp. pp. 2–26].

[12] We are indebted to Th. Peeters for this observation.

ing specific resources that are not found in most countries, oil being an example.[13] Consequently, greater effort will be required to generate explanatory variables that accurately reflect the influence of resource endowment on these disaggregated import (export) data.

THE THEORY AND MEASUREMENT OF TRADE FLOWS

Having completed our discussion of the determinants of import and export levels, we now turn to an analysis of trade flows. These flows will be denoted by V_{ij}, the value of the flow of goods from Country i to Country j. We can think of these flows as forming an $n \times n$ matrix of values, where n is the number of countries:

	V_1^M	V_2^M	$\cdots$	V_j^M	$\cdots$	V_n^M
V_1^X	0	V_{12}	.	V_{1j}	.	V_{1n}
V_2^X	V_{21}	0	.	V_{2j}	.	V_{2n}
$\vdots$	.	.	.	.	.	.
V_i^X	V_{i1}	V_{i2}	.	V_{ij}	.	V_{in}
$\vdots$	.	.	.	.	.	.
V_n^X	V_{n1}	V_{n2}	.	V_{nj}	.	0

The row and column totals, V_i^X and V_j^M, indicate the total value of exports and imports of the particular country in question. We would like to explain the trade flows, that is, the elements of the matrix.

There are two possible approaches that can be used for this purpose. We can assume that the values on the margins of the above matrix, V_i^X and V_j^M, are known, and use them as explanatory variables. Alternatively, we can use the more fundamental explanatory variables of the previous section, such as income and population, to explain jointly the levels of imports and exports, and the values of the trade flows. Most of the studies to be discussed have attempted the latter, more difficult task. We shall do likewise and instead of using the actual values of exports and imports as explanatory variables, we will use F_i to denote that the size of the foreign sector is being explained by

---

[13] Thus, Chenery's [3, p. 634] result for petroleum-product imports was

$$\log V_i^M = 0.88 + 1.0 \log Y_i - 0.44 \log N_i$$

with an adjusted R^2 of only 0.57.

the regression as well as the value of the trade flows. This point will be brought out more fully below.

Three models have been used to describe the trade flows.[14] The earliest appealed to physical laws of gravitation and electrical forces to arrive at the conclusion that the flow of goods from Country i to Country j equals the product of the potential trade or trade capacity measured by F, the value of the foreign sector at the two points ($F_i \times F_j$), divided by the resistance or distance (perhaps squared). While the economic meaning of such "gravity" models is not altogether clear, we will present below a specification similar to that implied by these models.

A second approach, employed by Linnemann [16], specifies a Walrasian general-equilibrium model, with each country having its own supply and a set of demands for the goods of all other countries. Solving for the flows, we would obtain the usual general-equilibrium result that each flow depends on everything else. But we would have some reason to believe that the particular flow V_{ij} would be most influenced by export-supply factors in Country i and import-demand factors in Country j. We might therefore write

$$V_{ij} = h(F_i, F_j)$$
$$= h[f(Y_i, E_i, U_i, R_i), f(Y_j, E_j, U_j, R_j)] \qquad (6.8)$$

We could also take the simple additional step of including a resistance variable R_{ij} to indicate the level of trade resistance specific to the flow from i to j.

The third description of trade flows is based on a probability model, which we have adapted from the work of Savage and Deutsch [21]. It is characterized by demanders being assigned to suppliers in a random fashion. There are three reasons why we prefer this (or this kind of) model. In the first place, the general-equilibrium model does not suggest the form of the function h in Equation (6.8). We will argue presently that this form can be represented by the simple product $F_i \times F_j$. Secondly, as noted below, statistical problems of heteroscedasticity and autocorrelation become clear when the probability model is used. Finally, the probability model will serve to tie these studies together with other work, especially that of Savage and Deutsch just mentioned.

Turning now to the details of the probability model, we will view world trade as being generated by thousands of small independent transactions.

---

[14] A brief discussion of some of these models can be found in Taplin [23]. Similar models have been used to explain other types of international and interregional flows, including migration, commuting, truck transportation, and tourism; see, for example, Glejser and Dramais [7] and the references cited therein. Waelbroeck [27] included relative prices in a model of trade flows for the Common Market countries for 1958 and presented for each country some calculations of the "elasticities of substitution" for six commodity groupings. This is an improper use of such a model, however, because as noted in Footnote 2, prices drop out of the reduced form of the general-equilibrium relationships under consideration.

Each transaction will be of a certain size β and will involve one exporting country and one importing country. Since Country i enjoys a share of world trade $f_i = F_i/T$, where T is total world trade, we will quite naturally assume that the probability that a particular transaction involves Country i as the exporter is f_i. In similar fashion, the probability that Country j is the home of the importer is f_j. For the moment we will assume that the selections of exporter and importer are independently performed and we will write the probability that the flow travels from i to j as

$$p_{ij} = f_i f_j \tag{6.9}$$

Let us assume further that all transactions are of size β, and that N of these transactions occur. We can then write total world trade as

$$T = N\beta \tag{6.10}$$

and calculate the expected flow from Country i to Country j: [15]

$$V_{ij} = N\beta f_i f_j = \frac{F_i F_j}{T} \tag{6.11}$$

This equation expresses the fact that Country i is prepared to export F_i worth of goods, which, because of the randomness in the assignment of suppliers to demanders, is distributed evenly among the importers proportional to the size of each demand F_j.[16]

[15] The text describes a multinomial probability distribution. Feller [5, p. 141] gives the expected value as

$$E(V_{ij}) = N\beta f_i f_j$$

with the corresponding regression equation given by

$$V_{ij} = N\beta f_i f_j + u_{ij} \qquad E(u_{ij}) = 0$$

The corresponding variance is (Feller [5, p. 214])

$$\text{Var}\,(u_{ij}) = \text{Var}\,(V_{ij}) = N\beta^2 f_i f_j (1 - f_i f_j) = \beta\, F_i F_j \left[\frac{1 - (F_i/T)(F_j/T)}{T}\right]$$

We observe that for $f_i f_j < 1/2$ the variance is an increasing function of $f_i f_j$. This situation is described as heteroscedasticity and will necessitate some alteration of ordinary least squares. (See Footnote 18.)
A second source of statistical difficulty stems from the correlation of the error terms. Ordinary least squares requires that the error terms be independently generated. In our model, however, flows with positive error terms (deviations from the expected value) will tend to be offset by negative errors elsewhere. The actual covariance is (Feller [5, p. 224, problem 20])

$$\text{Cov}\,(V_{ij}, V_{i'j'}) = N\beta^2 f_i f_j\, f_{i'} f_{j'}$$

[16] It should be pointed out that the probability model just presented is but one among many candidates. Its most glaring weakness is that it makes no allowance for the fact that p_{ii} and V_{ii} are zero, that is, that there is no trade flow internal to any country. We could conceivably generalize the model to include internal flows. Alternatively we could amend

(Footnote continued on next page)

Of course the assignment of suppliers to demanders is not a simple random process. Significant deviation from randomness will be induced by the same set of costs or resistance factors that were seen earlier to influence the total value of the foreign sector. For instance, as we choose pairs of countries that are farther and farther apart, their respective traders are less and less likely to make contact. This is due both to increased transport costs and to reduced business knowledge. Tariffs, language problems, and cultural differences will also play a part. Similarly, economic and political alliances such as customs unions may reduce the physical and psychic resistances to trade. We might think of these resistance factors as affecting the probability that traders of Countries i and j get together, in which case this requires an alteration of Equations (6.9) and (6.11) to

$$p_{ij} = f_i f_j g(R_{ij}) \qquad (6.12)$$

$$V_{ij} = N\beta f_i f_j g(R_{ij}) = \frac{F_i F_j g(R_{ij})}{T} \qquad (6.13)$$

where R_{ij} is a variable reflecting the diverse set of trade resistances between i and j.[17]

Equation (6.13) assumes the central theoretical role in the analysis of trade flows. We now turn to the empirical counterpart of that theory. The previous section has provided an extensive discussion of the determinants of the foreign sectors, F_i and F_j, and we will consequently direct the following

---

the model to restrict p_{ii} and V_{ii} to zero. This is what is done by Savage and Deutsch [21]. This requires the addition of some cumbersome but small variables to all the equations. We have avoided these complications in the belief that the essential features of the trade flows are contained in our presentation.

A second point worth mentioning is that the actual levels of imports and exports of each country are not fixed by our model, but are the result of the random assignment process. We might instead require that the assignment occur after the levels of imports and exports are fixed. We would then describe the assignment by a hypergeometric distribution rather than a multinomial distribution. The expected values would remain the same, but the variances would be somewhat reduced. (See Feller [5, p. 219].)

Another restrictive assumption is the requirement that the size of a transaction be fixed at β. A more realistic assumption is that β has a probability distribution. (See Savage and Deutsch [21].)

Finally, it may be that the assignment of exporter to importer is not independent of the assignments that have already occurred. It is natural enough to expect considerable resistance to the first flows from i to j, but once these flows are established, further flows are much more likely. This suggests that the flows among small countries will be much more skewed than among larger countries simply because the smaller countries will have overcome fewer of the initial resistances. Larger countries with large foreign sectors will be well beyond the influence of these forces. Pulliainen's [20] use of Y_I and Y_J (defined below) in Equation (6.20) can be interpreted as reflecting this influence.

[17] The variances and covariances reported in Footnote 15 can be altered accordingly to

$$\text{Var } (V_{ij}) = N\beta^2 f_i f_j \, g(R_{ij})[1 - f_i f_j \, g(R_{ij})]$$

$$\text{Cov } (V_{ij}, V_{i'j'}) = -N\beta^2 f_i f_j f_{i'} f_{j'} \, g(R_{ij}) g(R_{i'j'})$$

discussion particularly at the resistance factors, $g(R_{ij})$. First, however, we would like to illustrate the empirical link between the trade-flow regressions and the foreign-sector regressions of the previous section. Equation (6.13) includes two unmolested foreign-sector terms. This suggests that we should be able to read the foreign-sector expressions directly from the trade-flow equation. For example, Linnemann [16, p. 82] provides the following trade flow result: [18]

$$\log V_{ij} = \alpha_0 + 0.99 \log Y_i - 0.2 \log N_i + 0.85 \log Y_j$$
$$- 0.15 \log N_j + \log g(R_{ij}) \tag{6.14}$$

where $g(R_{ij})$ refers to resistance variables to be identified subsequently. Taking the F_i and F_j terms from this equation, we obtain

$$\log V_j^M = \log F_j = \alpha_0' + 0.85 \log Y_j - 0.15 \log N_j \tag{6.15}$$

$$\log V_i^X = \log F_i = \alpha_0'' + 0.99 \log Y_i - 0.2 \log N_i \tag{6.16}$$

These equations are almost identical to Glejser's results reported in Equations (6.5) and (6.6), a fact that tends to support our probability model and its consequent equation (6.13). Furthermore, this illustrates the fact that a regression of the form (6.14) explains the total value of the foreign sector as well as the levels of flows to and from individual countries.

Let us now focus our attention on the $g(R_{ij})$ term that appears in our theoretical model represented by Equation (6.13) and in a regression such as the one indicated in Equation (6.14). We have already mentioned a wide

---

[18] With the exception of Pöyhönen's [18] work, all the results to date have been fitted by ordinary least squares with a log-linear function. Footnotes 15 and 17 suggest that this is not the optimum fitting procedure. The model we have presented in Equation (6.13) can be written

$$V_{ij} = \frac{F_i F_j \, g(R_{ij})}{T} + u_{ij}$$

where u_{ij} is an error term with

$$E(u_{ij}) = 0$$

$$\text{Var}(u_{ij}) = N\beta^2 f_i f_j \, g(R_{ij})[1 - f_i f_j \, g(R_{ij})]$$

$$\text{Cov}(u_{ij}, u_{i'j'}) = -N\beta^2 f_i f_j f_{i'} f_{j'} \, g(R_{ij}) g(R_{i'j'})$$

The covariance terms can perhaps be neglected as they are surely smaller than the variance terms by a factor of one hundred (since no country has more than a tenth of world trade, $f_i f_j < 1/100$). Maximum likelihood estimation, assuming the u_{ij} are distributed normally, requires the minimization of

$$\sum_{ij} \frac{[V_{ij} - F_i F_j \, g(R_{ij})]^2}{F_i F_j \, g(R_{ij})[T^2 - F_i F_j \, g(R_{ij})]}$$

This compares with the log-linear ordinary least squares minimization of

$$\sum_{ij} [\log V_{ij} - \log F_i - \log F_j - \log g(R_{ij})]^2$$

variety of influences subsumed in $g(R_{ij})$, which will tend to impede or enhance trade between individual countries. While the existing empirical work does not do full justice to the rich theoretical possibilities of this term, the results that have been obtained are nevertheless interesting and provocative.

The simplest resistance factor is distance itself. Tinbergen [25, p. 273], for example, fitted a regression of the form (6.14) and obtained

$$g(R_{ij}) = D_{ij}^{-0.89} \qquad (6.17)$$

where D_{ij} is the distance from Country i to Country j. Distance is seen to have a significant depressing effect on trade with an elasticity less than unity.

Recognizing the simplistic nature of this specification, Tinbergen [25, p. 266] altered the resistance variables to

$$g(R_{ij}) = D_{ij}^{\alpha_3} A^{\alpha_4} P_C^{\alpha_5} P_B^{\alpha_6} \qquad (6.18)$$

where A is a dummy variable for neighboring or adjacent countries, and P_C and P_B are dummy variables indicating Commonwealth and Benelux preference. His actual estimates had the proper signs and reasonably small standard errors but the R^2 climbed only slightly.

The use of the dummy variables to reflect preference-group membership has interesting implications for the analysis of such groups. The estimated coefficient on the dummy variable can be used to calculate the extent to which intermember flows were augmented. For instance, Tinbergen found that Benelux association increased the flows between members by 10 percent. It is not clear, however, from such information whether the increase in inter-member flows was at the expense of the member-to-nonmember flows or whether it reflected a general increase in trade of the member nations. The answer to such a question can be gleaned from the work reported in the previous section on the foreign sector. That is, Glejser's [6] results indicated that Belgium enjoyed a 60 percent increase in her foreign sector due to membership in preference groups (including colonial preference). Such quantitative information may be useful therefore insofar as it yields conclusions as to the trade-diverting/trade-creating effects of customs unions.[19]

---

[19] Another approach to the analysis of customs unions, suggested by Linnemann [16, p. 179], is to observe that two countries will have a total trade with the rest of the world given by

$$F_{1+2} = \alpha Y_1^{\alpha_1} N_1^{\alpha_2} + \alpha Y_2^{\alpha_1} N_2^{\alpha_2} - 2\beta Y_1^{\beta_1} N_1^{\beta_2} Y_2^{\beta_3} N_2^{\beta_4} D_{12}^{-\delta}$$

which indicates the sum of the total trade of the two countries minus their internal trade. If, however, these countries were fully integrated, we would have (assuming the resulting GNP is simply the sum of the individual ones)

$$F_{1+2} = \alpha(Y_1 + Y_2)^{\alpha_1}(N_1 + N_2)^{\alpha_2}$$

Although full integration is unlikely, a comparison of these two values might prove useful as a guide to the static effects of a customs union on trade with the rest of the world.

The distance term discussed above has one troubling feature. As the distance shrinks to zero, the term $D_{ij}^{-\delta}$ explodes, indicating very heavy trading for countries that are close to each other. This point has led Pöyhönen [18] to his unique scaling of the distance term

$$g(R_{ij}) = (1 + \gamma D_{ij})^{-\delta} \tag{6.19}$$

This describes resistance to trade as being a constant resistance plus a part that increments with distance. Since the resistance term reflects costs, we can think of this formulation as allowing for both fixed and variable costs. If the value of γ is large, variable costs will dominate. If it is small, variable costs will not have a great influence. This specification converges to the earlier one $[g(R_{ij}) = D_{ij}^{-\delta}]$ as γ grows.[20] Though this specification is clearly preferred to the earlier one on the grounds of generality, it has a computational drawback because it cannot be linearized by applying logarithms, and ordinary least squares cannot be used for the estimation.[21] With this computational burden in mind, Pöyhönen found it necessary to revert to the first specification.

In a later article, Pöyhönen [19] presented some theoretical arguments that led to the specifications used by Pulliainen [20]. These authors argued, in effect, that individual countries are not natural units in determining trade flows. The proper unit is the market area, comprising many countries. While trade between these market areas is adequately described by the flow equation we have already discussed, a second allocation of the trade is necessary for the within-market-area distribution. Such a description is based on the notion that information and distribution come in bundles that refer to a whole market, thereby inducing a business decision that refers to the whole market. For example, a U.S. businessman typically decides to export to the South American market. He rarely would make the decision to export to Brazil alone, since the heavy fixed costs associated with gathering information, making the decision, and establishing a distribution network need be incurred only once for either decision.

These considerations suggest the following equation

$$V_{ij} = \frac{F_i}{F_I} F_I \left(\frac{F_J}{T}\right)\left(\frac{F_j}{F_J}\right) g(R_{IJ}, R_{ij}, R_{iJ}, R_{Ij}) \tag{6.20}$$

where F_I is the foreign sector of the market area to which Country i belongs and R_{IJ} is a general resistance between market areas I and J. This equation is

---

[20] The value of γ that Pöyhönen reported, 0.00157/nautical mile, is a relatively small number reflecting the importance of fixed costs. For instance, variable costs do not equal fixed costs up to a distance of 700 nautical miles. We should also observe that the adjacent-country variable used by Tinbergen [25] and reported in Equation (6.18) can be interpreted as reflecting the influence of fixed costs.

[21] Pöyhönen minimized the sum of squared residuals in logarithms:

$$\sum e_i^2 = \sum_{ij} [\log V_{ij} - \log \hat{c} - \log \hat{c}_i - \log \hat{c}_j - \hat{\alpha} \log Y_i - \hat{\beta} \log Y_j + \hat{\delta} \log(1 + \hat{\gamma} D_{ij})]^2$$

interpreted as follows. The center terms $F_I(F_J/T)$ are familiar and describe the flow of trade from Market area I to Market area J. That is, Area I is prepared to export F_I worth of goods, which is distributed evenly among the market areas proportional to their demands F_J. A share of this flow F_i/F_I originates in the ith country. Similarly, the flow from Country i to Market area J is distributed evenly among the members of the market area proportional to their demands F_j, a fact which is indicated by the term F_j/F_J. The variable R_{IJ} can be thought of as affecting the flow of goods from I to J, while the other resistance terms alter the distribution of that flow among the members of the market area.

We can now cancel the identical terms in Equation (6.20) to arrive at precisely the same equation as before with the exception of the new resistance variables. The market-area consideration, therefore, affects only the trade resistance factors.

Pulliainen's [20, p. 82] resistance variables were actually

$$g(R_{ij}) = D_{ij}^{-d} Y_I^e Y_J^f (1 + |\, C_i^o - C_j^o \,|)^g \tag{6.21}$$

where Y_I and Y_J are the aggregate gross-domestic products of Market areas I and J, and C_i^o and C_j^o are the long-range mean temperatures of Countries i and j. In light of the above discussion that the market-area consideration has an effect only on the resistance factors, it is surprising to find Y_I and Y_J as explanatory variables. Pulliainen offers the appealing explanation that increases in trade between the two markets associated with increases in Y_I and Y_J are accompanied by a reduction in trade resistance as distribution, information, and sales networks are established. To use our symbols, we would write

$$R_{IJ} = r_{IJ} Y_I^e Y_J^f \tag{6.22}$$

where r_{IJ} reflects resistances associated with other variables.

The other contribution of Pulliainen is the use of the temperature variable $(1 - |\, C_i^o - C_j^o \,|)$ to reflect differences in resource endowments associated with different mean temperatures. As the temperatures become more separated, the countries in question become less similar in resource base, export more dissimilar products, and may trade more. On the other hand, tastes may be molded by the domestic production, and the consequent dissimilarity of tastes may induce countries with dissimilar resources to trade less.

It should be recognized that the temperature-disparity variable does not reflect resistance to trade in the previous sense of a monetary or psychic penalty. Rather, it reflects the simple fact that pairs of traders will not do business unless the supplier and demander have the same good in mind. What this suggests is that we must find some way of dealing with differences in the commodity composition of trade. One way to handle this is in terms of the aggregate relation as above with variables that indicate dissimilarities in resource base. Alternatively, at least in principle, one may perform the analysis on disaggregated commodity classes. A third approach, suggested by Linnemann [16], is to use variables in the aggregate relation that indicate the interaction of i's export structure with j's import structure such as

$$C_{ij} = \sum_k \frac{V_{ik}^X}{V_i^X} \frac{V_{jk}^M}{V_j^M} \qquad (6.23)$$

where V_{ik}^X/V_i^X is the proportion in value terms of exports of Commodity k by Country i, and V_{jk}^M/V_j^M is the proportion of imports of the same good by Country j.

A similar interaction term C_{ij}^* results naturally from the aggregation over commodities

$$V_{ij} = \sum_k \frac{F_{ik}^X F_{jk}^M g(R_{ijk})}{T_k} \qquad (6.24)$$

where F_{ik}^X is the export supply of the kth commodity by the ith country, F_{jk}^M is the import demand of the jth country, R_{ijk} is the trade resistance specific to the kth commodity, and T_k is the world value of k-commodity trade. This equation can be altered as follows

$$
\begin{aligned}
V_{ij} &= F_i \frac{F_j}{T} g(R_{ij}) \sum_k \frac{F_{ik}^X}{F_i} \frac{F_{jk}^M}{F_j} \frac{g(R_{ijk})}{g(R_{ij})} \left(\frac{T_k}{T} \right)^{-1} \\
&= \frac{F_i F_j\, g(R_{ij}) C_{ij}^*}{T}
\end{aligned} \qquad (6.25)
$$

with

$$C_{ij}^* = \sum_k \frac{F_{ik}^X}{F_i} \frac{F_{jk}^M}{F_j} \frac{g(R_{ijk})}{g(R_{ij})} \left(\frac{T_k}{T} \right)^{-1}$$

We may first note with regard to the foregoing equations that the appropriate interaction term is not the simple inner product given in Equation (6.22), but rather a weighted inner product C_{ij}^*. The factor T/T_k weights the commodity in inverse proportion to its importance in world trade. The larger the commodity class, the smaller its weight. The other factor $g(R_{ijk})/g(R_{ij})$ works in the opposite direction. There is a presumption that resistance to trade is least [large $g(R_{ijk})$] for those commodities that form the bulk of world trade. Accordingly the larger commodity class should be given a somewhat larger weight. These two counteracting considerations may possibly make the unweighted inner product C_{ij} very close to the properly weighted term.

Secondly, there is some question as to whether the use of the commodity composition of imports and exports as explanatory variables is legitimate. As we noted earlier, the explanation of trade flows, given the levels of imports and exports, is presumably a much easier task than the explanation of the trade flows with only the more fundamental variables. Had we been concerned with the easier task, we would have used a relation such as

$$V_{ij} = \frac{V_i^X V_j^M g(F_{ij})}{T} \tag{6.26}$$

where V_i^X and V_j^M are the actual levels of exports and imports, rather than Equation (6.13) in our earlier discussion. While the use of the interaction term does not weaken the hypothesis to the extent that the use of V_i^X and V_j^M would, it nonetheless is open to question on the same grounds. More fundamental explanatory variables reflecting the interaction of resource endowments or tastes would seem to be more appropriate choices, for example, the temperature disparity variable discussed above.

The work we have been describing to this point, using such fundamental explanatory variables as income and population, should be thought of as testing both the theory of the total foreign sector and the theory of trade flows, since the two theories must be valid to produce a good fit. Suppose, however, that we wanted to test the flow theory alone; we could use a regression such as (6.26), in which the values of exports and imports are explanatory variables. An alternative is the use of dummy variables c_i and c_j

$$V_{ij} = c_i c_j g(R_{ij}) \tag{6.27}$$

This says that i and j have foreign sectors of size c_i and c_j, the determinants of which are not of concern. Thus, Equation (6.27) would provide a good fit quite independent of the validity of what is being posited in the theoretical description of the total foreign sector.

It is instructive to compare Equation (6.27) with a hybrid specification that Pöyhönen [18] and Pulliainen [20] have employed in their work

$$V_{ij} = c_i c_j Y_i^\alpha Y_j^\beta g(R_{ij}) \tag{6.28}$$

Equation (6.28) is the same as (6.27) except for the inclusion of the income terms, Y_i and Y_j. However, since (6.28) contains the dummy variables, c_i and c_j, this specification is a test only of the theory of trade flows.[22]

We may note, in conclusion, two other approaches that have been used to analyze trade flows. While these approaches may be of some interest in describing the structure of the trade matrices in question, they are cruder than what we have been discussing in the sense that no attempt generally is made

---

[22] It is worth noting that Pöyhönen calculated the coefficients on the income terms to be quite close to 0.5, in comparison with coefficients in the 0.8 to 1.0 range obtained by all other investigators, including Pöyhönen's own research associate, Pulliainen. The only satisfactory explanation of this phenomenon is the existence of a computational error. That is, the minimization of a value such as Pöyhönen's (see Footnote 21) necessarily involves an iterative technique. It is common for iterative techniques either to converge to a local minimum or to converge so slowly that the program feels convergence is complete long before the true values are reached. The fact that Pöyhönen's initial values are 0.5, therefore, makes 0.52 and 0.504 as final values very suspect.

to explain why, economically speaking, the distribution of trade flows is more skewed than would be assumed on the basis of a simple probability model. No resort is made, in other words, to variables such as distance, trade preferences, etc., which constitute the economic forces behind the observed flows.

The first approach is represented by the work of Savage and Deutsch [21], who developed a simple probability model to describe the generation of international flows. While our model described earlier in Equation (6.11) has been adapted from the Savage–Deutsch model, there are nevertheless two important differences to be noted. Their model takes into account the fact that there is no flow internal to any country; that is, they restrict p_{ii} and V_{ii} to zero. Secondly, they allow the size of a transaction (consignment, in their terminology) to vary with mean β and variance σ^2. Using this model, Savage and Deutsch estimated the expected flows from knowledge of the marginal totals, V_i^X, V_i^M, and explored for significant differences between the actual and expected flows, which they of course discovered.[23] The logical subsequent step of regressing these deviations on resistance variables was performed with some success by Linnemann [16, p. 183]. Closely related to the Savage and Deutsch approach is that of Uribe, Theil, and de Leeuw [26], which sought to predict trade flows from knowledge of the future import and export totals, V_i^X, V_i^M, with an adjustment for the fact that present flows do not conform to the hypothetical simple pattern such as that indicated by our Equation (6.11).[24]

[23] More specifically the authors assumed

$$p_{ij} = \begin{cases} SP_iQ_j & \text{for } i \neq j \\ 0 & \text{for } i = j \end{cases}$$

with the normalizing constant

$$S = (1 - \sum_k P_kQ_k)^{-1}$$

The numbers P_i and Q_j will be approximately the probabilities of having i as the origin and j as the terminal point. The authors then calculated the expected values of V_i^X and V_j^M as

$$E(V_i^X) = TSP_i(1 - Q_i)$$
$$E(V_j^M) = TSQ_j(1 - P_j)$$

where T is total world trade. These equations were then solved for estimates of P_i and Q_j, which were used to calculate the expected flows as

$$E(V_{ij}) = TSP_iQ_j$$

[24] A simple prediction of V_{ij} suggested by Uribe, Theil and de Leeuw, is

$$V_{ij} = \frac{V_i^X V_j^M}{T}$$

This prediction can be adjusted to allow for the divergence of the actual flow from the expected flow in a base period as follows

$$V'_{ij} = \frac{V_i^X V_j^M}{T} \times \frac{V_{ij0}}{V_{i0}^X V_{j0}^M / T_0}$$

That is, if V_{ij} in the base period V_{ij0} exceeds its expected value ($V_{i0}^X V_{j0}^M / T_0$), we will adjust our estimate of V_{ij} accordingly.

CONCLUSION

The review in this chapter has suggested a number of possibly fruitful areas for research into the factors determining the level and flow pattern of a country's foreign trade. The significance of such research must be understood in the context of seeking a broader understanding of the empirical basis of the pure theory of international trade. This is something a number of the studies cited have failed to make clear.

The starting point for investigation is to be found in the economic models depicted in Equations (6.2) and (6.8) and in the probability model of trade flows in Equation (6.11). The need for further theoretical refinement and empirical specification of these models should be evident from our discussion. It would appear especially worthwhile to attempt to give greater empirical content to the resource endowment, utility structure, and resistance variables represented in the models.

In particular, the relation between the cross-section and time-series analysis of the determinants of the size of a country's foreign sector should be investigated in order to see whether some typical growth path for this sector can be identified. This observation points toward a pooling of cross-section and time-series data in a single study. It is also important to be certain that the model used in analyzing a country's foreign sector is consistent with the model of international trade flows that has been used. In both types of investigation, the significance of such resistance factors as distance, market familiarity, and preference arrangements has been made clear. These are certainly factors that deserve more careful study.

REFERENCES

1. Balassa, B., "Patterns of Industrial Growth: Comment," *American Economic Review*, LI (June 1961), 394–97.

2. Centrum voor Economische Studien, Katholieke Universiteit te Leuven, "Application du Modèle Gravitationnel à la Structure des Echanges Internationaux de Biens d'Equipement," Parts I–III (mimeographed, 1967).

3. Chenery, H. B., "Patterns of Industrial Growth," *American Economic Review*, L (September 1960), 624–54.

4. Chenery, H. B. and L. Taylor, "Development Patterns: Among Countries and Over Time," *Review of Economics and Statistics*, L (November 1968), 391–416.

5. Feller, W., *An Introduction to Probability Theory and Its Applications*, Vol. I. New York: John Wiley and Sons, Inc., 1957.

6. Glejser, H., "An Explanation of Differences in Trade-Product Ratios Among Countries," *Cahiers Economiques de Bruxelles*, 5, No. 37 (1968).

7. Glejser, H. and A. Dramais, "A Gravity Model of Interdependent Flows" (mimeographed, July 9, 1968).

8. Goodman, L. A., "Statistical Methods for the Preliminary Analysis of Transactions Flows," *Econometrica*, 31 (January 1963), 197–208.

9. Hufbauer, G. C., "The Commodity Composition of Trade in Manufactured Goods," presented at the Universities–National Bureau Conference on Technology and Competition in International Trade (October 1968). New York: Columbia University Press, forthcoming.

10. Johnson, H. G., "Economic Development and International Trade," in R. E. Caves and H. G. Johnson, eds., *Readings in International Economics*. Homewood: Richard D. Irwin, Inc., 1968.

11. Johnston, J., *Econometric Methods*. New York: McGraw-Hill, 1963.

12. Keesing, D. B., "Population and Industrial Development: Some Evidence from Trade Patterns," *American Economic Review*, LVIII (June 1968), 448–55; B. Balassa, "Country Size and Trade Patterns: Comment," and D. B. Keesing, "Reply," *American Economic Review*, LIX (March 1969), 201–04.

13. Kindleberger, C. P., *Foreign Trade and the National Economy*. New Haven: Yale University Press, 1962.

14. Kuznets, S., "Quantitative Aspects of the Economic Growth of Nations: IX, Level and Structure of Foreign Trade: Comparison for Recent Years," *Economic Development and Cultural Change*, XIII (October 1964, Part II), 1–106.

15. Kuznets, S., "Quantitative Aspects of the Economic Growth of Nations: X. Level and Structure of Foreign Trade: Long-Term Trends," *Economic Development and Cultural Change*, 15 (January 1967, Part II), 1–140.

16. Linnemann, H., *An Econometric Study of International Trade Flows*. Amsterdam: North-Holland Publishing Co., 1966.

17. Maizels, A., *Industrial Growth and World Trade*. London: Cambridge University Press, 1965.

18. Pöyhönen, P., "A Tentative Model for the Volume of Trade Between Countries," *Weltwirtschaftliches Archiv*, Band 90 (1963, I), 93–100.

19. Pöyhönen, P., "Toward a General Theory of International Trade," *Ekonomiska Samfundets Tidskrift*, (No. 2, 1963), 69–77.

20. Pulliainen, K., "A World Trade Study: An Econometric Model of the Pattern of the Commodity Flows in International Trade in 1948–1960," *Ekonomiska Samfundets Tidskrift* (No. 2, 1963), 78–91.

21. Savage, I. R. and K. W. Deutsch, "A Statistical Model of the Gross Analysis of Transactions Flows," *Econometrica*, 28 (July 1960), 551–72.

22. Steuer, M. D. and C. Voivodas, "Import Substitution and Chenery's Patterns of Industrial Growth—A Further Study," *Economia Internazionale*, XVIII (February 1965), 47–82.

23. Taplin, G. B., "Models of World Trade," International Monetary Fund, *Staff Papers*, XIV (November 1967), 433–55.

24. Temin, P., "A Times-Series Test of Patterns of Industrial Growth," *Economic Development and Cultural Change*, 15 (January 1967), 174–82.

25. Tinbergen, J., *Shaping the World Economy: Suggestions for an International Economic Policy*. New York: The Twentieth Century Fund, 1962.

26. Uribe, P., H. Theil, and C. G. de Leeuw, "The Information Approach to the Prediction of International Trade Flows," *Review of Economic Studies*, XXXIII (July 1966), 209–20.

27. Waelbroeck, J., "On the Structure of International Trade Interdependence," *Cahiers Fconomiques de Bruxelles*, 4, No. 36 (1967).

28. Whitman, M. v. N., "Economic Openness and International Financial Flows," *Journal of Money, Credit, and Banking*, I (November 1969), 727–49.

Constant-Market-Share Analysis
of Export Growth

A country's exports may fail to grow as rapidly as the world average for three reasons: (1) Exports may be concentrated in commodities for which demand is growing relatively slowly; (2) exports may be going primarily to relatively stagnant regions; or (3) the country in question may have been unable or unwilling to compete effectively with other sources of supply. In this chapter we shall discuss a method of analysis designed to disentangle these effects.[1]

At the heart of the method of analysis is the assumption that a country's share in world markets should remain unchanged over time. The difference between the export growth implied by this constant-share norm and the actual export performance is attributed to the effect of competitiveness, and the actual growth in exports is divided into competitiveness, commodity-composition and market-distribution effects. This will be made clearer in the discussion below.

THEORY AND MEASUREMENT

Demand for exports in a given market from two competing sources of supply may be described by the following relationship:

$$\frac{q_1}{q_2} = f\left(\frac{p_1}{p_2}\right) \tag{7.1}$$

where q_i and p_i are the quantity sold and price of the commodity from the ith supply source. This relationship will be recognized as the basic form of

---

[1] This type of analysis was applied initially in the foreign-trade context by Tyszynski [26] in studying changes in the market shares of countries exporting manufactured goods from 1899–1950. For an earlier application in the study of industrial location, see Creamer [7].

the elasticity of substitution, which we treated at length and with some skepticism in Chapter 3. The various assumptions implicit in Equation (7.1) are unimportant, however, for present purposes.

Relationship (7.1) may be altered by multiplying by p_1/p_2 to obtain

$$\frac{p_1 q_1}{p_2 q_2} = \frac{p_1}{p_2} \times f\left(\frac{p_1}{p_2}\right) \qquad (7.2)$$

This implies

$$
\begin{aligned}
\frac{p_1 q_1}{p_1 q_1 + p_2 q_2} &= \left(1 + \frac{p_2 q_2}{p_1 q_1}\right)^{-1} \\
&= \left\{1 + \left[\frac{p_1 f(p_1/p_2)}{p_2}\right]^{-1}\right\}^{-1} \qquad (7.3) \\
&= g\left(\frac{p_1}{p_2}\right)
\end{aligned}
$$

which indicates that Country 1's share of the market in question will remain constant except as p_1/p_2 varies. This establishes the validity of the constant-share norm and suggests that the difference between export growth implied by the constant-share norm and actual export growth may be attributed to price changes. For want of a better term, the discrepancy between the constant-share norm and actual performance has been labeled the "competitiveness effect." Thus when a country fails to maintain its share in world markets, the competitiveness term will be negative and will indicate price increases for the country in question somewhat greater than its competitors.[2]

The constant-share norm will allow us to make several interesting calculations. Toward that end we will need the following definitions:

$V_{i.}$ = value of A's exports of Commodity i in Period 1.
$V'_{i.}$ = value of A's exports of Commodity i in Period 2.
$V_{.j}$ = value of A's exports to Country j in Period 1.

[2] Richardson [20] has pointed out, however, that this statement requires the additional assumption that the elasticity of substitution exceeds one in absolute value, a fact that is likely for reasonably fine categories of data.

The term competitiveness is perhaps misleading in this context since it brings with it an unwarranted emotional reaction. To be competitive is ordinarily a desirable thing. This is not necessarily the case in the present analysis as there are many economic reasons why a country might undergo a reduction in its share of a market and therefore incur the "uncompetitive" label. For instance, a small country might be exporting commodities to regions with very fast-growing demands and might not have the domestic capacity to maintain its market shares. Accordingly, the country ought to raise its asking price and be subjected to a reduction in its market share. Another country exporting to more stagnant regions would have little trouble maintaining its share and may have a positive competitiveness effect. Clearly, the first country is not less competitive than the second under the ordinary definition of the word. However, in terms of the present analysis, the first country would be designated less competitive. We shall return later in the chapter to a discussion of the determinants of the competitiveness effect.

$V'_{.j}$ = value of A's exports to Country j in Period 2.

V_{ij} = value of A's exports of Commodity i to Country j in Period 1.

 r = percentage increase in total world exports from Period 1 to Period 2.

r_i = percentage increase in world exports of Commodity i from Period 1 to Period 2.

r_{ij} = percentage increase in world exports of Commodity i to Country j from Period 1 to Period 2.

It follows from the above definitions that for Period 1

$$\sum_j V_{ij} = V_{i.} \qquad \sum_i V_{ij} = V_{.j} \tag{7.4}$$

and similarly for Period 2. In addition, the value of Country A's exports in Period 1 is given by

$$\sum_i \sum_j V_{ij} = \sum_i V_{i.} = \sum_j V_{.j} = V_{..} \tag{7.5}$$

The application of the constant-share norm will depend on the nature of the market that we have in mind when writing (7.1). At the first level of analysis, we may view exports as being completely undifferentiated as to commodity and region of destination. That is to say, exports may be viewed as a single good destined for a single market. If A maintained its share in this market, then exports would increase by $rV_{..}$, and we may write the following identity

$$V'_{..} - V_{..} = rV_{..} + (V'_{..} - V_{..} - rV_{..}) \tag{7.6}$$

We will refer to Equation (7.6) as a "one-level" analysis. It divides the growth in A's exports into a part associated with the general increase in world exports and an unexplained residual, the competitiveness effect.

We may instead argue that exports are in fact quite a diverse set of commodities and that when we write Equation (7.1), what we have in mind is the world market for a particular commodity class. For the ith commodity we may write an expression analogous to (7.6)

$$V'_{i.} - V_{i.} \equiv r_i V_{i.} + (V'_{i.} - V_{i.} - r_i V_{i.}) \tag{7.7}$$

which may be aggregated to

$$
\begin{aligned}
V'_{..} - V_{..} &\equiv \sum_i r_i V_{i.} + \sum_i (V'_{i.} - V_{i.} - r_i V_{i.}) \\
&\equiv (rV_{..}) + \sum_i (r_i - r)V_{i.} + \sum_i (V'_{i.} - V_{i.} - r_i V_{i.})
\end{aligned}
\tag{7.8}
$$
$$\quad (1) \qquad\qquad (2) \qquad\qquad\qquad (3)$$

This equation represents a "two-level" analysis, in which the growth of A's exports is broken into parts attributed to: (1) the general rise in world exports; (2) the commodity composition of A's exports in Period 1; and (3) an unexplained residual indicating the difference between A's actual export increase and the hypothetical increase if A had maintained its share of the exports of each commodity group.

The commodity-composition effect in identity (7.8) requires further comment. It has been defined by

$$\sum_i (r_i - r)V_i. \tag{7.9}$$

and is meant to indicate the extent to which A's exports are concentrated in commodity classes with growth rates more favorable than the world average. Thus, if world exports of Commodity i increased by more than the world average for all commodities, $(r_i - r)$ is positive. This positive number will receive a heavy weight when added to the other terms if $V_{i.}$ is relatively large. Accordingly the sum indicated by (7.9) would be positive if A had concentrated on the export of commodities whose markets were growing relatively fast and would be negative if A had concentrated in slowly growing commodity markets.

Finally, we may observe that exports are differentiated by destination as well as by commodity type. We have as yet made no allowance for the fact that some countries have easy access to rapidly growing regions while others are surrounded by relatively slow-growing neighbors. The appropriate norm in this case is a constant share of exports of a particular commodity class to a particular region. The identity analogous to (7.6) and (7.7) is

$$V'_{ij} - V_{ij} \equiv r_{ij}V_{ij} + (V'_{ij} - V_{ij} - r_{ij}V_{ij}) \tag{7.10}$$

which when aggregated yields

$$V'_{..} - V_{..} \equiv \sum_i \sum_j r_{ij}V_{ij} + \sum_i \sum_j (V'_{ij} - V_{ij} - r_{ij}V_{ij})$$

$$\equiv rV_{..} + \sum_i (r_i - r)V_{i.} + \sum_i \sum_j (r_{ij} - r_i)V_{ij}$$

$$\text{(1)} \qquad\qquad \text{(2)} \qquad\qquad\qquad \text{(3)} \tag{7.11}$$

$$+ \sum_i \sum_j (V'_{ij} - V_{ij} - r_{ij}V_{ij})$$

$$\text{(4)}$$

Identity (7.11) represents a "three-level" analysis in which the increase in A's exports is broken down into parts attributed to: (1) the general rise in world exports; (2) the commodity composition of A's exports; (3) the market distribution of A's exports; and (4) a residual reflecting the difference between the actual export growth and the growth that would have occurred if A had maintained its share of the exports of each commodity to each country.

The market distribution term in identity (7.11) may be interpreted in the same manner as the commodity-composition effect. It is defined by

$$\sum_i \sum_j (r_{ij} - r_i)V_{ij} \tag{7.12}$$

and is seen to be positive if A had concentrated its exports in markets that were experiencing relatively rapid growth. The term would be negative if A had concentrated in more stagnant regions.[3]

The interpretation of the competitiveness residual is not as straightforward as the other terms. A negative residual reflects a failure to maintain market shares. If export demand is described by relationship (7.1), then this residual is necessarily associated with a rise in relative prices, p_1/p_2. However, relationship (7.1) ignores the many other influences that will affect the saleability of a country's exports in foreign markets. In addition to: (1) the differential rates of export price inflation, the general competitiveness residual may reflect: (2) differential rates of quality improvement and the development of new exports; (3) differential rates of improvement in the efficiency of marketing or in the terms of financing the sale of export goods; and (4) differential changes in the ability for prompt fulfillment of export orders.[4]

---

[3] It should be mentioned that it is arbitrary whether one allows first for the effect of the commodity composition and then the market distribution, or vice versa. Had we allowed for the market distribution first, the center two terms in identity (7.11) would have been

(Market Effect)　(Commodity Effect)
$$\sum_j (r_j - r)V_{.j} \;+\; \sum_i \sum_j (r_{ij} - r_j)V_{ij}$$

Although the sum of the above terms is equal to the center terms in identity (7.11), the values which we would attribute to the commodity and market distributions will not be the same. That is,

Commodity Effect
$$\sum_i (r_i - r)V_{i.} \neq \sum_i \sum_j (r_{ij} - r_j)V_{ij}$$

Market Effect
$$\sum_i \sum_j (r_{ij} - r_j)V_{ij} \neq \sum_i (r_j - r)V_{.j}$$

According to Richardson's calculations [20], the effects may vary substantially, depending on which one is calculated first.

It should also be noted that other ways of expressing Equation (7.11) are possible. For instance, we might normalize by dividing by $V_{..}$

$$\frac{V'_{..} - V_{..}}{V_{..}} = r + \frac{\sum_i (r_i - r)V_{i.}}{V_{..}} + \frac{\left[\sum_i \sum_j (r_{ij} - r_i)V_{ij}\right]}{V_{..}} + \frac{\left[\sum_i \sum_j (V'_{ij} - V_{ij}) - r_{ij}V_{ij}\right]}{V_{..}}$$

This explains the percentage increase in exports, not the levels as we have done in the text. Tyszynski [26] actually used

$$\frac{V'_{..}}{V'_w} - \frac{V_{..}}{V_w} = \left(\frac{(r_i + 1)V_{i.}}{V'_w} - \frac{V_{..}}{V_w}\right) + \left(\frac{V'_{..}}{V'_w} - \frac{(r_i + 1)V_{i.}}{V'_w}\right)$$

where V_w is the total value of world trade. In this form the change in a country's share of world trade is set equal to the change that would have occurred if its share in each commodity class had been maintained, plus the competitiveness residual.

[4] See Fleming and Tsiang [9, pp. 219-22] for a more extended discussion of these factors.

It should be stressed that the factors just mentioned that bear upon the saleability of a country's exports are meant to describe the demand side of the phenomenon under study. The actual value taken on by the residual will of course result from the interaction of both demand and supply. As with the time-series analysis of demand, it may prove to be difficult to identify the separate influences of demand and supply. We may nonetheless list some supply factors that may affect one country's export-supply price vis-à-vis its competitors in world trade. These are: (1) differential rates of monetary inflation; (2) differential growth rates of available productive factors and the responsiveness of export supply to the domestic supply of these factors; (3) differential rates of productivity increases; and (4) the extent to which the country is concentrated in exports to very rapidly growing markets.[5]

The interpretation of the competitiveness residual is therefore clearly complicated by the nature of the general-equilibrium system that lies behind it. It is further complicated by the necessarily arbitrary selections of a base period and the level of disaggregation of the commodity and market groups. This also complicates the interpretation of the market and commodity effects. The analysis is thus quite inflexible in the sense that its implications may apply only to the specified time period with the particular breakdown of commodities and market groups. Possibly different conclusions will emerge on the relative importance of the various factors isolated if another choice of time period and level of aggregation is made.[6]

THE CHOICE OF "STANDARD"

We have indicated that the appropriate level of analysis and the extent of disaggregation by commodity and region depend on the market for which the elasticity-of-substitution relationship (7.1) is thought to hold. We have, however, taken for granted that the competing exports, q_2 in (7.1), are the

---

[5] See Ooms [18] for a mathematical model that indicates these points.

[6] The choice of a level of aggregation is not quite as arbitrary as the choice of base period is. We have pointed out that each "level" of analysis is based on a different view of export competition. The choice of a "level" of analysis as well as the degree of disaggregation within that "level" thus depends on whether the elasticity-of-substitution relationship is applicable to the particular submarket.

Richardson's calculations [20] suggest that quite different results may emerge when final–rather than initial–year weights are used and when disaggregation of both markets and especially commodities is introduced. His work also contains an extensive theoretical analysis of the underpinnings of the constant-market-share method. His conclusions regarding the method are on the whole rather negative in view of its comparatively weak theoretical foundation and the sensitivity of the empirical results to the different computing and data variations we have noted.

world total, and we have used world growth rates as a standard with which to judge export performance of a particular country. For much the same reason that the elasticity of substitution may not hold for various levels of aggregation, it may also not hold for one country vis-à-vis the rest of the world. Competition may be rather minor between various countries and regions and an appropriate choice of competing exports may be quite restricted. This suggests that the world standard may not provide an appropriate constant-shares norm. This leads to rather difficult problems in the selection of a more restricted standard. Apart from the theoretical question of the adequacy of the elasticity-of-substitution function vis-à-vis certain competitors, there also arise questions as to just what it does mean to establish such norms and what interpretations of the results are meaningful.

FURTHER IMPLICATIONS

Despite the foregoing reservations, the constant-market-share analysis poses an interesting and important question. This concerns the extent to which a country's exports are concentrated in commodities and markets that can be considered to be relatively slowly or rapidly expanding, and what the nature of the actual expansion of exports has been in the particular context. Presumably a country will prefer to be concentrated in commodities and markets that are rapidly expanding. For policymakers, this analysis may point the way to a preferred distribution of exports. The less developed countries in particular may be able to find support in terms of negative commodity and regional effects for their complaint about the slow expansion of their export markets.

Studies that have used this method have been retrospective in character. There is no reason, however, why the method could not be used for export projections. We could thus determine by how much a country's exports might increase or decrease due to currently existing favorable commodity or market distributions on the assumption of a continuation of the most recent trends in these markets. This of course assumes away the competitiveness effect, which may in fact be quite important in determining exports.

It may also be mentioned that this method should not be construed as a replacement for traditional least squares demand analysis. It has no probability basis and therefore cannot be used to make valid probability statements about demand parameters or about future events. The method may, however, be useful in conjunction with traditional analysis insofar as traditional least squares can be brought to bear on the analysis of the competitive residuals.[7] We may in the process be able to separate the demand influences from the supply influences, and determine the extent to which the residual depends on price or nonprice factors. In addition, such an analysis would provide a means with which to forecast the residuals and consequently allow us to make probability statements about future values of exports.

The competitiveness residual for any particular market is given by

$$V' - V\left(\frac{V' + V'_w}{V + V_w}\right) \tag{7.13}$$

where V, V_w, V', V'_w represent the value of exports to the market by country A and by the rest of the world in Periods 1 and 2.[8] If we divide this by $V' + V'_w$ and employ Equation (7.3), we obtain

$$\frac{V'}{V' + V'_w} - \frac{V}{V + V_w} = g\left(\frac{p'}{p'_w}\right) - g\left(\frac{p}{p_w}\right) \tag{7.14}$$

which relates a value easily calculated from the competitiveness residual to the relative price terms in each period. Accordingly, if we regress this value on the relative prices, we shall obtain an estimate of the function g. In addition to the relative price variables, we should include any of the demand factors discussed earlier that are likely to influence the saleability of exports. We would then be able to assess the relative importance of the price and nonprice factors. Unfortunately, however, data on these nonprice factors may be lacking. Furthermore, we have only one residual (one data point) for each market. Extra data points may of course be obtained by repeating the analysis over time. This amounts roughly to estimating the elasticity of substitution for the particular market. Alternatively one can assume that the function g in (7.14) is the same for all markets and a cross-section regression may be used.[9]

The supply side of the phenomenon may also be analyzed by a regression of the change in relative prices on such variables as the differential rates of monetary inflation, the differential rates of growth of factors, and the differ-

---

[7] It is interesting in this context that Junz and Rhomberg [12] have used the method to indicate the importance of the commodity and market effects in deciding on the level of aggregation to employ in regression analysis of factors determining market shares. They found the commodity effect to be negligible and thus adjusted the data only for the market effect. However, since they employed only three commodity classifications in their analysis, it is by no means clear that the commodity effect would have remained negligible if more disaggregated classifications had been used. In any event, as Kreinin [13, p. 511] and Magee [15, pp. 34–35] have pointed out, the real problem that Junz and Rhomberg wished to avoid was having to collect price data for the disaggregated commodity classes.

[8] That is, in terms of our previous notation

$$r = \frac{V' + V'_w}{V + V_w} - 1$$

[9] See, for example, Junz and Rhomberg [12] and Kreinin [13], who have regressed the residual on the change in relative prices. This is appropriate, however, only when the g function in Equation (7.14) is linear. The estimate thus obtained should not be labeled, as

ential rates of productivity increase. The combination of the demand-side regression and the supply-side regression would allow us to explain and/or predict the value of the competitiveness residual.

CONCLUSION

The constant-share norm provides a useful tool for analyzing export performance by allowing achieved export growth to be separated into commodity, market-distribution, and competitiveness effects. While the competitiveness residual results from the complex interaction of demand and supply, the problem of identifying the separate influences of the demand and supply sides is essentially the same as the simultaneity problem of ordinary regression analysis discussed in Chapter 2. As we have seen, regression analysis may be applied to the residuals to attack this problem.

Quite apart from the competitiveness residual, the analysis provides useful information concerning the extent to which the country in question is exporting to markets with relatively unfavorable or favorable growth rates. This kind of information may be of interest to the authorities concerned with export policies.

A NUMERICAL ILLUSTRATION

A numerical illustration of the constant-market-share analysis is to be found in Table 7.1. The notation is essentially the same as we have been using. The data refer to total world exports (excluding Italy) and to Italian exports for 1955 and 1959. There are seven SITC commodity groups ($i = 1 \ldots 7$) and ten market groups ($j = 1 \ldots 10$) specified. All the relevant calculations are shown, except the cross classifications of world exports and Italian exports by market destination and commodity groups. The analysis of the change in Italian exports between 1955 and 1959 is indicated at the bottom of the table.

---

by the aforementioned authors, an elasticity of substitution. But the estimate may be related to the elasticity of substitution e through Equations (7.14) and (7.3) as

$$e = \frac{\partial f/f}{\partial(p_1/p_2)/(p_1/p_2)} = e_g\left(\frac{1}{1-g}\right) - 1$$

where

$$e_g = \frac{\partial g/g}{\partial(p_1/p_2)/(p_1/p_2)}$$

TABLE 7.1

Illustration of the Constant-Market-Share Analysis of Changes in Italian Exports, 1955-59 †

(Millions of Dollars)

Market	(1) (2) Actual World Exports 1955	1959	(3) Actual Italian Exports 1955 ($V_{.j}$)	(4) 1959 ($V'_{.j}$)	(5) (2)÷(1)−1 (r_j)	(6) (5)×(3) ($r_j V_{.j}$)	(7) 0.239×(3) ($rV_{.j}$)	(8) ($\sum_i r_{ij}V_{ij}$)*
1. North America	15450	20520	176	380	0.328	58	42	60
2. Latin America	6920	7580	190	257	0.095	18	45	29
3. EEC	15334	19763	434	797	0.289	125	104	161
4. EFTA	15960	18330	432	648	0.148	64	103	76
5. Other W. Europe	3480	3810	181	192	0.095	17	43	21
6. Austr., N.Z. & So. Africa	3780	3660	46	55	−0.032	−1	11	−3
7. Japan	2120	3000	12	11	0.415	5	3	0
8. Other Asia & Africa	14000	17110	288	400	0.222	64	69	57
9. Eastern Europe	7360	11700	59	120	0.590	35	14	40
10. All Other	5660	6120	38	54	0.081	3	9	0
Total	90064	111593	1856	2914	0.239	388	443	441
			$\left(\sum_{i=1}^{7}\sum_{j=1}^{10} V_{ij}\right)$	$\left(\sum_{i=1}^{7}\sum_{j=1}^{10} V'_{ij}\right)$	(r)	$\left(\sum_{j=1}^{10} r_j V_{.j}\right)$	$\left(\sum_{j=1}^{10} rV_{.j}\right)$	$\left(\sum_{i=1}^{7}\sum_{j=1}^{10} r_{.j}V_{.ij}\right)$

Commodity	(1) (2) Actual World Exports 1955	1959	(3) Actual Italian Exports 1955 ($V_{i.}$)	(4) 1959 ($V'_{i.}$)	(5) (r_i)	(6) ($r_i V_{i.}$)	(7) ($rV_{i.}$)	(8) ($\sum_j r_{ij}V_{ij}$)

TABLE 7.1 (Continued)

			$\left(\sum_{i=1}^{7}\sum_{j=1}^{10} V_{ij}\right)$	$\left(\sum_{i=1}^{7}\sum_{j=1}^{10} V'_{ij}\right)$	(r)	$\left(\sum_{i=1}^{7} r_i V_{i\cdot}\right)$	$\left(\sum_{i=1}^{7} r V_{i\cdot}\right)$	$\left(\sum_{i=1}^{7}\sum_{j=1}^{10} r_{ij}V_{ij}\right)$
1. SITC 0 & 1	17779	20769	412	536	0.168	69	98	75
2. SITC 2 & 4	16529	17994	130	140	0.089	12	31	3
3. SITC 3	9728	11445	166	214	0.177	29	40	18
4. SITC 5	4569	6389	127	208	0.398	51	50	51
5. SITC 7	16821	23981	371	758	0.426	158	89	156
6. SITC 6 & 8	23349	29498	650	1058	0.263	171	155	138
7. SITC 9	1289	1517	—	—	0.177	—	—	—
Total	90064	111593	1855	2914	0.239	490	443	441

Analysis

Italian exports in 1959 2914
Italian exports in 1955 1856
                         1058

Change in exports   100.0%

1. Due to increase in world trade:	$\sum_{i=1}^{7} rV_{i\cdot}$	443	41.9
2. Due to commodity composition:	$\sum_{i=1}^{7} r_i V_{i\cdot} - \sum_{i=1}^{7} rV_{i\cdot}$	47 **	4.4
3. Due to market distribution:	$\sum_{i=1}^{7}\sum_{j=1}^{10} r_{ij}V_{ij} - \sum_{i=1}^{7} rV_{i\cdot}$	−49 **	−4.6
4. Due to increased competitiveness:	$\sum_{i=1}^{7}\sum_{j=1}^{10} V'_{ij} - \sum_{i=1}^{7}\sum_{j=1}^{10} V_{ij} - \sum_{i=1}^{7}\sum_{j=1}^{10} r_{ij}V_{ij}$	617	58.3

* r_{ij} was first computed from: the cross classification of actual world exports by market destination and commodity groups and then multiplied by V_{ij}, the cross classification of actual Italian exports by market destination and commodity groups for 1955.

† Based on R. M. Stern, *Foreign Trade and Economic Growth in Italy* (New York: Frederick A. Praeger, 1967), pp. 33–42 and 161–63.

** If the order of these two influences is reversed, the effect of market distribution is then: $\sum_{j=1}^{10} r_j V_{\cdot j} - \sum_{j=1}^{10} rV_{\cdot j} = -5$ and the effect of commodity composition becomes 53.

REFERENCES

1. Armington, P. S., "A Theory of Demand for Products Distinguished by Place of Production," International Monetary Fund, *Staff Papers*, XVI (March 1969), 159–76.

2. Armington, P. S., "The Geographic Pattern of Trade and the Effects of Price Changes," International Monetary Fund, *Staff Papers*, XVI (July 1969), 179–201.

3. Awad, F. H., "The Structure of World Export Trade, 1926–1953," *Yorkshire Bulletin*, II (July 1959), 19–37.

4. Balassa, B., "Recent Developments in the Competitiveness of American Industry and Prospects for the Future," in U.S. Congress, Joint Economic Committee, *Factors Affecting the United States Balance of Payments*. Washinton: U.S. Government Printing Office, 1962, pp. 27–54.

5. Baldwin, R. E., "The Commodity Composition of Trade: Selected Industrial Countries, 1900–1954," *Review of Economics and Statistics*, XL (February 1958, Supplement), 50–71.

6. Baldwin, R. E., "Implication of Structural Changes in Commodity Trade," in U.S. Congress, Joint Economic Committee, *Factors Affecting the United States Balance of Payments*. Washington: U.S. Government Printing Office, 1962, pp. 57–72.

7. Creamer, D., "Shifts of Manufacturing Industries," in *Industrial Location and Natural Resources*. Washington: U.S. National Resources Planning Board, 1943.

8. DeVries, B. A., *The Export Experience of Developing Countries*. World Bank Staff Occasional Papers, No. 3. Baltimore: Johns Hopkins Press, 1967, pp. 18–31.

9. Fleming, J. M. and S. C. Tsiang, "Changes in Competitive Strength and Export Shares of Major Industrial Countries," International Monetary Fund, *Staff Papers*, V (August 1958), 218–48.

10. Haberler, G., "Introduction" to the Papers and Abstracts of Papers at a Universities–National Bureau Committee for Economic Research Conference on Problems in International Economics, *Review of Economics and Statistics*, XL (February 1958, Supplement), 3–9.

11. Houston, D. B., "The Shift and Share Analysis of Regional Growth: A Critique," *Southern Economic Journal*, 33 (April 1967), 577–81.

12. Junz, H. B. and R. R. Rhomberg, "Prices and Export Performance of Industrial Countries, 1953–63," International Monetary Fund, *Staff Papers*, XII (July 1965), 224–69.

13. Kreinin, M. E., "Price Elasticities in International Trade," *Review of Economics and Statistics*, XLIX (November 1967), 510–16.

14. Lamfalussy, A., *The United Kingdom and the Six*. Homewood: Richard D. Irwin, Inc., for the Yale University Growth Center, 1963, esp. pp. 47–58 and pp. 137–40.

15. Magee, S., "Theoretical and Empirical Studies of Competition in International Trade: A Review," an unpublished study for the Council of Economic Advisers (1968).

16. Maizels, A., *Industrial Growth and World Trade*. Cambridge: Cambridge University Press, 1963.

17. Narvekar, P. R., "The Role of Competitiveness in Japan's Export Performance, 1954–58," International Monetary Fund, *Staff Papers*, VIII (November 1960), 85–100.

18. Ooms, V. D., "Models of Comparative Export Performance," *Yale Economic Essays*, 7 (Spring 1967), 103–41.

19. Organization for Economic Co-operation and Development, F. G. Adams, et al., *An Econometric Analysis of International Trade*. Paris: OECD, 1969.

20. Richardson, J. D., *Constant-Market-Shares Analysis of Export Growth*. Doctoral dissertation, University of Michigan, 1970.

21. Romanis, A., "Relative Growth of Exports of Manufactures of United States and Other Industrial Countries," International Monetary Fund, *Staff Papers*, VIII (May 1961), 241–73.

22. Spiegelglas, S., "World Exports of Manufactures, 1956 vs. 1937," *The Manchester School*, XXVII (May 1959), 111–39.

23. Stern, R. M., *Foreign Trade and Economic Growth in Italy*. New York: Fredcrick A. Praeger, 1967, Chap. 2.

24. Svennilson, I., *Growth and Stagnation in the European Economy*. Geneva: United Nations, 1954.

25. Tims, W. and F. M. Meyer Zu Schloctern, "Foreign Demand and the Development of Dutch Exports," *Cahiers Economiques de Bruxelles*, No. 15 (1962).

26. Tyszynski, H., "World Trade in Manufactured Commodities, 1899–1950," *The Manchester School*, XIX (September 1951), 272–304.

27. Wells, S. J., *British Export Performance: A Comparative Study*. Cambridge: Cambridge University Press, 1964, esp. pp. 5–9.

Estimating
the Welfare Effects of
Trade Liberalization

We shall be concerned in this chapter with measuring the static welfare effects an economy may experience as the result of trade liberalization. These effects will arise as an economy adjusts to trade liberalization by altering its domestic pattern of consumption and production to the dictates of international prices and in the process more fully reaps the benefits of specialization according to its comparative advantage.

In actuality, trade liberalization will of course have a variety of complicated effects on an economy. In the short run, there may be important adjustment problems arising from the required transfer of resources among the different productive sectors. These problems may include balance-of-payments deficits or surpluses and unemployment of productive factors probably concentrated in particular industries and regions. Longer-run effects may include an alteration of the international flow of direct investment, domestic redistribution of income, revitalization of sluggish domestic industries due to economies of scale, and improved dissemination of technology. Evidently, then, the static welfare effects we shall treat are but a part of a host of complicated responses to trade liberalization.

We shall begin by examining the welfare effect of a prohibitive tariff in the case when exports and imports are treated in the aggregate as individual goods. Thereafter, we shall treat the case of a nonprohibitive tariff. We shall then explore the multigoods case, making allowance for the possibility of changes in the terms of trade and tariffs on imported inputs. Following our theoretical exposition will be a discussion of some of the measurement problems that arise in assessing the welfare effects of trade liberalization. We shall have occasion finally to indicate how the analysis may be related to the effects of customs unions and trade preferences.

THE WELFARE EFFECT OF A PROHIBITIVE TARIFF

A tariff on importables will raise the internal price of the importable good, and thus drive a wedge between the external price ratio and the internal price ratio. When the tariff becomes sufficiently high, international trade will cease. Such a prohibitive tariff is compared with free trade in Figure 8.1,

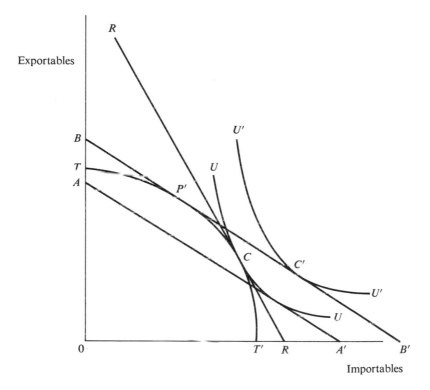

FIGURE 8.1

Welfare Effect of a Prohibitive Tariff

where TT' is the production possibilities curve, UU and $U'U'$ are community indifference curves, and AA' and BB' are international trading lines. Free trade and competitive conditions require that the international price line be tangent to both the production possibilities curve and the community indifference curve, thus requiring production at P' and consumption at C'. Under the assumption of an infinitely elastic offer curve, the imposition of a tariff on importables will cause the internal price line to be steeper than the international price line. Consumption and production will adjust to maintain their tangencies with the internal price line, thus increasing the production and reducing the consumption of importables. When the internal price line is RR, both production and consumption are at C and trade with the rest of the world ceases. The loss in utility induced by the prohibitive tariff is reflected by the movement from $U'U'$ to UU, which may be measured at the international price ratio in terms of the exportable good as AB, the amount of the exportable good that could be surrendered and still maintain the pre-trade level of utility.

The length AB is associated with the notion of consumer surplus and can be calculated under a rather strict assumption as a triangle under an ordinary import-demand function. To refresh the reader's memory on this point, we shall briefly review the argument that leads to the measurement of such triangles.[1] Referring to Figure 8.2, suppose an individual enters the

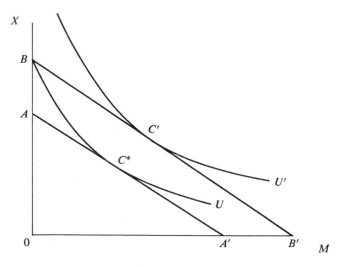

FIGURE 8.2

Welfare Gain in a Simple Exchange Situation

market place with OB of good X and a utility level U. Trading at the competitive price indicated by the straight line BB', he adjusts his consumption to point C' and enjoys a utility increment that may be measured by AB, the

[1] For other descriptions see Friedman [12] or Patinkin [26].

amount of good X he could surrender and still be as well off as he was in the pretrade situation.

It is convenient to break up the length AB into smaller segments x_i, as in Figure 8.3. If we let P' be the slope of the utility curve at C^* and let P_i be

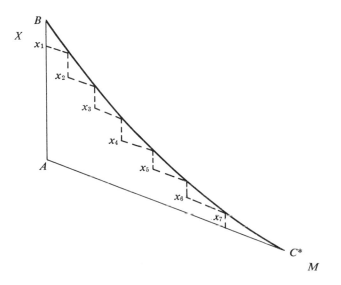

FIGURE 8.3

Measurement of Welfare Gain: A

the slope of the utility curve in segment i, we may then calculate the length x_i as depicted in Figure 8.4 as

$$x_i = P_i \Delta M_i - P' \Delta M_i \qquad (8.1)$$

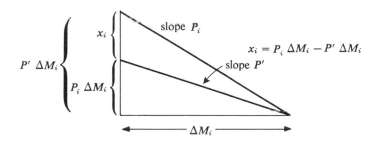

FIGURE 8.4

Measurement of Welfare Gain: B

The length AB is just the sum of these segments: [2]

$$AB = \sum_i x_i = \sum_i (P_i \Delta M_i - P' \Delta M_i) \tag{8.2}$$

We may now define a compensated demand curve Dd in Figure 8.5, which indicates the amount that would be purchased if consumption were constrained to the initial utility level by compensating variations in money income. The height of such a curve is simply the slope P_i of the utility curve at the relevant point. The segment x_i is thus the rectangular area as indicated,

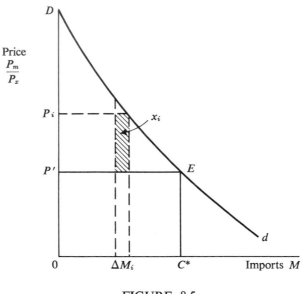

FIGURE 8.5

Compensated Demand Curve

and the length AB is represented by the triangular area $P'ED$. We thus have the consumer surplus measured in terms of the good X as a triangular area under a compensated demand curve.

[2] More precisely

$$AB = \int_{M'}^{M''} \left[\frac{\partial X}{\partial M}(M) - \frac{\partial X}{\partial M}(M'') \right] dM$$

where M' and M'' are the initial and final values of M and $(\partial X/\partial M)(M)$ is the slope of the particular utility curve evaluated at M.

Unfortunately there are no observations available to us which would disclose the nature of the compensated demand curve. We would require for this purpose that a compensating variation of income be made that in turn would require a knowledge of the unknown utility structure. What is observed, however, is the ordinary demand curve indicating purchases of importables as a function of money income and prices. If the compensated and ordinary demand curves are related in some known way, the compensated curve could be constructed from the observable ordinary demand function. One way to relate the two demand curves is to assume that importables have a zero income elasticity of demand. Under this assumption the purchases of M depend only on relative prices, and thus compensating variations in income do not alter the amount purchased, and, correspondingly, the ordinary and compensated demand curves are identical. Accordingly, under the assumption of zero income effect, triangles under ordinary demand curves will provide a measure of the consumer surplus rendered by the exchange possibilities of liberalized trade.

This analysis is appropriately thought to apply to a single individual who behaves consistently to maximize some ordinal preference map. Whether it can be aggregated to the level of a national economy is questionable on two counts. In the first place, we will have to construct a community indifference map by aggregating individual preferences. This will involve problems of income distribution and, implicitly, interpersonal comparisons of utility. Secondly, we will have to assume that the community behaves in a fashion that seeks to maximize the indifference map. Otherwise empirical observations will disclose nothing about the true indifference structure.

To summarize, we have seen that if the community has a consistent utility map and obtains maximum utility as indicated by that map, the surplus rendered by the exchange possibilities of international markets can be measured by the area under a compensated demand curve reflecting the amount of the export good that could be surrendered with no loss in welfare. When the observed demand curve is inelastic to income changes, it will correspond with the compensated demand curve and the welfare gain is simply the appropriate triangle under the ordinary demand curve. The assumptions implicit in this welfare analysis are clearly quite restrictive. We shall return subsequently to discuss the likely impact of departures from them.

Our discussion thus far has been confined to the simplest possible type of exchange situation. Let us introduce some further complexities. In particular, we shall now make allowance for adjustments in production as well as consumption, as in Figure 8.1, in the context of assessing the welfare impact of a nonprohibitive tariff.

THE WELFARE EFFECT OF A NONPROHIBITIVE TARIFF

Figure 8.6 illustrates the effect of a nonprohibitive tariff. As before, the international price lines are AA' and BB' and the internal price lines are RR' and SS' with importables relatively more expensive. Production and consumption adjust with the tariff to P and C to maintain the tangency conditions with respect to the internal price lines. Trading in international markets occurs at the international price ratio, and the line PC is parallel to AA'. The loss of utility due to the imposition of the tariff may be measured by AB, the amount of the exportable good that could be surrendered with no loss in utility.

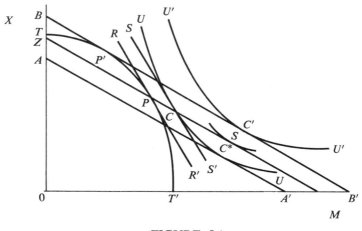

FIGURE 8.6

Welfare Effect of a Nonprohibitive Tariff

It is convenient to separate the exchange surplus Ab into two segments, AZ and ZB. We may associate the segment AZ with the adjustment of consumption, and ZB with the adjustment in production. It is clear that if production is fixed at P, AZ is the amount of the exportable good that consumers could be deprived of and still be as well off as they were with the tariff. Similarly with consumption fixed at C, producers could be deprived of the amount ZB and still would be able to satisfy the consumption requirements.

We may now adapt the previous analysis of the simple exchange to this more complex situation. A consumer who enters the market with the bundle indicated by C will trade to S, which is exactly analogous to the consumer of

Figure 8.2 who traded from B to C'. Accordingly, we may define a compensated demand curve that maintains real income at level U. This is the dd curve in Figure 8.7 with the triangle GHJ measuring the length AZ. In an analogous fashion, a producer entering the market with bundle P would adjust to P'. The curve ss in Figure 8.7 is thus defined as the production of M constrained to the production possibilities curve TT', and the triangle DFE measures the exchange surplus ZB.[3]

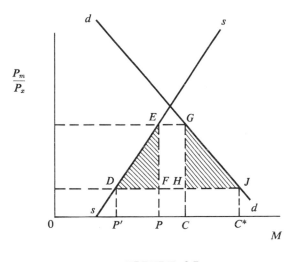

FIGURE 8.7

Welfare Triangles

While dd is properly defined as a compensated demand curve, for measurement purposes we will again assume that the import good enjoys a zero income effect and that, as a consequence, the ordinary demand curve corresponds with the compensated one. This has the further desirable property of making the compensated demand curve dd independent of the initial tariff level (i.e., the particular utility curve from which it was calculated). It should be noted that the supply curve will not require a similar assumption, since production will be constrained under competitive conditions to fall on the transformation curve. Empirical observations will thus disclose directly the nature of the supply curve.

[3] This analysis is due to Johnson [16]. The area under the supply curve is often referred to as producer's surplus. Mishan [24] argues that any separation of consumer's surplus from producer's surplus is "arbitrary and erroneous." We have avoided such terminology here.

The welfare triangles DEF and GHJ may be calculated as follows (noting that ΔC is negative)

$$
\begin{aligned}
\frac{1}{2} \Delta P \, \Delta \frac{P_m}{P_x} &- \frac{1}{2} \Delta C \, \Delta \frac{P_m}{P_x} \\
&= \frac{1}{2} \left[\frac{\Delta(P_m/P_x)}{(P_m/P_x)} \right]^2 \left[\frac{(\Delta P - \Delta C)/(P - C)}{\Delta(P_m/P_x)/(P_m/P_x)} \right] (P - C) \frac{P_m}{P_x} \qquad (8.3) \\
&= \frac{1}{2} \left(\%\Delta \frac{P_m}{P_x} \right)^2 \eta_I V_I
\end{aligned}
$$

where V_I is the value of imports expressed in units of the exportable good, η_I is the elasticity of the import excess-demand function, and $\%\Delta P_m/P_x$ is the percentage change in prices due to tariff reduction.[4] The import excess-demand function relates imports (consumption minus production) to relative prices. This is the same function whose estimation was discussed in Chapter 2, and the elasticities calculated by that route are appropriate for use here.

The Multigood Case   The multigood case is considerably more complicated, as it involves potential consumption and production adjustments in many directions even for the comparatively simple instance of a change in a single tariff. As Johnson [17, p. 332] has pointed out, two possibilities will greatly aggravate the situation: (1) changes in relative prices of nontraded goods, and (2) substitutions between imports and domestic goods and among domestic goods. However, Johnson has argued that these complications may be neglected either because of a negligibly small group of nontraded goods or because welfare losses and welfare gains of these adjustments will tend to cancel. In that event the appropriate welfare measure is simply: [5]

$$
\frac{1}{2} \sum_i \left(\Delta \frac{P_m}{P_x} \right)_i (\Delta P_i - \Delta C_i) \qquad (8.4)
$$

The foregoing formula is not so simple as it might appear, however, since the ΔP_i and ΔC_i are production and consumption adjustments that occur as a result of all the price changes, including the own price $[\Delta(P_m/P_x)]_i$. Only when cross effects are neglected can this be modified as in (8.3) to

$$
\frac{1}{2} \sum_i \left(\%\Delta \frac{P_m}{P_x} \right)_i^2 \eta_i V_i \qquad (8.5)
$$

where η_i is the elasticity of the import excess-demand function, and V_i is the value of imports of commodity i expressed in terms of the numeraire export good.

[4] This formula may be easily modified when production of the importable good goes to zero with the tariff reduction. See Johnson [17, p. 333].

[5] See Johnson [17, p. 341]. Stern [27] has used this formula to calculate the welfare effect of the U.S. tariff.

When the international supply is infinitely elastic, as would be the case if we were dealing with a relatively small country vis-à-vis the world market, the percentage change in prices due to tariff elimination is simply the proportional tariff rate t_i, and we may modify (8.4) and (8.5) to

$$\sum_i \frac{1}{2} t_i \frac{P_m}{P_x} \Delta(P_i - C_i) \tag{8.4'}$$

and

$$\sum_i \frac{1}{2} t_i^2 \eta_i V_i \tag{8.5'}$$

Furthermore, in the multigood case it is convenient to use a composite good such as money GNP as the numeraire X, in which case the V_i terms assume their monetary values, as the welfare gain does. In such cases the welfare gain is often expressed as a percent of GNP for interpretative purposes.

Terms-of-Trade Changes Another complication we will need to consider is the effect of a change in the terms of trade. If the international offer curve is not infinitely elastic, that is, if world demand for exportables (or world supply of importables) is not infinitely elastic, tariff reduction will result in excess supply of the country's goods in world markets and/or excess demand for importables. Price adjustment will cheapen the country's goods

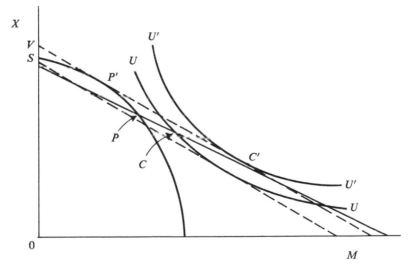

FIGURE 8.8

The Impact of Terms-of-Trade Changes

and reduce the welfare gain from tariff reduction. This possibility is graphed in Figure 8.8, where the elimination of tariffs has cheapened exportables so that the new terms of trade are represented by the dotted lines. The welfare increase is thus given by SV, which may be negative. This complication applies only to Formulas (8.4') and (8.5') specifically because the proportional tariff rates t_i no longer reflect the percentage change in prices from tariff elimination. Formulas (8.4) and (8.5) continue to hold, but with the caveat that the terms must include price adjustments from terms-of-trade changes.[6]

Imported Inputs   Finally, we must acknowledge the fact that tariffs apply to materials and unfinished goods as well as to finished goods. The opportunity cost theory embodied in our diagrams does not allow for such tariffs. What we can do at least in principle is seek to define a "uniform tariff equivalent" as the tariff rate that if applied uniformly to all imports would yield the same restriction as the existing tariff structure. Such a rate could then be used to assess the welfare gains. We must not be deceived of course into thinking that this represents a solution to the problem, since there are acute difficulties in measuring a "uniform tariff equivalent."[7] From an applications standpoint, the problem of tariffs on inputs thus remains substantially unresolved.

STATISTICAL ESTIMATION OF WELFARE EFFECTS

The formulas just presented involve tariffs, import values, and elasticities. Tariff and import value data are of course available, but detailed (disaggregated) estimates of elasticities are not. Researchers have in practice provided educated guesses as to the elasticities, but these should be viewed with con-

---

[6] As Johnson [17, p. 330] has pointed out, this gain can no longer be thought of as the amount of exportables that could be extracted with no loss in income since this would involve a terms-of-trade change. Rather the extraction of goods must be "divided between importables and exportables in accordance with the country's marginal propensity to import."

Kreinin's [22] calculations suggest to him that about half of a tariff reduction accrues to the foreign suppliers in the form of increased prices. Basevi [5] has constructed a model that includes the terms-of-trade effect, and he calculates an efficiency *gain* from the U.S. tariff structure ranging from $258 to $558 million. This compares with Stern's [27] estimate (ignoring the terms-of-trade effect) of a *loss* ranging from $258 to $448 million, neither of which is very large when compared with U.S. GNP.

[7] In Basevi's [5, p. 850] words: "Estimates . . . are subjected to a high degree of guesswork." See Balassa [2] for relevant estimates and formulas in the context of his work on effective protection.

siderable skepticism. A formula which has been used to assist the guesswork is

$$\eta = \frac{P}{M} \epsilon^S + \frac{C}{M} \epsilon^D \qquad (8.6)$$

where ϵ^S and ϵ^D are the (positive) elasticities of the domestic supply and demand curves and P, C, M are domestic production, consumption and imports.[8] This formula will provide improved estimates only to the extent that ϵ^S and ϵ^D can be more accurately guessed than η itself. There is no particular reason to believe that this will be the case.

An additional difficulty is introduced when quotas are used instead of tariffs. In this case researchers have attempted to estimate a tariff equivalent to the quota defined as the tariff that would provide the same degree of protection as the quota. They have taken this to be the deviation between the protected home market price and the prevailing international price, a calculation which assumes competitive conditions.

CUSTOMS UNIONS AND TRADE PREFERENCES

The welfare analysis of customs unions and trade preferences is essentially the application of the ideas expressed earlier to a multicountry framework. In the absence of terms-of-trade effects this amounts simply to performing the calculations for more than one country. The endogenous inclusion of the terms-of-trade effects in a multicountry trade liberalization scheme involves complicated calculations that have not in practice been made. Rather, researchers provide guesstimates of the likely terms-of-trade changes and apply the welfare formulas straightforwardly. For example, Balassa and Kreinin [4] guess that the effect of trade liberalization under the "Kennedy Round" would increase European export prices of manufactured goods by one-third of the tariff reduction. Ignoring the welfare effects of the decrease in EEC and EFTA discrimination due to such reduction, they computed the welfare

[8] For the U.S., Stern [27, p. 463] assumed representative elasticities to be −0.25 and zero for crude materials, foodstuffs, and animals, −0.40 and 0.20 for manufactures, −0.50 and 0.25 for nondurable finished manufactures, and −1.00 and 0.50 for durable finished manufactures. Balassa [2, p. 601] assumed the following demand and supply elasticities for his commodity categories: intermediate products whose main inputs are natural raw materials, −0.2 and 0.1; intermediate goods at higher levels of fabrication, −0.3 and 0.2; consumer goods, −1.0 and 0.8; and investment goods, −0.3 and 0.3. Basevi [5, p. 849] used the following estimates of Floyd [11]: supply elasticities of exports and imports, 4.5 and 6.1; and demand elasticities for exports and imports, a high of −9.9 and −2.7 and a low of −5.1 and −1.5. Floyd's estimates reflected ostensibly an upward adjustment of empirically estimated elasticities to take account of the simultaneity bias.

effects listed in Table 8.1. It will be noted that these effects are all relatively small.[9]

TABLE 8.1

Estimated Direct Welfare Effects of Trade
Liberalization in the Kennedy Round †
(Millions of Dollars)

	Cost of Protection	Terms-of-Trade Effects	Total
United States	+69	−63	+ 6
Canada	+39	− 7	+32
Common Market	+39	+61	+100
United Kingdom	+30	+ 9	+39
Continental EFTA	+12	+ 7	+19
Japan	+15	− 7	+ 8
Industrial Countries	+204	—	+204

† Adapted from B. Balassa and M. Kreinin, "Trade Liberalization under the 'Kennedy Round': The Static Effects," *Review of Economics and Statistics*, XLIX (May 1967), 136.

CONCLUSION

In conclusion, we may review the variety of assumptions implicit in the foregoing analysis. They are:

(1) Competitive conditions that assure that production occurs on the transformation curve.

(2) The existence of a community indifference map, which is actually used when the level of imports/exports is decided on. Otherwise the observed demand curve is quite irrelevant for assessing welfare gains.[10]

[9] It is interesting to quote Corden [6, p. 51] in this connection:

. . . the reason for the cost or benefit of these changes turning out to be so small is that imports are rarely more than 20 per cent of a country's G.N.P., that any particular trade policy rarely affects more than, say, one-quarter of these imports, and that (income distribution apart) the social costs of foregoing these imports and producing similar goods at home instead, or the social gain from ceasing to protect, is usually less than the value of these duty-free imports simply because tariffs are usually less than 100 per cent.

[10] A perhaps more fruitful approach is to assume a particular utility structure as Johnson [17] does. Welfare gains under such a scheme would remain potential unless redistributive programs were adopted. The actual gain would of course not be assessed since the community would not consume to maximize the assumed utility function.

(3) Zero income elasticity of the imported good.

(4) Negligible substitutions in production and consumption among non-traded and between nontraded and import goods.

(5) Negligible substitutions in production and consumption of import goods.

(6) Infinitely elastic supply of international goods and, consequently, constant terms of trade.

With a suitably complicated analysis, (4), (5), and (6) may be dropped, although only (6) has been dropped in actual practice.

In addition to this long list of assumptions, the import-demand elasticities and any terms-of-trade changes that have been incorporated are in general merely guesses. Can we, then, place any faith at all in the estimate obtained? It should be clear from our theoretical analysis that there is a real surplus to be gained through the international exchange of goods and services and that tariffs tend to eat into that surplus. The numerical value of that surplus and its response to tariff policy should thus be an important parameter of commercial policy. In the absence of perfect information, policymakers will consequently have to make do with what is available.

That the estimates provide an accurate assessment of the surplus is highly doubtful. However, the formulas used do provide high estimates when tariff rates are high and when imports are highly responsive to price adjustments. Clearly, this is as it should be. Thus, while the formulas may not be perfectly accurate, they may be taken to provide an order-of-magnitude approximation. Furthermore, inasmuch as the same assumptions are applied to all countries with perhaps equal validity, the calculated welfare gains may provide a reasonably accurate ranking of the countries involved. In any case, the welfare estimates do seem to enjoy at least a slight preference over pure guesswork.[11]

REFERENCES

1. Balassa, B., ed., *Studies in Trade Liberalization*. Baltimore: Johns Hopkins Press, 1967.

2. Balassa, B., "Tariff Protection in Industrial Countries: An Evaluation," *Journal of Political Economy*, LXXIII (December 1965); reprinted in R. E. Caves and H. G. Johnson, eds., *Readings in International Economics*. Homewood: Richard D. Irwin, Inc., 1968, pp. 579–604.

[11] Corden [6, p. 51] concludes in this regard:

It seems quite probable that as the "unimportance of international trade," or at least the relative unimportance of most changes in trade policies, is more fully appreciated we will see a general rehabilitation of partial techniques in trade theory at the expense of the more elegant but less directly applicable general-equilibrium techniques.

3. Balassa, B., "Tariff Reductions and Trade in Manufactures Among the Industrial Countries," *American Economic Review*, LVI (June 1966), 466–72.

4. Balassa, B. and M. E. Kreinin, "Trade Liberalization under the 'Kennedy Round': The Static Effects," *Review of Economics and Statistics*, XLIX (May 1967), 125–37.

5. Basevi, G., "The Restrictive Effect of the U.S. Tariff," *American Economic Review*, LVIII (September 1968), 840–52.

6. Corden, W. M., *Recent Developments in the Theory of International Trade*. Special Papers in International Economics, No. 7. Princeton: International Finance Section, Princeton University, 1965.

7. Corden, W. M., "The Calculation of the Cost of Protection," *Economic Record*, XXIII (April 1957), 29–51.

8. Corden, W. M., "The Structure of a Tariff System and the Effective Protective Rate," *Journal of Political Economy*, LXXIV (June 1966), 221–37.

9. Dean, G. W. and N. R. Collins, "Trade and Welfare Effects of EEC Tariff Policy: A Case Study of Oranges," *Journal of Farm Economics*, XLVIII (November 1966), 826–46.

10. Flanders, M. J., "Measuring Protectionism and Predicting Trade Diversion," *Journal of Political Economy*, LXXIII (April 1965), 165–69.

11. Floyd, J. E., "The Overvaluation of the Dollar: A Note on the International Price Mechanism," *American Economic Review*, LV (March 1965), 95–107.

12. Friedman, M., "The Marshallian Demand Curve," *Journal of Political Economy*, LVII (December 1949); reprinted in *Essays in Positive Economics*. Chicago: University of Chicago Press, 1953, pp. 47–99.

13. Harberger, A. C., "Taxation, Resource Allocation, and Welfare," in *The Role of Direct and Indirect Taxes in the Federal Revenue System*. A Conference Report of the National Bureau of Economic Research and the Brookings Institution. Princeton: Princeton University Press, 1964.

14. Harberger, A. C., "The Measurement of Waste," *American Economic Review*, LIV (May 1964), 58–76.

15. Hause, J. C., "The Welfare Costs of Disequilibrium Exchange Rates," *Journal of Political Economy*, LXXIV (August 1966), 333–52.

16. Johnson, H. G., "The Costs of Protection and Self-Sufficiency," *Quarterly Journal of Economics*, LXXIX (August 1965), 365–72.

17. Johnson, H. G., "The Cost of Protection and the Scientific Tariff," *Journal of Political Economy*, LXVIII (August 1960), 327–45.

18. Johnson, H. G., "The Welfare Costs of Exchange-Rate Stabilization," *Journal of Political Economy*, LXXIV (October 1966) 512–18.

19. Krause, L. B., "United States Imports and the Tariff," *American Economic Review*, XLIX (May 1959), 542–51.

20. Kreinin, M. E., "'Price' vs. 'Tariff' Elasticities in International Trade: A Suggested Reconciliation," *American Economic Review*, LVII (September 1967), 891–94; G. D. Wood, Jr., "Comment," and M. E. Kreinin, "Reply," *American Economic Review*, LIX (March 1969), 198–200.

21. Kreinin, M. E., "Trade Creation and Diversion in a Customs Union—A Graphical Presentation," *Kyklos*, XVI (Fasc. 4, 1963), 660–61.

22. Kreinin, M. E., "Effect of Tariff Changes on the Prices and Volumes of Imports," *American Economic Review*, LI (June 1961), 310–24.

23. Kreinin, M. E., *Alternative Commercial Policies—Their Effect on the American Economy*. East Lansing: Institute for International Business, 1967.

24. Mishan, E. J., "What is Producer's Surplus?" *American Economic Review*, LVIII (December 1968), 1269–82.

25. Officer, L. H. and J. R. Hurtubise, "Price Effects of the Kennedy Round on Canadian Trade," *Review of Economics and Statistics*, LI (August 1969), 320–33.

26. Patinkin, D., "Demand Curves and Consumer's Surplus," in C. F. Christ, ed., *Measurement in Economics*. Stanford: Stanford University Press, 1963.

27. Stern, R. M., "The U.S. Tariff and the Efficiency of the U.S. Economy," *American Economic Review*, LIV (May 1964), 459–70.

28. Wonnacott, R. W. and P. Wonnacott, *Free Trade Between the United States and Canada*. Cambridge: Harvard University Press, 1967.

Index of Names
and Authors

A

Adams, F. G., 54, 182
Allen, R. G. D., 51
Almon, S., 25-27, 40, 51
Armington, P. S., 182
Arndt, S. W., 105
Awad, F. H., 182

B

Balassa, B., 140, 150 n.3, 168-69, 182, 194 n.7, 195-98
Baldwin, R. E., 182
Ball, R. J., 34-35, 51
Bank of Canada, 131 n.2
Bannerji, H., 51, 74
Basevi, G., vi, 194 n.6-7, 195 n.8, 198
Bell, P. W., 80 n.3, 105
Black, S. W., 80, 104-05
Board of Governors of the Federal Reserve System, 101, 105, 140
Boissonneault, L., 16 n.13, 24, 35, 55, 123-24, 141
Borts, G. H., 105
Branson, W. H., 9 n.5, 12 n.8, 51, 94 n.13, 103 n.23, 104-05
Brookings Institution, 122
Brown, A. J., 74
Bruno, M., 136 n.2, 140
Bryant, R. C., vi, 99, 104-05

C

Canterbery, E. R., 105

Centrum voor Economische Studien, 168
Chenery, H. B., 136 n.2, 137 n.3, 139-40, 152-55, 157, 168
Cheng, H. S., 28 n.25, 51
Choudry, N. K., 51
Cohen, B. J., 105
Collins, K., vi
Collins, N. R., 198
Corden, W. M., 196 n.9, 197 n.11, 198
Corlett, W. J., 31 n.29, 54, 57 n.1, 61 n.6, 75
Council of Economic Advisors, 122
Creamer, D., 171 n.1, 182
Cross, J., vi

D

DaCosta, G. C., 34, 51, 74
Davis, T. E., 16 n.13, 51
Dean, G. W., 198
DeLeeuw, C. G., 167, 170
Detomasi, D. D., 51
Deutsch, K. W., 158, 160 n.16, 167, 170
DeVries, B. A., 182
Dramais, A., 158 n.14, 169
Duesenberry, J. S., 35, 55
Dutta, M., 34, 52

E

Eckstein, P., 136 n.2, 137 n.3, 139-40
Ely, J. E., 51
Evans, M. K., 140-41

201

F

Fei, J. C. H., 140
Feige, E. L., 102 *n*.21 & 2, 105
Feller, W., 159-60, 159 *n*.15, 169
Ferguson, C. E., 52
Flanders, M. J., 198
Fleming, J. M., 74, 175 *n*.4, 182
Floyd, J. E., 105, 195 *n*.8, 198
Forte, F., 107
Fortucci, P., 141
Friedman, M., 186 *n*.1, 198
Fromm, G., 140

G

Gehrels, F., 52
Ginsburg, A. L., vi, 17 *n*.15, 48-49,
    52, 67 *n*.15, 68-72, 74
Glejser, H., 155-56, 158 *n*.14, 162, 169
Goldberger, A. S., 7 *n*.1, 38 *n*.35, 48,
    52, 104 *n*.25, 105
Goodman, L. A., 169
Gray, H. P., 52, 107
Griliches, Z., 52
Grubel, H. G., 105
Gruber, W., 106

H

Haberler, G., 182
Haq, W., 52
Harberger, A. C., 31 *n*.29, 52, 74, 198
Harley, C. K., 35, 52
Hause, J. C., 198
Heckerman, D. G., 96, 107
Heien, D. M., 52
Helliwell, J., 106, 141
Hendershott, P. H., 80 *n*.4, 99, 104-05,
    107
Henderson, M., 53
Hicks, J. R., 65, 67, 75
Houston, D. B., 182
Houthakker, H. S., 16 *n*.12 & 14,
    28 *n*.24, 35, 52
Hufbauer, G. C., 146 *n*.1, 169
Hurtubise, J. R., 199

I

Ingram, J. C., 106
Islam, N., 52

J

Johnson, H. G., 154 *n*.7, 169, 191 *n*.3,
    192, 194 *n*.6, 196 *n*.10, 198
Johnston, J., 7 *n*.1, 15 *n*.9, 25, 33 *n*.30,
    52-53, 104 *n*.25, 106, 146 *n*.2, 169
Jorgenson, D. W., 25-26, 53
Junz, H. B., 75, 178 *n*.7 & 9, 183

K

Kaliski, S. F., 36, 53, 75
Keesing, D. B., 169
Kemp, M. C., 53
Kenen, P. B., 80, 106
Kindleberger, C. P., 91, 106, 169
Klein, L. R., 53, 140
Koo, A. Y. C., 53
Koyck, L. M., 15 *n*.11, 53
Krause, L. B., 53, 198
Kravis, I. B., 8 *n*.3, 53
Kreinin, M. E., 53, 75, 178 *n*.7 & 9,
    183, 194 *n*.6, 195-96, 198-99
Kubinski, A., 75
Kuznets, S., 155 *n*.8, 156 *n*.11, 169

L

Laffer, A. B., 96, 106-07
Lamfalussy, A., 183
Leamer, E. E., 92 *n*.11, 97 *n*.18,
    104 *n*.26, 106
Lee, C. H., 106
Lerner, A., 29 *n*.26
Leven, J. H., vi, 90 *n*.10, 96 *n*.16, 106
Lewis, W. A., 17 *n*.15, 53
Linnemann, H., 150 *n*.3, 153, 158,
    161, 162 *n*.19, 165, 167, 169
Lipsey, R. E., 8 *n*.3, 53
Liu, T. C., 127, 141
Lovell, M. C., 53

M

MacDougall, G. D. A., 75
Magee, S. P., 16 *n*.12, 16 *n*.14, 28 *n*.24,
    35, 52-53, 178 *n*.7, 183
Maizels, A., 141, 169, 183
Marshall, A., 29 *n*.26
Marwah, K., 34-35, 51
Mauer, L. J., 106
Meyer zu Schloctern, F. M., 183

Miller, N. C., vi, 93 n.12, 106
Mills, F. C., 8 n.3, 54
Mishan, E. J., 191 n.3, 199
Moore, L., 54
Morgan, D. J., 31 n.29, 54, 57 n.1, 61 n.6, 75
Morrissett, I., 57 n.1-2, 75
Murakami, A., 54

N

Narvekar, P. R., 183
Neisser, H., 34, 54
Nerlove, M., 23 n.22, 54
Nicholson, R. J., 75
Nurkse, R., 106

O

Office of Business Economics, 129
Officer, L. H., 199
Ooms, V. D., 75, 176 n.5, 183
Orcutt, G. H., 1, 28 n.24, 29-30, 32-34, 40, 54
Organization for Economic Co-operation and Development, 54, 124, 141, 183

P

Patinkin, D., 186 n.1, 199
Peeters, Th., vi, 156 n.12
Pincus, J., 138, 140-41
Polak, J. J., 16 n.14, 54, 62 n.8, 75
Polasck, M., 52
Pöyhönen, P., 161 n.18, 163, 166, 169
Prachowny, M. F. J., vi, 16 n.12, 16 n.14, 54, 94 n.14, 106, 125-28, 141
Prais, S. J., 33 n.30, 54
Preeg, E. H., 54, 75
Pullianen, K., 155-56, 160 n.16, 163-64, 166, 169

R

Ranis, G., 140
Rao, S. V., 54
Reimer, R., 54
Rhomberg, R. R., 7 n.2, 16 n.13, 24, 35, 54-55, 75, 94 n.14, 106, 123-24, 141, 178 n.7 & 9, 183

Richardson, J. D., vi, 172 n.2, 175 n.3, 176 n.6, 183
Robinson, T. R., 55
Romanis, A., 183
Roy, P. N., 55

S

Salant, W. S., 141
Sasaki, K., 55
Savage, I. R., 158, 160 n.16, 167, 170
Scaperlanda, A. E., 106
Scott, M. FG,, 55
Shinkai, Y., 75
Smith, W. L., 67 n.14, 74
Spiegelglas, S., 183
Stein, J. L., 80, 94, 96-97, 103-04, 107
Stern, R. M., v, 55, 59 n.4, 62 n.8, 69 n.16, 74-75, 92 n.11, 97 n.18, 104 n.26, 106, 181, 183, 192 n.5, 194 n.6, 195 n.8, 199
Steuer, M. D., 155, 170
Stevens, G. V. G., 107
Stoll, H., 107
Strout, A. M., 140
Suits, D. B., 7 n.1, 15 n.9, 26 n.23, 55, 69 n.16, 114, 141
Svennilson, I., 183
Swamy, D. S., 55

T

Taplin, G. B., 158 n.14, 170
Taubman, P., 140
Taylor, L., 155, 168
Taylor, W. B., 55
Temin, P., 170
Theil, H., 141, 167, 170
Tims, W., 183
Tinbergen, J., 75, 162, 163 n.20, 170
Tower, E. L., 107
Tsiang, S. C., 74, 175 n.4, 182
Turnovsky, S. J., 55
Tyszynski, H., 171 n.1, 175 n.3, 183

U

United Nations, 136, 142
U. S. Congress, Joint Economic Committee, 142
U. S. Department of Commerce, 100, 107, 124, 142

University of Michigan, 142
Uribe, P. H., 167, 170

V

Vanek, J., 142
Vernon, R., 92, 107
Voivodas, C., 155, 170
Von Böventer, E., 55

W

Waelbroeck, J., 158 n.14, 170
Waud, R. N., 102 n.21 & 2, 107
Wells, S. J., 183
Wemelsfelder, J., 55
Whitman, M. v. N., 93 n.12, 106, 170

Wilkinson, B. W., 55
Willett, T. D., vi, 107
Winter, S., vi
Wolf, C., vi
Wonnacott, P., 199
Wonnacott, R. J., 199
Wood, G. D., 199

Y

Yoshihara, K., vi

Z

Zarembka, P., 19 n.19, 55
Zelder, R. E., 167 n.13, 75
Zupnick, E., 59 n.4, 62 n.8, 75

Index of Subjects

A

Aggregation of data
in constant-market-share analysis, 176
and import-demand functions, 33,
42-48
in international capital movements,
99
and model building, 115
and price elasticity estimates, 33, 47
and price indexes, 41-48
in trade flow model, 165
in two-gap import-demand function,
139
Almon technique, 26-27

B

Balance of payments, models relating
to
Brookings, 122-123, 130-31
Federal Reserve — MIT, 130
Keynesian model, 120-21
Michigan econometric model, 128
model of world economy, 119-20
OBE, 129
Prachowny, 125-28
Rhomberg-Boissonneault, 123-24
Wharton, 129
Bayesian inference, 38
Brookings Report, 122-23

C

Capacity utilization, 14

Capital controls; see International
capital movements
Capital movements; see International
capital movements
Capital-output ratio, 133
CMS analysis; see Constant-market-
share analysis
Cochran-Orcutt iterative technique, 28
Compensated demand curve, 188
Competitiveness in international trade;
see CMS analysis
Conditional forecast, 111
Confidence intervals, 37
Constant-market-share analysis
aggregation, 176
commodity effect, 174
competitive effect, 172, 175
elasticity of substitution, 171, 178
market effect, 174
theory of, 171
Consumer surplus, 186
Covered interest arbitrage, 81
Credit rationing, 98
Cross section analysis
in estimation of elasticity of substitution, 69
in general equilibrium model, 145,
153
Customs unions
impact on trade flows, 155, 162, 195
welfare effects of, 195-96

D

Decision forecast, 113

Demand for exports; *see* Export demand
Demand for imports; *see* Import demand
Direct foreign investment; *see* International capital movements
Distributed lags; *see* Time dimension
Dummy variables
  in analysis of curvilinearity, 48-49
  in elasticity of substitution, 69-71
  in import demand function
    representing *unusual* periods, 15
    representing seasonal variations, 15
    with interaction terms, 50
    representing customs unions, 162
Durables, import demand for, 13

E

Econometric forecasting
  model building
    endogeneous variables, 110, 114-16
    exogeneous variables, 110, 114-16
    estimation problems, 116
    policy analysis, 117
    reduced form, 110
    structural form, 110
  conditional forecast, 111
  decision forecast, 113
  forecast error, 114
  informative forecast, 112
  interval forecast, 112
  balance of payments; *see* Balance of payments
  point forecast, 112
  policy analysis, 111, 117-18
    impact analysis, 117
    policy multiplier, 117
  unconditional forecast, 111
Elasticity of substitution
  defined, 56
  in CMS analysis, 172, 178
  estimation of
    simultaneous equation bias, 63
    using time-series and cross-section analysis, 69-71
  interpretation and use of results, 64, 73
  derivation of price elasticities, 65
  theoretical derivation of, 57-60
  time-series and cross-section analysis

    estimation techniques, 69-70
    interpretation of results, 70
Elasticity pessimism, 29
Endogeneous variables; *see* Econometric forecasting
Errors in measurement, 32-33
Exogeneous variables; *see* Econometric forecasting
Expected return; *see* International capital movements
Expectations formation, 93, 102
Export demand; *see also* Import demand, 10
  explanatory variables, 16
  lack of data, 16
  in two-gap model, 139
Export-import gap; *see* Two-gap models

F

Federal Reserve – MIT model, 130
First differences, 28
Forecasting; *see* Econometric forecasting
Foreign exchange reserves, 15
Foreign investment, direct; *see* International capital movements
Forward market, 81
Functional form, 17-18, 48
  for capital movements, 84, 102

G

General equilibrium analysis; *see* Trade dependence
Gravity model; *see* Trade interdependence

H

Harrod-Domar production function, 133, 136

I

Import demand
  dependent variable, 8-9
    current value of, 9
    deflated value of, 8
    and price indexes, 8
  estimation bias, 29

Import demand *(cont.)*
  explanatory (independent) variables,
      9-17
    capacity utilization term, 14
    credit for financing imports, 16
    distributed lags in, 15, 19
    domestic supply variables, 11
    and durables and nondurables, 13
    dummy variables, 15
    foreign exchange reserves, 15
    income term, 9
    and money illusion, 10
    price indexes as price term, 11
    and raw materials, 12
    and unfinished goods, 12
  functional form in, 17-18
  reporting results, 36-40
  results of studies, 35
  special problems in estimation
    data aggregation, 33, 42-48
    errors in measurement, 32-33
    magnitude of price changes, 34
    multicollinearity, 36
    simultaneity, 30
    time dimension distortion, 21, 34
  time dimensions in; *see* Time dimen-
      sion, 19-28
  and two-gap models, 137
Import supply, 7
Income elasticity, estimates of, 35
Index numbers; *see* Aggregation, 41,
      101
Inferior security, 78
Informative forecast, 112
Interest arbitrage
  covered, 81
  pure, 87
International capital movements
  measurement problems
    capital controls, 97
    credit rationing, 98
    disaggregation, 99
    functional form, 84, 102
    index numbers, 101
    lag structure, 102
    net worth variables, 92
    risk and expected return proxies,
        92
    simultaneous equation bias, 103
    speculative periods, 96
    trade variables, 94
  theory

    direct investment, 91
    flow models, 77, 80
    long-term portfolio investments, 91
    portfolio-adjustment models, 78
    short-term portfolio investment
      determinants of, 82
      expected return from, 83
      functional form, 84
      risk of, 83
    speculation
      expected return from, 84
      influence on capital flows, 85
      risk of, 84
    stock models, 78, 80
    trade arbitrage, 87
      demand for, 88
      and pure interest arbitrage, 87
      supply of, 89
    trade credit, 90, 94
Investment-savings gap; *see* Two-gap
      models

K

Kennedy Round; *see* Welfare effects of
      trade liberalization
Keynesian model, *see* Balance of pay-
      ments

L

Laspeyres price index, 42ff.
Less-developed countries; *see* Two-gap
      models
Long-term portfolio investment; *see*
      International capital movements

M

Market areas and trade interdepend-
      ence, 163
Marshall-Lerner condition, 29
Michigan econometric model, 128
Model building; *see* Econometric fore-
      casting
Money illusion, and import demand,
      10, 45
Multicollinearity
  and data interpretation, 23, 38
  and demand functions for inter-
      national capital movements,
      101

Multicollinearity *(cont.)*
  and distributed lags in import-
    demand function, 23

N

Nondurables, import demand for, 13

O

Office of Business Economics econo-
    metric model, 129

P

Paasche price index, 42
Point forecast, 112
Policy analysis with econometric
    models, 111, 117-18
Policy multipliers, 117
Prachowny econometric model, 125
Price elasticities
  derived from elasticity of substitu-
    tion, 64-69
  results of studies, 35
  special problems in estimation; *see*
    Import demand
Price indexes
  and aggregation, 42-48
  deflating imports and exports, 8
  as explanatory variable in import
    demand equation, 11, 42
  Laspeyres, 42ff.
  Paasche, 42
  use of unit value indexes for, 15
Producer surplus, 191
Pure interest arbitrage, 87

Q

Queues, 14

R

Raw materials, import demand for, 12
Reduced form of model, 110
Reporting results, 36-40
Resistance to international trade, 151,
    162
Resource endowment and international
    trade, 149

Results of econometric studies
  balance-of-payments forecasts, 124,
    130
  constant-market-share analysis, 179
  import-demand functions, 35
  two-gap models, 139
  welfare effects of Kennedy Round,
    195
Rhomberg and Boissonneault econo-
    metric model, 123-24
Risk; *see* International capital move-
    ments

S

Savings function; *see* Two-gap models
Seasonal adjustment, 15
Short-term portfolio investment; *see*
    International capital movements
Significance tests, 37
Simultaneous equation bias
  in elasticity of substitution measure-
    ment, 63
  in import demand functions, 30
  in international capital movements,
    103
  and price elasticity estimates, 29-31
Sombart law, 156
Speculation; *see* International capital
    movements
Statistical significance tests, 37
Stock-adjustment models
  of import response lags, 23-25
  of international capital movements,
    80
Structural form, 110
Supply of securities; *see* International
    capital movements

T

Tariffs; *see* Welfare effects of trade
    liberalization
Time dimension
  distributed lags in import demand
    functions, 19-28
  Almon technique, 26
  first differences, 28
  geometric decay, 24
  Jorgenson approach, 26
  polynominal lags, 26

Time dimension *(cont.)*
    rational distributed lags, 26
    and stock-adjustment process,
      23-25
    distributed lags in international capi-
      tal movements, 80, 93, 102
    and price elasticity bias, 21
Trade arbitrage and trade credit; *see*
    International capital movements
Trade dependence
    cross-section data, 145, 153
    customs unions, 155
    preferences, 155
    resistance to trade, 151
    Sombart law, 156
    theory of, 147
Trade flows; *see* Trade interdependence
Trade interdependence
    customs unions, 162
    gravity model, 158
    probability model, 158
    market areas, 163
    resistance factors, 162
    Walrasian model, 158
Trade liberalization; *see* Welfare effects
    of trade liberalization
Trade sectors; *see* Trade dependence
Two-gap models, 133-40
    import-export gap, 134

gap estimates, 138
savings-investment gap, 134
savings function, 137

U

Unconditional forecast, 111
Underdeveloped countries; *see* Two-
    gap models
Unfinished goods, import demand
    for, 12
Uniform tariff equivalent, 194
Unit value indexes, 15

W

Walrasian model of trade flows, 158
Welfare effects of trade liberalization
    customs unions and trade prefer-
      ences, 195
    dynamic vs. static considerations,
      184
    imported inputs, 194
    Kennedy Round, 195
    nonprohibitive tariffs, 190-92
    prohibitive tariffs, 185
    terms-of-trade effect, 193
    uniform tariff equivalent, 194
Wharton econometric model, 129